Pointing the Finger

Pointing the Finger

Islam and Muslims in the British Media

Julian Petley and Robin Richardson

ONEWORLD

OXFORD

A Oneworld Paperback Original

Published by Oneworld Publications 2011

ISBN 978-1-85168-812-8 (Paperback)
ISBN 978-1-85168-813-5 (Hardback)

Typeset by Glyph International
Cover design by vaguelymemorable.com
Print and bound in Great Britain by Bell & Bain, Glasgow
Front cover cartoon © Andrzej Krauze / Guardian News & Media Ltd 2006

Oneworld Publications
185 Banbury Road, Oxford, OX2 7AR, England

Learn more about Oneworld. Join our mailing list to
find out about our latest titles and special offers at:
www.oneworld-publications.com

Mixed Sources
Product group from well-managed
forests and other controlled sources
www.fsc.org   Cert no. TT-COC-002769
© 1996 Forest Stewardship Council
FSC

Contents

CONTENTS

Contributors to *Pointing the Finger*

Claire George received her PhD from Durham University in 2005 and completed an MA in Journalism at Brunel University in 2008. She is an active Anglican whose work strongly supports building greater understanding between different faiths.

Justin Lewis is Head of the School of Journalism, Media and Cultural Studies at Cardiff University. He joined Cardiff in 2000, having worked for twelve years in the United States at the University of Massachusetts. He has written numerous books about the media, culture and politics, including *Constructing Public Opinion* (2001) and *Citizens or Consumers: What the media tell us about political participation* (2005).

Paul Mason is a Senior Lecturer in the School of Journalism, Media and Cultural Studies at Cardiff University. He has written extensively in the field of law, crime and media. He is co-author of *Nine Years of UK Anti-Terrorism Legislation: an audit of civil liberties* (2010), which was written for the legal research group Adduce, and *Images of Islam*, which accompanied a Channel Four *Dispatches* programme (2007). He is currently training as a barrister.

Kerry Moore is a Lecturer in Journalism in the School of Journalism, Media and Cultural Studies at Cardiff University, and co-editor of *Migrations and the Media* (forthcoming). Her research interests focus on exploring racism in political and media discourse, and she has recently completed her PhD, which examines discourses of asylum under New Labour.

Hugh Muir is a journalist at the *Guardian* and the author of numerous articles on the issues of race, racism and Islamophobia. He was responsible with, Laura Smith, for the interviews and research underlying *Islamophobia: issues, challenges and action* (2004).

Julian Petley is Professor of Screen Media and Journalism in the School of Arts at Brunel University, chair of the Campaign for Press and Broadcasting Freedom and a member of the board of Index on Censorship. His most recent books are *Censorship: a beginner's guide* (2009) and the co-authored *Television News, Politics and Young People: generation disconnected?* (2010).

Robin Richardson is a director of the Insted educational consultancy. His previous roles include director of the Runnymede Trust and chief inspector of education in the London borough of Brent. He acted as consultant and editor for the Commission on the Future of Multi-Ethnic Britain chaired by Lord Parekh (1998-2000), wrote *Islamophobia: a challenge for us all* (1997), and edited *Islamophobia: issues, challenges and action* (2004).

Laura Smith is a journalist, writer and communications consultant who has written for the *Guardian, Independent* and the London *Evening Standard*. She was shortlisted for a Race in the Media award in 2001 and was responsible, with Hugh Muir, for the interviews and research underlying *Islamophobia: issues, challenges and action* (2004).

Introduction

Julian Petley and Robin Richardson

In his book *Only Half of Me: being a Muslim in Britain* (2006), journalist Rageh Omaar recalls a brief episode he witnessed on a London bus. It was a cold and dark afternoon, 'the kind of winter's day when it seems the sun has struggled to rise at all'. He was sitting on the lower deck and suddenly became aware of eight teenage schoolgirls clattering and tumbling down from the top deck, shouting to each other and talking loudly on their mobile phones. They were full of gaiety and laughter and were from a range of backgrounds. Some were of Somali heritage. Omaar writes:

> The Somali girls switched back and forth, in and out, from a thick London accent to Somali. One of them turned to her white friend and screeched: 'Those bacon crisps are disgusting! Just keep that minging smell away from me girl, I tell ya!' and then fell about laughing. They discussed each other's clothes and another girl in their class, then one of the Somali girls shouted, '*Bisinka*! did you really say that?' In one breath she went from a Somali Muslim word, *Bisinka*, which means 'By God's mercy' or 'With God's help', and which Somalis say

when something shocking happens, to English. None of her friends, black, white or Muslim, batted an eyelid.

(Omaar, 2006: 211–12)

The vignette evokes a multicultural society at ease with itself. Elsewhere in his book, however, Omaar is well aware of conflicts and problems. He is not starry-eyed – references to 7 July and 21 July 2005 run through his book with grim frequency. But he also takes pains to accentuate common ground and shared interests, the aspects of modern city life that are ordinary, positive and hopeful. Amid vivid reminders of linguistic, religious, cultural and ethnic differences and interactions, none of the school students he saw on the bus was in any way fazed – 'none … batted an eyelid'. Cultural differences can be threatening and can cause deep discomfort and anxiety – for Muslims, Omaar stresses, as well as for everyone else. But that is not the whole story. It is possible to realise, he says, that 'our worlds are not in conflict'.

Implicitly throughout, and from time to time directly, Omaar attends to the texts, talk and imagery through which relations between Muslims and non-Muslims are represented – and not represented – in the British media. Being a journalist himself he knows well the practical context in which journalists work: commercial competition between papers and between channels; the bottom lines of ratings and circulation figures; the relentless pressure of deadlines; the political expectations and requirements of proprietors and editors; the pressure to entertain, simplify and please rather than to inform, challenge and educate; the inevitability of inaccuracy and distortion even with the best will in the world; the continual emphasis on immediacy, sensation, novelty, human interest. Despite his personal knowledge of the daily pressures under which journalists work, Omaar believes the media could do a better job. In effect, though not in so many words, he proposes that the following questions about the media should be asked:

Do the media promote informed debate about the building and maintenance of multicultural democracy and, within this context, about relations between Muslims and non-Muslims? Or do they promote a bias against understanding by oversimplifying, giving insufficient information about the background to the news and pandering to readers' anxieties and prejudices?

How community-sensitive is media reporting about multiculturalism and British Muslim identities? Is it likely to foster anxiety, fear or hostility within particular communities – for example, in the views and expectations that non-Muslims have of Muslims, and that Muslims have of non-Muslims? And what is likely to be its impact on public policy, and on perceptions of public policy, for example in relation to preventing violent extremism and to foreign affairs?

Does media coverage hinder or promote mutual understanding, and increase or decrease a sense of common ground, and of shared belonging and civic responsibility, and of safety and security?

How accountable to a range of different communities are the media, for example through publishing letters and articles which present a range of views, quoting a range of opinions, standpoints and sources, and correcting errors?

These are also the questions underlying the chapters in this book. The recurring themes can be summarised as follows:

The dominant view in the UK media is that there is no common ground between the West and Islam, and that conflict between them is accordingly inevitable.

Muslims in Britain are depicted as a threat to traditional British customs, values and ways of life.

Alternative world views, understandings and opinions are not mentioned or are not given a fair hearing.

Facts are frequently distorted, exaggerated or oversimplified, and sometimes even invented.

The tone of language is frequently emotive, immoderate, alarmist or abusive.

The coverage is likely to provoke and increase feelings of insecurity, suspicion and anxiety among non-Muslims.

The coverage is at the same time likely to provoke feelings of insecurity, vulnerability and alienation among Muslims, and in this
way to weaken the government's measures to reduce and prevent
extremism.

The coverage is unlikely to help diminish levels of hate crime and
acts of unlawful discrimination by non-Muslims against
Muslims.

The coverage is likely to be a major barrier preventing the success
of the government's community cohesion policies and programmes.

The coverage is unlikely to contribute to informed discussion and
debate among Muslims and non-Muslims about ways of working
together to maintain and develop Britain as a multicultural, multifaith democracy.

The book draws in part on a study conducted in 2006–7 for the
Greater London Council (Insted Consultancy, 2007). Subsequently,
several of the chapters in the report were revised, expanded and
updated, and several further chapters were added. Two members of
the original team acted as editors.

The pattern of the book is as follows. First (chapters 2 and 3),
there are theoretical introductions, respectively concerned with definitions and with the concept of narrative. Chapter 2 notes that there
is an international cluster of terms and phrases referring to negative
feelings and attitudes towards Islam and Muslims. The most widely
known member of the cluster is 'Islamophobia'. But competing with
it in certain contexts, countries and international organisations, and
among academic observers, there are several other terms. They
include 'anti-Muslim racism', 'intolerance against Muslims', 'anti-
Muslim prejudice', 'hatred of Muslims', 'anti-Islamism', 'anti-Muslimism', 'Muslimophobia', 'demonisation of Islam' and 'demonisation
of Muslims'. Such differences in terminology reflect, but they do not
exactly correspond to, differences of understanding and focus. The
chapter reviews the history and meanings of the term 'Islamophobia',
the objections that have been made to it and the alternatives that

have been proposed. It acknowledges that such discussion may seem unduly and even self-indulgently theoretical, a modern equivalent of speculating how many angels can perch on a pinhead. It is nevertheless important. How a problem is conceptualised fundamentally affects how it is addressed. The concept of Islamophobia (or whatever) is by no means as unproblematic as is sometimes thought. If media coverage of 'Islam' and 'Muslims' is to be adequately critiqued and improved, it is necessary at some stage, and preferably at the outset, to elucidate thorny conceptual and semantic issues. In the light of its discussion of the diversity of terminology, the chapter proposes a working definition: *a shorthand term referring to a multifaceted mix of discourse, behaviour and structures which express and perpetuate feelings of anxiety, fear, hostility and rejection towards Muslims, particularly but not only in countries where people of Muslim heritage live as minorities.*

The principal manifestations of Islamophobia include negativity and hostility in the media and the blogosphere, in the publications of certain think-tanks, and in the speeches and policy proposals of certain political leaders. As already mentioned, negativity in the media, and in particular the press, is the subject-matter of this book. It is relevant at the outset to note that there are other manifestations of Islamophobia as well. They include hate crimes on the streets against both persons and property, and desecration of Muslim cemeteries, cultural centres and religious buildings; harassment, abuse and rudeness ('the unkindness of strangers', as the term might be) in public places; unlawful discrimination in employment practices and the provision of services; non-recognition of Muslim identities and concerns, and removal of Muslim symbols in public space; and the absence of Muslims from public life, including politics and government, senior positions in business and commerce, and culture and the arts.

Chapter 3 makes four distinctions: between two aspects of narrative, 'histories' and 'stories'; between dominant and alternative worldviews; between content and form; and between open and closed forms of engaging, thinking, talking and writing. The distinction between content and form is introduced with a recollection of some words by the journalist Peregrine Worsthorne who, many years ago, claimed that Islam was 'once a great civilisation worthy of being argued with' but now 'has degenerated into a primitive enemy fit only to be sensitively subjugated' (*Sunday Telegraph*, 3 February 1991). He made two distinctions in this claim, the one to do with content ('great civilisation'/'primitive enemy') and the other with regard to forms of thinking, engaging and relating ('argued with'/'subjugated'). To see an individual or a group or a civilisation as 'worthy of being argued with' is necessarily to be open-minded towards them. The hallmarks of open-mindedness in the media, or indeed anywhere else, are itemised in chapter 3 and the chapter then draws to an end by citing some reflections from Edward Said.

'There is a difference', wrote Said in the 2003 preface of his magisterial *Orientalism*, first published in 1978, 'between knowledge of other peoples and other times that is the result of understanding, compassion, careful study and analysis for their own sakes, and on the other hand knowledge – if that is what it is – that is part of an overall campaign of self-affirmation, belligerence and outright war'. He continued by urging 'that the terrible reductive conflicts that herd people under falsely unifying rubrics like "America", "The West" or "Islam" and invent collective identities for large numbers of individuals who are actually quite diverse, cannot remain as potent as they are, and must be opposed, their murderous effectiveness vastly reduced in influence and mobilising power.' He concluded with words which are particularly relevant to the role and responsibility of the media in modern societies:

> Rather than the manufactured clash of civilisations, we need to concentrate on the slow working together of cultures that overlap, borrow from each other, and live together in far more interesting ways than any abridged or inauthentic mode of understanding can allow. But for that kind of wider perception we need time and patient and sceptical inquiry, supported by communities of interpretation that are difficult to sustain in a world demanding instant action and reaction.
>
> (2003: xiv)

This volume as a whole, it is hoped and intended, is a contribution to the kind of community of interpretation to which Said was referring.

With the conceptual groundwork laid in the first three chapters, the book then moves into the realm of empirical analysis. For the most part, the focus of the subsequent chapters is firmly on the British press, but chapter 6 also examines an episode of the BBC TV series *Panorama* and shows how press and television agendas on the subject of Muslims and Islam in Britain can sometimes coincide.

Chapter 4 sets the overall scene by examining the representation of British Muslims in the national press from 2000 to 2008. Its main findings are that, first, overall, thirty-six per cent of stories about British Muslims were about terrorism. In recent years, however, increasing numbers of stories have focused on religious and cultural differences between Islam on the one hand and British or Western culture on the other (twenty-two per cent of stories overall) and Islamic extremism (eleven per cent overall). In sum, it was found the bulk of coverage of British Muslims – around two-thirds – focused on Muslims as a threat in relation to terrorism, or as a problem with terms of differences in values, or as both. Second, the language used about British Muslims reflects the negative or problematic contexts in which they tend to appear. Four of the five most common discourses used about Muslims in the British press associate Islam/ Muslims with threats and problems or with opposition to dominant British values. So, for example, the idea that Islam is dangerous, backward or irrational is present in twenty-six per cent of stories. By contrast, only two per cent of stories contained the proposition that Muslims supported dominant moral values. Third, it was found that the most common nouns used in relation to British Muslims were *terrorist, extremist, Islamist, suicide bomber* and *militant*, with very little use of positive nouns such as *scholar*. The most common adjectives used were *radical, fanatical, fundamentalist, extremist* and *militant*. Indeed, references to radical Muslims outnumbered references to moderate Muslims by seventeen to one. Fourth, the visual representation of Muslims reflects the portrayals described in the content analysis.

There was a widespread use of police mugshots in the portrayal of Muslim men (with all the negative associations that these carry), while Muslims were commonly photographed outside police stations or law courts, this being very much in keeping with the high proportion of terrorism-related stories about British Muslims. Fifth, Muslims were often identified simply *as* Muslims rather than as individuals or members of other groups with distinct identities. So, for example, Muslims were much less likely than non-Muslims to be identified in terms of their job or profession, and much more likely to be unnamed or unidentified. Finally, decontextualisation, misinformation and a preferred discourse of threat, fear and danger, while not uniformly present, were strong forces in the reporting of British Muslims in the UK national press in the period under examination.

Chapter 5 examines a particular cluster of stories about Muslims and Islam, namely those that revolve around the increasingly common press trope that 'Britishness is being destroyed', and that British society and the British way of life are under threat. Blame for this is frequently laid at the door of 'foreigners' of one kind or another, but also identified as responsible is the pernicious influence of home-grown 'political correctness'. Such stories now abound in the British press, and this chapter examines four typical ones. These concern:

the alleged banning of piggy banks by a building society in a
    Lancashire town
the alleged banning of Christmas by a local council in London
the use of BP (Before Present) instead of BC (Before Christ) at
    a museum in the West Country
the police and Crown Prosecution Service taking a ten-year-old boy
    to court for playground bullying in Salford.

Each story illustrates the claim that 'common sense' is being threatened by the 'PC brigade'. More specifically, in the treatment of each story the attack on 'political correctness' is combined with an attack on Muslims – either explicitly or implicitly. In fact, the reportage of all four incidents involved very serious factual inaccuracies and distortions. These were uncovered by interviews with, and statements by, people who were directly involved in the stories themselves. The research concluded that the claims of 'political correctness' were unsubstantiated, and that the underlying fears that these stories address (and doubtless help to fuel) stem from rapid social and economic changes, in particular those caused by globalisation. The presence of Muslims in modern Britain, in this context, is little more than a convenient scapegoat.

The media frequently give the impression that there is a single, homogeneous 'Muslim community' in Britain, and that the government should have dealings only with organisations that are representative of that community. The problem is, however, that Muslims in Britain are extremely heterogeneous, and that different sections of the Muslim population are represented by a very wide range of different groups. When forced to confront this fact, the media frequently argue that people of Muslim heritage can be divided into two contrasting groups: good/bad, 'moderate'/'extremist', 'Sufi'/'Islamist' and so on. But this is not only misleading, it can also lead to the demonisation of certain Muslims and Islamic organisations. Chapter 6 examines in considerable detail a campaign in which the media (and not only the press) played a key role in attempting to demonise, and thus to sideline, one such organisation, the Muslim Council of Britain (MCB). The chapter argues that the media profoundly misunderstood both the heterogeneity of the Muslim population of Britain and the nature and function of the MCB. In playing a leading role in the attempted discrediting of the MCB, it greatly contributed to a situation in which the government eventually found itself increasingly at odds with many Muslim organisations, and able to talk officially only to those which it itself had established and which thus lacked legitimacy with many Muslims. In turn, this led it into a 'rebalancing' of its relationship with Muslim communities which emphasised counter-terrorist and 'anti-extremist' imperatives in a way that many have criticised as thoroughly self-defeating and counter-productive.

The disturbances in northern cities in 2001 gave rise to substantial discussion in the media about how young people of Muslim background should be assimilated into British norms and values. The discussion was massively amplified four years later at the time of the London bombs, when it was widely argued that multiculturalism had failed. Influential speeches were made by Gordon Brown, at that time Chancellor of the Exchequer, about the 'golden thread' in British history concerned with values said to be distinctly British, and by the then chairman of the Commission for Racial Equality, who in a famous phrase claimed the country was 'sleepwalking towards segregation'. New government policies were introduced relating to promoting community cohesion, preventing violent extremism (PVE) and promoting British identity in the education system, and in the creation and development of citizenship tests and ceremonies. In due course, in March 2010, a House of Commons select committee in effect acknowledged that the PVE programme had been based on dangerously inadequate assumptions and expectations. For many years these assumptions had been expressed and taken for granted throughout most of the media.

The situation of Muslims in Britain was frequently referred to in these discussions, but as often as not the references were implicit rather than explicitly emphasised, for multiculturalism mutated during the decade into a coded term for referring to Muslims and British Islam. This happened in intellectual and centre-left circles as well as more widely.

Chapter 7 reviews the ways in which the media portrayed discussions about multiculturalism, cohesion and Britishness in the period 1999–2009. As case studies, it takes three iconic episodes: the debates in summer and autumn 2005 occasioned by the London bombs; the introduction and implementation of the PVE programme; and the development of a 'Britishness curriculum', as the term might be, in the national curriculum in schools. (It should be noted that PVE is also discussed in the final section of chapter 6.)

Chapters 8 and 9 examine press representations of two specific issues: that of Muslim women who choose to wear a particular form of veil, and a speech given in February 2008 by the Archbishop of Canterbury about Sharia law. The authors of chapter 8 note that the press seem to find it impossible to discuss Muslim women without raising the question of the veil, and doing so in an almost entirely negative fashion. Their chapter examines the link between definitions of the Muslim veil which have emerged since 9/11 in the broader context of the 'War on Terror', and the mobilisation of a particular image of the veil forged in that moment, in support of exclusionary domestic politics and attacks on civil liberties. They argue that in press and much political discourse, the notion of the veil always stands for 'un-freedom' for Muslim women and, by association, in Europe today, has come to stand as a threat to non-Muslim women and to the 'Western values' that are purported to protect gender freedom.

Chapter 9 examines the considerable gulf between what the Archbishop of Canterbury actually said about Sharia law and the way in which this was represented by the press. In so doing it exposes the ignorance of many journalists (including, strikingly, various religious correspondents) about both Islam and Christianity. The way in which this chapter shows how the Archbishop's words were interpreted (entirely wrongly) as an attack on British values links it with chapter 5, but what is also particularly interesting about this analysis is how it brings out the considerable hostility not simply to Islam but to liberal values expressed by many press commentators on this affair.

Chapter 10 moves away from textual analysis in order to examine the institutions that produce newspaper articles in the first place. In particular, it asks: if you're of Muslim heritage, what is it like to work as a reporter on a mainstream newspaper? Are you treated differently? Is there any opportunity to influence your paper's policies and practices? Interviews with journalists from Muslim backgrounds reveal a wide range of experiences and perceptions, told almost entirely in their own words. The interviews lead to the conclusion that if media coverage of Islam and Muslims is to improve, then the make-up of the journalistic workforce on newspapers should more accurately reflect the proportion of Muslims living in Britain.

This, the authors argue, would have distinct advantages all round, since Muslim journalists: (1) are more likely to deal with Islam and Muslim-related issues with sensitivity, fairness and awareness of complexity; (2) are more likely to establish a rapport and to win trust when dealing with Muslim members of the public; (3) can advise and challenge colleagues, including senior editors, about the ways certain stories should and should not be covered; (4) can have an impact on the organisational culture of the paper, making it more open-minded and self-critical.

It is important, however, that senior managers in news organisations should understand that there is a wide range of opinion, outlook and practice among journalists of Muslim backgrounds, as with people of Muslim backgrounds more generally. For example, not all practise the religion, and no single individual should be treated as a representative or ambassador. They should also recognise that journalists of Muslim backgrounds are professionally journalists who happen to be Muslims rather than Muslims who happen to be journalists. Finally, they should resist pressures to limit people's career prospects by pigeon-holing and typecasting them into a narrow range of work.

Although the various contributors to this book are extremely critical of the way in which the media, and especially the press, habitually represent Muslims and Islam, the book concludes on a constructive and positive note by suggesting ways in which media coverage might be improved. As the book attempts to demonstrate, where Muslims and Islam are concerned, anxiety is the key issue, and the professional responsibility of journalists is to promote informed debate, as distinct from pandering to prejudice and provoking anxiety by being alarmist. But how can responsible journalism be fostered? The principal themes that need to be considered here include:

Freedom of expression: there is an important distinction to be made between having a right and exercising that right responsibly.
Dealing with anxiety: particularly at a time of rapid and extremely unsettling social and cultural change, journalists should do their

utmost to explain these changes rather than to fan the fears and resentments that these changes bring in their wake.

Religious literacy: increased understanding is needed of the range of ways in which religion may affect a person's values and perspectives.

Critical literacy: interpretative skills need to be developed so that readers, viewers and listeners can question media portrayals of issues and engage in debate.

Making complaints: the public needs to be encouraged to make complaints to the appropriate authority, to engage in debate and to express critical opinion on media matters about which they feel strongly.

Codes of professional practice need to be further developed to promote public accountability in the media.

Specifically with regard to Muslims, Islam and the media:

News organisations should review their coverage of issues and events involving Muslims and Islam, and should consider drawing up codes of professional conduct and style guides about use of terminology.

News organisations should take measures, perhaps within the framework of positive action in equalities legislation, to recruit more journalists of Muslim heritage who can more accurately reflect the views and experiences of Muslim communities.

News organisations should also consider how best to give Muslim staff appropriate professional support and to prevent them being pigeon-holed as specialists in minority issues rather than concerned with the full spectrum of an organisation's output.

Organisations, projects and programmes concerned with race relations should see and treat anti-Muslim prejudice as a form of discrimination, and as serious as other forms of discrimination.

The Commission for Equality and Human Rights (CEHR) should focus explicitly on, among other concerns, combating anti-Muslim prejudice, both in society generally and in the media in particular.

The Department for Communities and Local Government (DCLG) should give a higher profile to combating anti-Muslim prejudice in the media and the general climate of public opinion.

The Press Complaints Commission's terms of reference should be amended so it can consider distorted and inaccurate coverage of groups and communities as well as of individuals, and can consider complaints from third parties.

Throughout his book, Rageh Omaar asks and considers whether 'Islam' and 'the West' are inherently incompatible with each other. Inverted commas are necessary, since both terms are shorthand for immensely complex and variegated realities. Also, the realities are interrelated and merge with each other. Picturing the world as consisting of two large monolithic entities with little or nothing in common is arguably part of the problem. There are both Muslims and non-Muslims who consider that the two worldviews are incompatible and that violent conflict is inevitable – in a famous phrase, there is a clash of civilisations. However, it is appropriate to return to the scene on a London bus with which this chapter began – the cheerful acceptance of difference and diversity, accompanied by celebration of common ground, with no one batting an eyelid. Omaar ends his book by noting that 'Muslims are unfamiliar to and seen as alien by so many people in this country' and that 'their experiences as individuals are rarely heard'. And yet, he continues:

> Without allowing these voices in politics, on our streets, in our schools, in our newspapers and on television, we are lost. It is only when the voice of the individual is lifted above the waves of condemnation that all of us can begin to see more clearly, and perhaps start to realise, that our worlds are not in conflict after all.
>
> (2006: 215)

This report is frequently about, to use Omaar's phrase, 'waves of condemnation'. However, it also contains the voices of individuals. An aspiration throughout is to assert and to show that, despite frequent evidence and claims to the contrary, 'our worlds are not in conflict after all'.

1

The Demonisation of Islam and Muslims

Concepts, Terms and Distinctions

Robin Richardson

Diversity of terminology

There is an international cluster of terms and phrases referring to negative feelings and attitudes towards Islam and Muslims. The most widely
known member of the cluster is 'Islamophobia'. But competing with it
in certain contexts, countries and international organisations, and among
academic observers, there are several other terms. They include 'anti-
Muslim racism', 'intolerance against Muslims', 'anti-Muslim prejudice',
'hatred of Muslims', 'anti-Islamism', 'anti-Muslimism', 'Muslimophobia',
'demonisation of Islam' and 'demonisation of Muslims'.

There is a similar range of contested terms in other languages, not
just in English. In German, for example, there is a contest between
Islamophobie and *Islamfeindlichkeit,* the latter implying hostility, not fear.
In French, the contest is in part between *islamophobie* on the one hand
and *racisme anti-arabe* or *racisme anti-maghrébin* on the other, the latter
two phrases indicating that the phenomenon is primarily to be seen
as a form of anti-immigrant racism directed towards communities

from parts of the former French Empire, not primarily to do with religion or culture. The Scandinavian term *Muslimhat* translates literally into English as 'Muslim hatred', though more accurately as 'hatred of Muslims', with echoes of legal usage in English terms such as 'incitement to hatred' and 'hate crimes'.

Such differences in terminology reflect, but they do not exactly correspond to, differences of understanding and focus. For example, they reflect different views of causes, influences, drivers and key features, and therefore different kinds of proposals and practical agendas, and different approaches to media analysis. Also, the different terms may be used to distinguish between different manifestations of the phenomena under discussion, so that the term 'anti-Muslim racism' is used to refer to hate crimes, and to harassment, rudeness and verbal abuse in public spaces, whereas the term 'Islamophobia' refers to discourse and mindsets in the media, including the broadsheets as well as the tabloids (Sivanandan, 2010). Underlying the diversity of terminology, key questions include the following:

Is 'phobia' a more apposite term than terms such as 'fear', 'suspicion', 'worry' or 'anxiety', and in any case are the essential causes of fear (however named) primarily or solely inherent in Islam and Muslims or are there other significant factors at play which, in point of fact, have little or even nothing to do with Islam and Muslims? If so what are these other factors, and how should they be dealt with? Or are the dominant emotions that need to be named more accurately identified as hostility and hatred, not fear?

Where are the phenomena that are feared or hated mainly located, both objectively and in perception and imagination? Primarily in one's own country or continent? Or primarily out there in the wider world, and if so in which countries or continents in particular? Or are they located everywhere in the world, without differentiation?

Are the phenomena that are feared or hated primarily to do with 'Muslims' or primarily to do with 'Islam'? Namely, is it ethno-religious groups and communities ('Muslims') towards which

2

there are feelings of animosity and anxiety, or is it a culture, civilisation or religion ('Islam')? Or is this distinction invalid?

How does one identify and describe legitimate criticisms or anxieties
on the one hand and hate-filled or irrational criticisms and anxieties on the other?

Questions such as these may seem unduly and even self-indulgently
theoretical, a modern equivalent of speculating how many angels can
perch on a pinhead. It is nevertheless important to ask them. How a
problem is conceptualised fundamentally affects how it is addressed.
The concept of Islamophobia (or whatever) is by no means as unproblematic as is sometimes thought. If media coverage of 'Islam' and
'Muslims' is to be adequately critiqued and improved it is necessary at
some stage, and preferably at the outset, to elucidate thorny conceptual
and semantic issues. What exactly are we gazing at, grappling with? The
discussion in this chapter starts with consideration of the term
'Islamophobia' and then continues with notes on the various alternative phrases that have been proposed in recent years as more apposite.
Later in the chapter there will be discussion of underlying causes and
of contributory and exacerbating factors.

'Islamophobia'

The first known use in print of the French word *islamophobie* appears
to have been in a book entitled *La Politique musulmane dans l'Afrique
Occidentale Française* by Alain Quellien, published in Paris in 1910
(Ezzerhouni, 2010). The context was a criticism of the ways in which
French colonial administrators viewed the cultures of the countries
now known as Benin, Burkina Faso, Côte d'Ivoire, Guinea, Mali,
Mauritania, Niger and Senegal. The word then appeared in reviews of
Quellien's book in academic journals, and in a biography of Mohammed
by Alphonse Etienne Dinet (1861–1929), a French painter and convert
to Islam who lived for most of his adult life in southern Algeria. His
book was completed in 1916 and, when published some two years

later, was dedicated to the memory of Muslim soldiers in the French army who had died in the First World War (Vakil, 2008). In an English version of his book, the word *islamophobie* was translated as 'feelings inimical to Islam', not as Islamophobia.

The first use of the word in English in print appears to have been in an article by Edward Said in 1985, where he referred in passing to 'the connection ... between Islamophobia and antisemitism' and criticised writers who do not recognise that 'hostility to Islam in the modern Christian West has historically gone hand in hand' with anti-semitism and 'has stemmed from the same source and been nourished at the same stream' (1985: 8–9). The next recorded use of the word in English was in the American journal *Insight* on 4 February 1991, referring to hostility of the government of the Soviet Union towards its own Muslim citizens and regions: 'Islamophobia also accounts for Moscow's reluctance to relinquish its position in Afghanistan, despite the estimated $300 million a month it takes to keep the Kabul regime going' (cited by *Oxford English Dictionary*, as reported by the Commission on British Muslims and Islamophobia, 1997). In the UK the first known use of the word in print occurred in a book review in the *Independent* on 16 December 1991 (reprinted in Modood, 1992: 75–6). Modood noted there is a view that *The Satanic Verses* was 'a deliberate, mercenary act of Islamophobia' but indicated that his own view was that, 'while Islamophobia is certainly at work, the real sickness is militant irreverence'.

In October 2002 the House of Lords Select Committee on Religious Offences in the UK was informed in oral evidence that the English word had first been coined by Dr Zaki Badawi, at that time principal of the Muslim College in London, or else by Fuad Nahdi, founding director of the magazine *Q-News* (House of Lords, 2002). If indeed the word was coined by either of these it would have been in the late 1980s. The context would have included the campaigns led by *MuslimWise*, the predecessor of *Q-News*, and by the An-Nisa Society, a community organisation based in Brent in northwest London, to counter anti-Muslim hostility not only in society at large but also, and more especially, among people working in the field of race relations. The latter included the Commission for Racial Equality (CRE) nationally and race equality councils locally. Also, it included race equality officers and units in local government. All these were perceived to be insensitive and indifferent to the distinctive forms of ignorance, intolerance, discrimination and violence experienced by Muslims. The failure of the CRE and of race equality professionals more generally to take serious account of Islamophobia was itself an example, it was argued, of institutional Islamophobia.

The word has increasingly been used since about 2000 in the deliberations and publications of international organisations, including the United Nations, the Council of Europe, the European Union (EU) Agency for Fundamental Rights (FRA, previously the European Monitoring Centre, EUMC) and the Organization of the Islamic Conference (OIC). The word is now widely used in the UK media, though occasionally it still appears in inverted commas, to imply the meaning is not clear, or – in the author's view – not as clear as others claim. A further implication of the inverted commas is the claim there is in reality no such thing as Islamophobia: it is merely the figment of a paranoid or politically motivated imagination; or constructed out of a desire to perpetuate a siege mentality and sense of victimhood among Muslims; or to put an end to legitimate criticism; or to engage in lazy abuse (Malik, 2005; Phillips, 2006). Incidentally, the word is much commoner in Europe than in the United States. In 2007 it was used hundreds of times in the *Guardian* but on only twenty-six occasions in the *New York Times* (Cesari, 2006).

The disadvantages of the term 'Islamophobia' are significant (Allen, 2010; Vakil, 2008). Some of them are primarily about the echoes implicit in the concept of 'phobia'. Others are about the implications of the term 'Islam'. For convenience, they can be itemised as follows.

Medically, 'phobia' implies a severe mental illness of a kind that affects only a tiny minority of people. Whatever else anxiety about Muslims may be, it is not merely a mental illness and does not merely involve a small number of people.

To accuse someone of being insane or irrational is to be abusive and, not surprisingly, to make them defensive and defiant. Reflective dialogue with them is then all but impossible.

To label someone with whom you disagree as irrational or insane is to absolve yourself of the responsibility of trying to understand, both intellectually and with empathy, why they think and act as they do, and of seeking through engagement and argument to modify their perceptions and understandings.

The concept of anxiety is arguably more useful in this context than the concept of phobia. It is widely recognised that anxiety may not be (though certainly may be) warranted by objective facts, for human beings can on occasion perceive dangers that do not objectively exist, or anyway do not exist to the extent that is imagined. Also it can sometimes be difficult to identify, and therefore to name accurately, the real sources of an anxiety.

The use of the word 'Islamophobia' on its own implies that hostility towards Muslims is unrelated to, and basically dissimilar from, forms of hostility such as racism, xenophobia, sectarianism, and such as hostility to so-called fundamentalism (Samuels, 2006). Further, it may imply there is no connection with issues of class, power, status and territory; or with issues of military, political or economic competition and conflict.

The term implies there is no important difference between prejudice towards Muslim communities within one's own country and prejudice towards cultures and regimes elsewhere in the world where Muslims are in the majority, and with which 'the West' is in military conflict or economic competition.

The term is inappropriate for describing opinions that are basically anti-religion as distinct from anti-Islam. 'I am an Islamophobe,' wrote the journalist Polly Toynbee in the *Independent*, 23 October 1997, in reaction to the Runnymede 1997 report, adding: 'I am also a Christophobe. If Christianity were not such a spent force in this country, if it were powerful and dominant as it once was, it would still be every bit as damaging as Islam is in those theocratic states in its thrall … If I lived in Israel, I'd feel the same way about Judaism.'

The key phenomenon to be addressed is arguably anti-Muslim hostility, namely hostility towards an ethno-religious identity within European countries (including Russia), rather than hostility towards the tenets or practices of a worldwide religion. The 1997 Runnymede definition of Islamophobia was 'a shorthand way of referring to dread or hatred of Islam – and, therefore, to fear or dislike of all or most Muslims' (Commission on British Muslims and Islamophobia, 1997: 1). In retrospect, it would have been as accurate, or arguably indeed more accurate, to say 'a shorthand way of referring to fear or dislike of all or most Muslims – and, therefore, dread or hatred of Islam'.

Despite its disadvantages, the term 'Islamophobia' looks as if it is here to stay – it cannot now be discarded from the lexicon. Not least, this is because it has acquired legitimacy and emotional power among people who are at the receiving end of anti-Muslim hostility and prejudice, and is therefore capable of mobilising opposition and resistance. Further, people at the receiving end of religious intolerance may turn to their religious tradition for solace and moral support, and this strengthens their sense that it is their religion that is primarily under attack (Birt, 2009b). 'It has been observed,' say Peter Gottschalk and Gabriel Greenberg, 'that movements against discrimination do not begin until a commonly understood label evolves that brings together under one banner all forms of that particular prejudice.' They continue:

> Resistance to gender discrimination coalesced under the term 'sexism'. The civil rights movement gained momentum when harnessed to the notion of 'racism' that encapsulated the variety of innate prejudices and institutional obstacles in a white dominated society. The concept of 'antisemitism' has provided a powerful tool to object to anti-Jewish sentiment that was once, like the denigrations of women and blacks, considered normal and left largely unchallenged by people fitting the norm. Increasingly, and particularly among Muslims, 'Islamophobia'

provides a term to similarly draw attention to a normalised prejudice and unjustified discrimination. Undoubtedly this term will elicit the same unease among and even backlash from some of those whose notion of normal it challenges, just as its historical predecessors have and still do.

(2008: 11)

Since the word 'Islamophobia' is now here to stay, the task is to define as clearly as possible what one means by it, and does not mean, and to complement or replace it with other terms when appropriate. It is helpful to recall in this respect that it is recognisably similar to terms such as homophobia, xenophobia and europhobia, none of which imply mental illness, and that it not infrequently happens, in the history of language, that words are coined that are less than ideal. The word 'antisemitism', for example, is lexically nonsensical since there is no such thing as semitism; and in any case not all Jewish people are so-called Semites, nor are all so-called Semitic people Jewish. The word has been current long enough now, however, for it to be generally accepted as unproblematic. The same kind of acceptance is apparently being accorded to 'Islamophobia', despite the problems and disadvantages outlined above. It is nevertheless apposite to note and discuss some of the alternative terms that have been proposed, in particular 'anti-Muslim racism' and 'intolerance against Muslims'.

'Anti-Muslim racism'

In its discussion of racism, the Commission on the Future of Multi-Ethnic Britain (2000) emphasised that 'hostility which uses skin colour and physical appearance as markers of supposed difference does not represent the whole picture'. It continued:

There is also hostility using markers connected with culture, language and religion. The plural term 'racisms' is sometimes used to highlight such complexity. For anti-black racism is different, in terms of its historical and economic origins, and in its contemporary manifestations, stereotypes and effects, from anti-Asian racism. Both are different from, to cite three further significant examples, anti-Irish, anti-Gypsy and anti-Jewish racism. European societies, it is sometimes said, are multi-racist societies. Specific words have been invented over the years for certain types of racism directed at particular groups – the term antisemitism originated in the mid-nineteenth century, and more recently the terms orientalism and Islamophobia have been coined to refer, respectively, to anti-Asian racism in general and anti-Muslim racism in particular.

(2000: 59–60)

An obvious objection to the term 'anti-Muslim racism' is that Muslims are not a race and that therefore hostility towards them cannot be a form of racism. But, as is well known, the human species is a single race and distinctions between so-called races have no basis in science. From a scientific point of view it is as nonsensical to say that Africans, Asians or Chinese are races as to say that Muslims are. In legal parlance in the UK, the term 'racial group' means 'a group of people defined by their race, colour, nationality (including citizenship) or ethnic or national origin'. This is an extremely broad definition and clearly encompasses groups that are not normally thought of as races. If the term 'religious' were to be added, or if the term 'ethnic' were understood to encompass 'ethno-religious', then certainly Muslims would be defined in UK law as a racial group and the full force of race relations legislation would be brought to bear against hostility towards them.

Either way it would need to be understood that Muslim identity is not necessarily or universally to do with holding distinctive beliefs or engaging in specific practices – it can be primarily to do with a sense of belonging, or of being perceived to belong, to a broad cultural tradition. In this way, and to this extent, the term 'Muslim' in

England, Scotland and Wales can be similar to the terms 'Protestant' and 'Catholic' in Northern Ireland. Also in other parts of the world, including Nigeria, Lebanon and South Asia, the term refers to identity and belonging, not necessarily personal belief and piety. 'The South Asia I am from', writes Tariq Modood, 'is contoured by communal religious identities. It has nothing to do with belief. If you assert "I am an atheist", people will still think it meaningful to ask, "Yes, but are you a Muslim, a Hindu?" ' (2005: 16). It follows that hostility towards a certain ethno-religious community has nothing necessarily to do with hostility towards any specific religious beliefs. A key distinction must be drawn, this is by way of saying, between 'belief' on the one hand and 'affiliation' or 'association' on the other. Anti-Muslim racism, like antisemitism, sectarianism and factionalism throughout the world, attacks certain people because of their affiliation, or assumed affiliation, not because of their beliefs. Such affiliation, unlike belief, is not chosen. 'No one chooses to be born into a Muslim family,' writes Modood in the *Guardian* (21 January 2005). 'Similarly, no one chooses to be born into a society where to be a Muslim creates suspicion, hostility, or failure to get the job you applied for.'

It is relevant in this connection to note that the European Commission against Racism and Intolerance (ECRI) emphasises entirely explicitly that, so far as combating intolerance is concerned, the categories of race and religion are in certain respects interchangeable. Their definition of racism is: 'the belief that a ground such as race, colour, language, religion, nationality or national or ethnic origin justifies contempt for a person or a group of persons, or the notion of superiority of a person or group of persons' (ECRI, 2003: 5).[1] It is unfortunate that European anti-discrimination legislation, unlike ECRI, sees 'race' on the one hand and 'religion or belief' on the other as entirely separate strands, each with separate legal terminology and mechanisms of enforcement. In Britain, the Equality and Human Rights Commission (EHRC) draws a distinction between 'belief' and 'the believer', as if the latter term is an accurate way of referring to anyone associated in any way with a religious tradition, regardless of whether they are observant or pious (EHRC, 2009: 8).

Intolerance

The Organisation for Security and Co-operation in Europe (OSCE) uses the term 'intolerance and discrimination against Muslims' in its documents, as does the International Helsinki Federation for Human Rights, and focuses in particular on situations in OSCE states where people of Muslim heritage live as minorities — hence intra-national relationships, essentially, not international ones. The inclusion of the term 'discrimination' is a valuable reminder that there is a behavioural component as well as an attitudinal one. In international English, though not in UK English, the term 'discrimination' refers to a wide range of behaviour, including hate crimes of various kinds, not only actions that are unlawful under equal opportunities legislation.

'Tolerance' was originally a political or legal term which referred to permitting and protecting, as distinct from forbidding, persecuting and eliminating, opinions different from those of the majority in any one situation or country. The word 'intolerance', accordingly, refers in the first instance to the denial of rights and freedoms to certain minority groups and communities. In the course of time, however, the two words have developed new meanings and implications, for they now refer not only to legal and political systems but also to the attitudes, feelings and opinions of individuals which underlie such systems. In consequence, the term 'intolerance' is now close in meaning to words such as 'bias', 'bigotry', 'hatred', 'hostility', 'meanness', 'narrow-mindedness', 'prejudice', 'racism' and 'xenophobia'. It is frequently used in this wider meaning in the policy documents of international organisations, including not only the Organisation for Security and Co-operation in Europe but also the Council of Europe, the European Commission against Racism and Intolerance, the EU Agency for Fundamental Rights, the Organization of the Islamic Conference and the United Nations. As a concept describing the attitudes and mindsets of individuals, the word 'tolerant' has become increasingly close in meaning to words such as 'fair', 'generous', 'open-minded', 'patient', 'sympathetic' and 'understanding'; the noun 'tolerance', accordingly, implies not just putting up with or enduring opinions different from one's own but also, and more especially, a readiness to engage and interact with such opinions and to learn from them, and to seek ways of living and working with others not only in peaceful coexistence but also in active partnership and cooperation.

'Tolerance', to summarise, has both a narrow and a broad meaning. Narrowly, it refers to permitting. Broadly, it means active readiness to engage and work cooperatively on equal terms. In both its meanings it locates the OSCE's project in the centuries-old and European-wide history of relationships between majorities and minorities with regard to religion. Iconic events in this history include the Edict of Nantes (1598) in France and the law of toleration of all religions (1773) under Catherine the Great in Russia. Within Britain, the terms 'intolerance' and 'tolerance' recall struggles over many centuries for emancipation and civil rights by Jews and Roman Catholics. The OSCE's wide perspective in time and space valuably directs attention to issues of rights, recognition, reasonableness and coexistence.

In the light of the discussions in the previous paragraphs, a broad definition of Islamophobia can be formulated as follows, to explain how the word 'Islamophobia' is used in this book:

> A shorthand term referring to a multifaceted mix of discourse, behaviour and structures which express and perpetuate feelings of anxiety, fear, hostility and rejection towards Muslims, particularly but not only in countries where people of Muslim heritage live as minorities.

The principal manifestations of Islamophobia include: negativity and hostility in the media and the blogosphere, in the publications of certain think-tanks and influence-leaders, and in the speeches and policy proposals of certain political leaders; hate crimes on the streets against both persons and property, and desecration of Muslim cemeteries, cultural centres and religious buildings; harassment, abuse and rudeness ('the unkindness of strangers', as the term might be) in public places; unlawful discrimination in employment practices and the provision of services; non-recognition of Muslim identities and concerns, and removal of Muslim symbols in public space – 'the best Muslim for us is the Muslim we cannot see', as Tariq Ramadan put it in the *Guardian* (29 November 2009); the absence of Muslims from public life, including politics and government, senior positions in business and commerce, and culture and the arts.

Islamophobia, as defined and exemplified above, is similar to the following, but is not in all respects the same:

racism, xenophobia and xenoracism, particularly the forms of racism directed against the communities which migrated to western Europe after the Second World War from the Caribbean, North Africa, South Asia, sub-Saharan Africa and Turkey; towards the communities which formed from 1990 onwards as a result of movements of refugees and people seeking asylum; and the even more recent communities formed by migrant workers within the EU;

prejudices against Arab and other Muslim cultures which developed in the Iberian peninsula and south-east Europe from the eighth century of the common era onwards, linked in due course to orientalism – the ways in which knowledge about Muslims and Islam was constructed and transmitted from about 1750 onwards, both in academia and in popular representations – and the colonisation of most Muslim-majority regions of the world by European powers, including Russia;

the demonising of military and economic rivals, particularly since the first Gulf War and the invasions of Iraq and Afghanistan, and in relation to political and military support for the state of Israel;

fears, insecurities, scapegoating and moral panics relating to national identity which arise essentially from globalisation, multiculturalism and pluralism, not specifically from encounters with Muslims or Islam;

the pursuit, prosecution and punishment of terrorist organisations which claim legitimacy by, in part, using language, symbols and concepts associated with Islam;

critiques of Islamic theology, jurisprudence and political philosophy;

critiques of the human rights records of certain countries where Islam is a feature of the dominant culture.

Of the manifestations of Islamophobia mentioned above, it is negativity in the media (and in particular the press) that is the subject-matter of this book. It is described and illustrated at length in later chapters. First, in this opening chapter, it is relevant to note certain causal and contextual factors that underlie, exacerbate and reinforce Islamophobia but are not Islamophobic in themselves. In particular there is consideration of globalisation, moral panics and the legacy of history. More briefly, there are notes on social exclusion, secularism, the demonising of rivals and the use of Islamic discourse and symbols to justify violent extremism.

Causal, contextual and exacerbating factors

The Commission on the Future of Multi-Ethnic Britain, chaired by Bhikhu Parekh in the period 1998–2000, noted that racisms in the modern world arise in part from what it called the 'unsettling' of nation-states caused by globalisation. The reference was not only or primarily to post-war immigration but to industrial restructuring and consequent unemployment and under-employment; loss of control on the part of national governments in relation to the movement of global capital and investment; the increasing importance of supra-national institutions and the emergence of non-state actors such as al-Qaida in possession of formidable military resources and capacity to mobilise support for their use; the influence of the internet and blogosphere, similarly undermining the capacity of governments and other traditional arbiters to mould hearts and minds; the growth of local identities and loyalties; postmodernism, and moral and social pluralism combined with lack of deference towards tradition and elders; and, not least, the salience of ecological factors which make a mockery of human-made borders and boundaries, and compel cooperation and a *modus vivendi* whether humans like it or not. In unsettled and unsettling situations human beings look around for scapegoats or, in a different metaphor, for lightning conductors with which to name and channel their anxiety and ensuing anger. Muslims are not the causes of the anxieties; they may nevertheless be blamed for them. Liz Fekete refers strikingly to this phenomenon across Europe in the title of her recent book about Islamophobia: *A Suitable Enemy* (2009). Tariq Ramadan, in a discussion of the Swiss referendum on minarets in the *Guardian* (29 November 2009), comments:

> While European countries and citizens are going through a real and deep identity crisis, the new visibility of Muslims is problematic ... At the very moment Europeans find themselves asking, in a globalising, migratory world, 'What are our roots?', 'Who are we?', 'What will our future look like?', they see around them new citizens, new skin colours, new symbols to which they are unaccustomed.

The search for and construction of suitable enemies involves the spreading of moral panic, namely intensity of feeling expressed by a large number of people about a specific group of people who appear to threaten the social order at a given time:

> A condition, episode, person or group of persons emerges to become defined as a threat to societal values and interests; its nature is presented in a stylised and stereotypical fashion by the mass media; the moral barricades are manned by editors, bishops, politicians and other right-thinking people; socially accredited experts pronounce their diagnoses and solutions; ways of coping are evolved or (more often) resorted to; the condition then disappears, submerges or deteriorates and becomes more visible ... [P]ublic concern about a particular condition is generated, a symbolic 'crusade' mounted, which with publicity and actions of certain interest groups, results in ... moral enterprise [or] the creation of a new fragment of the moral constitution of society.

> (Cohen, 2002 [1972]: 1)

Ethical responsibility for journalists lies in seeking to acknowledge and understand anxiety but not pandering to it, not inflaming it into panic, not creating bogey figures. It is in competition with commercial responsibility, however, for consumers of the media enjoy a certain frisson of anxiety – as the authors of chapter 4 of this book note, the news value of a story about Muslims is 'enhanced by the hint of menace'. 'If the media was doing its job,' said a reporter quoted in chapter 10, 'it would help Britain's two million Muslims to be able to develop a kind of reasoned, questioning attitude within itself ... But instead it's far easier and a more potent story to paint a picture of this kind of green peril on your doorsteps.'

Painted as a 'green peril', Muslims are the latest incarnation of folk devils in a lineage which since the 1950s has included teddy boys, mods and rockers, punks, video nasties, recreational drug-taking, yardies, African-Caribbeans, welfare scroungers, dangerous dogs, teenage mothers, trendy teachers, asylum-seekers, Gypsies and travellers, and immigrants of many kinds. Moral panics have some or all of the following features in common:

the construction of folk devils seen as the embodiment of all that is negative and deviant and, in some cases, wholly evil;

criticism of officials in the civil service, local government and public services ('bureaucrats'), in churches and other voluntary sector organisations ('do-gooders' and 'bleeding hearts') and in academia ('ivory towers'), for not understanding the seriousness of threats by which society is apparently faced;

a linking together of apparently disparate threats, implying they have a single cause and all are symptoms of the same underlying malaise;

an increased sense of 'us' and 'them', with no similarities, commonalities or shared interests between the two;

a strengthened sense of self-righteousness and moral indignation in the majority of the population – namely, an idealising of 'us' accompanies, and is reinforced by, the demonising of 'them';

exaggeration, distortion and sensationalism in the media – objective molehills are made into subjective mountains;

a pervasive sense of crisis and collective nightmare, 'one damn thing after another', and of social and cultural change out of control.

And, as a consequence of all the above:
appeals and greater support for more restrictive and punitive laws, and curtailments of civil liberties.

The construction of folk devils is assisted by folk memories. General Henri Gouraud (1867–1946) was the commander of the French army in the Middle East during the First World War and the first governor of Syria and Lebanon under the French mandate. It is said that when he arrived in Damascus in July 1920 he went directly to the Umayyad Mosque and stood at the tomb of Salah al-Din, the inspirational Muslim leader whose armies defeated the Europeans in the Third Crusade. He announced: 'Nous revoilà, Saladin!' – 'We're back, Saladin!' or 'Here we are again!' It is said further that he added: 'My presence here consecrates the Cross over the Crescent.' The story well illustrates the power of folk memories to affect and interpret the present. It does not, however, demonstrate that there is a single unbroken story of mutual animosity, even though frequently over the centuries the Crusades (1095–1291) have been used by both Muslims and non-Muslims as a template that explains essential and supposedly irreconcilable differences between them.

Other iconic events over the centuries which have possessed the power to focus strong feelings of anger and hostility include the Battle of Tours (732), the account of the battle of Roncevaux given in *The Song of Roland* (eleventh century), the rise of the Ottoman Turks as an imperial power and the conquest of Constantinople (1453) and the siege of Vienna (1529), the Reconquista, and the European (including Russian) empires of the eighteenth and nineteenth centuries leading in due course to wars and movements against them of resistance, liberation and decolonisation. Modern Islamophobia is not merely a continuation of previous antagonisms. It does, however, use imagery and ideas from them, and is strengthened by them.

In addition to anxieties about national identity and security arising from globalisation, factors affecting the development and influence of modern Islamophobia include the following:

A high proportion of Muslim communities in European countries where they have settled relatively recently are affected by poverty, unemployment and social exclusion. Intolerance against Muslims is in part generated by a desire to justify or excuse this state of affairs. To say this is to recall a famous dictum about the history of racism: 'Slavery was not born of racism. Rather, racism was the consequence of slavery.' It can happen that negative attitudes are sometimes generated by the desire to explain and justify unequal power relations and discriminatory practices, but are not themselves the main cause of inequalities and discrimination.

The electoral success of political parties that use anti-Muslim slogans and messages in their propaganda may mean that more mainstream parties fail to distance themselves explicitly and in a high-profile way from such intolerance against Muslims. There is a lack of political will to address their concerns, and insufficient attention is paid in race equality programmes, organisations and activities to the specific features and consequences of intolerance against Muslims.

It frequently happens in times of war that states demonise their enemies and idealise themselves, in order to mobilise public opinion in their own country. The invasions of Iraq and Afghanistan, for example, have been in part justified within the general climate of public opinion by claims about Islam as a threat.

Muslim citizens, particularly those belonging to the younger generation, may feel demoralised and depressed, for they see no future for themselves in the society in which they were born. Human beings have a basic need for self-confidence, self-respect and self-esteem. The sources of these are relationships with others, and the perceptions of oneself that one receives from others. Disrespect and intolerance from wider society can lead to feelings of alienation, disaffection and anger among young Muslims, and these in their turn may lead or contribute to educational failure and to unemployment. Such feelings are exacerbated if there is a perceived or real bias in employment opportunities, and also if there is a perceived or real bias in criminal justice systems, with the consequence that

Muslims are more likely than non-Muslims to be stopped, questioned and searched by police officers, and if they are perceived to receive harsher punishments than non-Muslims for similar offences.

Muslim citizens or residents are prevented from playing a full part in the political, cultural and economic activities of their societies. This not only has consequent disadvantages for themselves, as mentioned above, but also for society more generally. For example, Muslim approaches to personal, moral and social life do not get an adequate hearing. Democratic debates, critical thinking and dialogue about mutual understanding and common citizenship are rendered increasingly difficult. It is difficult for Muslim communities to engage in self-criticism, particularly in public.

A significant minority of young Muslims may be attracted, because of their disaffection and sense of injustice, towards violent extremism. At the same time government measures to win 'the hearts and minds' of Muslim communities in the overall tasks of preventing violent extremism, may be hindered.

Concluding note

In autumn 2009 a referendum in Switzerland called for the banning of minarets. 'What is happening in Switzerland,' asked Tariq Ramadan in the *Guardian* (29 November 2009), 'the land of my birth?' After all, he mused, there are only four minarets in Switzerland – 'so why is it that it is there that this initiative has been launched?' He continued:

Every European country has its specific symbols or topics through which European Muslims are targeted. In France it is the headscarf or burka; in Germany, mosques; in Britain, violence; cartoons in Denmark; homosexuality in the Netherlands – and so on. It is important to look beyond these symbols and understand what is really happening in Europe in general and in Switzerland in particular: while European countries and citizens are going through a real and deep identity crisis, the new visibility of Muslims is problematic – and it is scary.

The campaign against the minarets, commented Ramadan, was fuelled by just these anxieties and allegations. Voters were drawn to the cause by a manipulative appeal to popular fears and emotions. For example, posters featured a woman wearing a burka with the minarets drawn as weapons on a Swiss flag. The claim was made that Islam is fundamentally incompatible with Swiss values. 'The Swiss majority', said Ramadan, 'are sending a clear message to their Muslim fellow citizens: we do not trust you and the best Muslim for us is the Muslim we cannot see.'

The stand-up comedian Ken Dodd used to observe sadly sometimes in his act that what he likes about the British is that they are not foreigners. Such world-weariness can raise a wry smile. But differences of nationality and language, as also differences of age, gender, ethnicity and social class, are inescapable. Human beings never exist outside cultural and social locations, and therefore outside situations and relationships of unequal power, and outside historical circumstances. No one is totally unaccommodated – or, it follows, unaccommodating. On the contrary, everyone is embedded in a cultural tradition and in a period of history, and in a system of unequal power relations. Everyone, therefore, is engaged in unending tasks and struggles to accommodate and adjust to others. How talk and text in the media help modern societies to understand and to live with differences of perception and of value-system is crucial. The Ken Dodd response to such differences is certainly beguiling. But removing differences of perception and values from the world is psychologically not beneficial, morally not desirable and politically not possible. Demonisation is not an option.

2

Big Pictures and Daily Details

The Content and Form of Narratives

Robin Richardson

Histories and stories

The West's war against terror, wrote the defence correspondent of the *Daily Telegraph* in October 2001, 'belongs within the much larger spectrum of a far older conflict between settled, creative productive Westerners and predatory, destructive Orientals'. On 11 September, he said, 'the Oriental tradition … returned in an absolutely traditional form. Arabs, appearing suddenly out of empty space like their desert raider ancestors, assaulted the heartlands of Western power, in a terrifying surprise raid'. His words were a vivid and dramatic summary of the way the Western media both reflected and shaped how the events of 9/11 were seen.

It is frequently the case, both for those who report events and for those who read or hear about them in the media, that something seems to erupt suddenly from empty space, or as if from a desert where normally nothing happens, nothing ever grows. Always metaphorically, and sometimes – as in September 2001 – literally, such events are experienced as surprise raids. The first priority for the human mind, when confronted with a surprise raid, is to place it within a narrative, so that it is connected to more familiar experiences and begins to make sense, and so that any further such events can be better anticipated, and actions to deal with them are maximally effective. In this instance a key element in the narrative is that 'predatory, destructive Orientals' are intrinsically violent and have no reason, other than that they are intrinsically violent, for acting in hostile or defensive ways towards the West. The narrative is about relationships and comparisons, it is important to note, not just about so-called Orientals – it is about 'us-and-them', as the term might be, not simply about 'them'.

In relation to 'the West' and 'the Muslim world' there is a range of competing and overlapping narratives. (Inverted commas signal that both terms are shorthand for immensely complex and variegated realities. Also, the realities are interrelated and reciprocally affect each other. Picturing the world as consisting largely of two large monolithic entities with little or nothing in common is arguably part of the problem.) A narrative, it can be said, consists of a history on the one hand and a collection of stories on the other. In a different metaphor, there is a big picture and a set of vivid details. This chapter continues with consideration of the distinction between history and story. Then, based broadly on an idea first mooted by a historian of contemporary events (Timothy Garton Ash, in the *Guardian*, 15 September 2005), it notes eight competing big pictures of us-and-them and focuses on two of these pictures in particular. In relation to these two, it delineates what it calls the default position, namely the assumptions that are taken for granted unless a conscious effort is made to alter them, in the media's portrayal of relationships – both international and intra-national – between 'the West' on the one hand and Muslim countries and communities on the other. Next, it cites several opinion surveys conducted in Western countries in recent years which show that the default position is widespread. It draws to an end by considering the principal components of an alternative narrative about 'the West' and 'the Muslim world', and by considering the *form* of narratives as distinct from their content.

Histories

A history, as the term implies, is an account of how we got to where we are; it explains or seeks to explain patterns of cause and effect, and who or what is to blame. It provides a stock of metaphors, analogies and vivid imagery, as in the extract about 9/11 cited above, and a recurring concern is to establish – again, as in the example cited above – the distinctive features of 'us' and 'them', self and other, insider and outsider, allies and enemies, victims and aggressors, those who 'really' belong in our society or civilisation and those who do not (Ansari, 2004; Philo and Berry, 2004; van Dijk, 2000). Further, histories recall glories to inspire, humiliations to avenge, acts of heroism and martyrdom to be emulated and grievances to redress. Even more significantly, they provide explanations and justifications for current policies and actions – it is not rare, as is well known, for histories to be revisited and revised, to align them to new concerns, intentions and programmes in the present. A history, therefore, is not only about the past, for it shapes expectations of what is likely to happen next. In a familiar metaphor, it helps build a radar system on the look-out for anomalies and threats in the objective world. If the sense of history is inaccurate, there is a danger that practical policies in the present will be self-defeating. In the current context this has been acknowledged implicitly, and to an extent explicitly, in major speeches by Western leaders (Miliband, 2009; Obama, 2009), by the House of Commons Communities and Local Government Committee (2010), and by the Leadership Group on US–Muslim Engagement (2009 [2008]).

Stories, in the sense the word is being used here, are individual items in newspapers and on TV and radio. They are interesting in themselves but also help to keep histories and big pictures alive. Some – most, indeed – come and go: they are here today, gone tomorrow. Some, though, run for two or three days, or for a bit longer, particularly if they move from one paper to another, and backwards and forwards between print media, TV and radio. Some stories, most certainly, are so momentous and so obviously true that they are incorporated overnight into history – 9/11, obviously, and 7/7. But most are not at all as momentous as those. Most illustrate and recall history, in the manner of a vivid case study – they revivify and reinforce history, but they do not enter it, except in the minds and memories of the individuals most directly affected, or if there's something about the story that causes particular individuals continually to return to it in their minds' eyes and ears, and to dwell on it. 'I cannot forget', writes a newspaper columnist, 'the story of the Brownie leader in Bradford who was stoned in the street by Asian youths who snarled "Christian bitch" at her' (Peter Hitchens, in the *Mail on Sunday*, 11 July 2004).

Through its sense of history and its stock of vivid case studies a narrative handles four questions: What's the problem? What's the background? What's the solution? What do we want? The last of these is about our notion of the good life, and the kind of society that nourishes the good life. The questions are asked both implicitly and explicitly. With regard to the first of these questions ('What's the problem?') Timothy Garten Ash suggested in the above-mentioned *Guardian* article there are six principal narratives or perspectives – six big pictures – in competition with each other in relation to the West and Islam. They are not, he stresses, mutually exclusive. On the contrary, there are overlaps among them and in practice, for any one person at any one time, the narrative they find most plausible is likely to be complemented and qualified by at least one of the others. It is logically impossible, however, for someone to operate with all six with equal assurance. Introducing the six narratives, he said:

> Four years after the 11 September 2001 terrorist attacks on New York and Washington, which were perpetrated in the name of Allah, most people living in what we still loosely call the west would agree that we do have troubles with Islam. The vast majority of Muslims are not terrorists, but most of the terrorists who threaten us claim to be Muslims. Most countries with a Muslim majority show a resistance to what Europeans and Americans generally view as desirable modernity, including the essentials of liberal democracy. Why? What's

the nub of the problem? Here are six different views often heard in the west, but also, it's important to add, in Muslim countries ... As you go down the list, you might like to put a mental tick against the view you most strongly agree with. It's logically possible to put smaller ticks against a couple of others, but not against them all.

Briefly summarised, and with additional brief comments, the six narratives are set out below, together with two more.

1. *Religion.* The problem is religion in general, which is merely ignorance, superstition and wishful thinking. The sooner human beings stop being religious the safer the world will be.

2. *Islam.* The problem is a particular religion: Islam. It is backward, barbaric and intolerant and supports the oppression of women. Islam is stuck in the Middle Ages. It needs a reformation, based on science and modern thinking.

3. *Islamism.* The problem is Islamism, namely an interpretation of Islam that has its intellectual roots in organisations such as the Muslim Brotherhood founded in Egypt after the First World War and subsequently developed by Sayyid Qutb in Egypt and Maulana Maududi in Pakistan. Alternative phrases or words instead of Islamism include political, militant or radical Islam; Islamic activism; Qutbism; jihadism; extremism; and fundamentalism. Islamism is a political ideology of hate.

4. *West Asia/Middle East.* The problem lies in the specific history of West Asia, particularly the history of Arab nations. Key events and factors of the last 100 years include the Sykes–Picot Agreement of 1916 for the dismemberment of the Ottoman Empire, the Balfour Declaration and in due course the creation of the state of Israel, processes of decolonisation and globalisation, tensions and conflicts within and between Arab countries and between Arab countries and Iran, the Sunni/Shi'a rift, and the emergence of oil-rich economies.

5. *The West.* The problem is 'the West'. From the Crusades to colonisation, and from moral and military support for Israel to the recent invasions and occupations of Afghanistan and Iraq, Western powers have oppressed Muslim countries and cultures, and have developed forms of anti-Muslim hostility, Islamophobia and orientalism in order to justify their own behaviour. This has provoked, understandably, much bitterness and anti-Western hostility in return.

6. *Alienation.* The problem lies in the alienation of young people of Muslim heritage born and educated in European countries. They are marginalised and excluded by processes of religious and racist discrimination, and demoralised and depressed by the torrent of anti-Muslim stereotypes they see in the media. Some turn to an ideology of nihilism and terrorism, intermixed with Islamism (see above), as a rhetoric of self-justification.

7. *Conflicts of material interest.* The problem is not in the first instance to do with differences of culture, religion, ideology or civilization. Rather, it is to do with conflicts of material interest. Globally, the key conflicts are around power, influence, territory and resources, particularly oil. Within urban areas in Europe they are around employment, housing, health and education. Such conflicts become 'religionised' or 'culturalised' – each side celebrates and idealises its own traditions and cultural heritage, including religion, and denigrates and demonises the traditions of the other.

8. *Anxieties about national identity and security.* The attacks on 9/11 were a vivid reminder that the governments of nation-states – even of extremely powerful nation-states, most notably the United States – are unable to guarantee the security of their citizens. At the same time they cannot control, to the extent that they did in the past, economic, cultural and ecological borders. The resulting insecurities lead to scapegoating and moral panics, with Muslims as a convenient target, but not the real cause.

Of the eight big pictures summarised above, it is the second ('the problem is Islam') and the third ('the problem is Islamism') that are dominant in the media as a whole, though with different nuances between and within different papers, programmes and channels. Garton Ash comments that sometimes what is said in so many words is not necessarily the same as what a speaker really thinks. Nor is it necessarily what they intended to say, or what is actually heard and understood by others. Of the third big picture, for example ('the problem is Islamism, not Islam'), he says that this is the official view of George Bush and Tony Blair, but continues:

> Well, they would say that, wouldn't they? They're not going to insult millions of Muslim voters and the foreign countries upon which the west relies for its imported oil. But do they really believe it? I have my doubts. Put them on a truth serum, and I bet they'd be closer to 2 ['the problem is Islam'].

In countries where Muslims live as minorities, there are certain recurring stereotypes in the general climate of anti-Muslim opinion. Sometimes these are expressed outright. Often, however, they are simply assumed and taken for granted, part of common sense. So to speak, they are the default position which is widely assumed if it is not explicitly denied. Six of the most frequent sets of negative stereotypes in the default position are as follows:

1. *All the same.* Muslims are seen as all much the same as each other, regardless of their ethnicity, nationality, social class, geographical location and political outlook, and regardless of how observant and religiously oriented they are, or are not. With regard to terrorism and violent extremism, for example, it is imagined there is a 'slippery slope' between moderates and extremists, with even the most moderate Muslims being potential extremists.
2. *All religiously motivated.* It is thought that the single most important thing about a 'Muslim' is that he or she has certain

religious beliefs and engages in certain religious practices. Accordingly, it is thought that everything a Muslim does is motivated by religion. So if a Muslim engages in violence, for example, this must be because their religion advocates violence. If a Muslim-majority country is economically backward or abuses human rights this too, it is thought, must be much more due to the prevailing religious tradition of the country than to any other factor.

3. *All totally other.* Muslims are seen as totally other – they have few or no interests, characteristics, needs, concerns or values in common with non-Muslims, and this was as true in the past as it is in the present. In short, the values of Muslims and non-Muslims are incompatible with each other. Among other things, this means Muslims are not seen as possessing any relevant and valuable insights, perspectives and achievements from which non-Muslims may learn and benefit.

4. *All inferior.* Muslims are seen as culturally, intellectually, politically and morally inferior to non-Muslims – quick to take offence, prone to irrationality and violence, hypocritical in the practice of their religion, sexist and oppressive in their treatment of women, homophobic in their views of sexual identities, intolerant towards worldviews different from their own, fundamentalist and narrow-minded, disinclined or unable to engage in reasoned debate, and hostile and full of hate towards 'the West' for no good reason. It is allegedly a sign of Muslim inferiority and backwardness that the governments of certain Muslim-majority countries have little respect for democracy and human rights, and that economic and social development has been slight. The only language Muslims understand, it is said, is the language of force and violence.

5. *All a threat.* Muslims are seen as a threat to non-Muslims. Globally, they may attack non-Muslim countries, as on 9/11, and they are a threat to the existence of Israel. Within non-Muslim countries they are a treacherous and disloyal fifth

column or enemy within, in active collusion or tacit sympathy with international terrorism, engaged in a clash of civilisations and in a global conspiracy and jihad against 'the
West'. In addition, they are a threat to non-Muslim cultures,
societies and values, intending the 'Islamisation' of Europe
and turning the continent into 'Eurabia'. Further, it is
claimed they are a demographic time-bomb, and will fairly
soon be a numerical majority in certain European cities and
countries.

6. *All impossible to work with*. As a consequence of the previous
   five perceptions, it is believed there is no possibility of cooperation and partnership between 'them' and 'us', Muslims
   and non-Muslims, working as equals on tasks that require
   mediation, negotiation, compromise and partnership.

The six assumptions listed above are sometimes articulated entirely
explicitly. A particularly vivid example came in an article published
in summer 2004 under the pseudonym of 'Will Cummins' in the
Sunday Telegraph. Cummins' principal claim was that all Muslims are
the same and that all are different from non-Muslims. He chose,
however, to express these claims by saying that all Muslims are the
same in the sense that all dogs are the same. This example inevitably
implied, even though logically it did not inherently entail, the claim
that Muslims are inferior to non-Muslims, a lower order of being.
Not all people who broadly share the underlying assumptions listed
above would approve of the offensive and extreme form of self-
expression Cummins used:

All Muslims, like all dogs, share certain characteristics. A dog is
not the same animal as a cat just because both species are comprised of different breeds. An extreme Christian believes that
the Garden of Eden really existed; an extreme Muslim flies
planes into buildings – there's a big difference.

(*Sunday Telegraph*, 25 July 2004)

29

Another strong statement that all Muslims are the same and all are different from non-Muslims is to be found in Samuel Huntington's influential book *The Clash of Civilizations*. 'The underlying problem for the West,' he writes, 'is not Islamic fundamentalism. It is Islam, a different civilization whose people are convinced of the superiority of their culture and are obsessed with the inferiority of their power' (Huntington, 1996: 217–18). A more recent and even more virulent expression of the view that there is a continuum or slippery slope between so-called moderates and so-called extremists. appeared in autumn 2009 in an article published in the United States (cited in Kumar, 2010). Recalling the vivid American phrase 'going postal', describing the phenomenon of violent rage in which a worker – archetypically a postal worker – suddenly snaps and guns down his colleagues, the author proposed a new phrase should be coined, 'going Muslim'. It would describe 'the turn of events where a seemingly integrated Muslim-American – a friendly donut vendor in New York, say, or an officer in the U.S. Army at Fort Hood – discards his apparent integration into American society and elects to vindicate his religion in an act of messianic violence against his fellow Americans.' The article continued:

> The difference between 'going postal', in the conventional sense, and 'going Muslim', in the sense that I suggest, is that there would not necessarily be a psychological 'snapping' point in the case of the imminently violent Muslim; instead, there could be a calculated discarding of camouflage – the camouflage of integration – in an act of revelatory catharsis.

To repeat, such explicit and virulent expressions of anti-Muslim hostility are rare in the mainstream media. They are to be found in the propaganda of certain political parties, however, claiming that 'Western' values such as freedom of speech, democracy and rights for women are incompatible with Islam, that Islam is a cancer eating away at Western freedoms and democracy, and that there are similarities between the Qur'an and Nazi literature. Explicit statements of the six themes are also widespread on websites and in the blogo-sphere, on radio chat-shows and phone-in programmes, in the pub-lications of certain think-tanks, and in responses to opinion polls and surveys. They are generally implicit rather than explicit throughout the print media, and on radio and television. A Manichean view of human affairs – the notion that all of life is a cosmic battle between good and evil, heroes and villains – is celebrated in much popular fiction (Al-Shaikh-Ali, 2009), and throughout comics and computer games. So are many other hard-and-fast, black-and-white distinc-tions and dichotomies. Such views give strength and credence to many kinds of hostility and distrust, including hostility and distrust towards Muslims.

Within the context of the six themes summarised above, more specific allegations are made about British Muslims, and more gener-ally about Muslims elsewhere in Europe. The principal allegations include the following:

Failure to integrate. Muslims do not wish to integrate into European societies, it is said, but prefer to live in separate, self-segregated communities and neighbourhoods. Failure to integrate leads to failure in the educational system and failure to obtain economic well-being. There is in consequence much bitterness and a deep sense of alienation, a victim mentality, and a false, self-deceiving perception that mainstream society is unjust and Islamophobic. These feelings and perceptions then lead to additional failure in education and employment, and the vicious spiral continues.

Unreasonable demands. Muslims are accused of making unreasonable demands on European societies, expecting the Judeo-Christian traditions of these societies to be modified, changed or jettisoned so they won't be offended or inconvenienced. Among other mat-ters, the demands are about dress codes in public places (particu-larly the burka, which seems to symbolise antagonism to the state and to established customs of openness), the building of mosques in towns and cities, the use of community languages in public, the establishment of faith schools and after-school religious classes.

31

Mixed loyalties. Muslims in Europe supposedly owe their principal loyalty to the worldwide *Ummah*, not to the country where they live. They therefore cannot be depended on to support their country's foreign policies, or even its sports teams. In relation to international situations, for example in Iraq, Israel/Palestine and Afghanistan, they are a fifth column or enemy within.

Support for extremism. The sense of alienation and lack of loyalty mentioned above are believed to combine to make Muslim communities in Europe a breeding ground for extremism. It is true that only a small minority of them actually engage in acts of violence but there is a general climate of tacit support and sympathy for extreme measures, whether these are committed within Europe or elsewhere. In well-known metaphors, 'ordinary' Muslims constitute the pond in which extremists swim, and the hinterland from which they emerge. All Muslims are on a single continuum, at one end of which there is readiness to support, or even to engage in, terrorist acts.

Obscurantism. It is claimed that Islamic theology has never gone through the kinds of critical review and reformation that were the hallmarks of the Enlightenment in Europe. Scriptures are not subjected to textual criticism; doctrines and moral teachings are not seen in historical context; multiple interpretations of a text are not acceptable; received tradition is paramount.

Incompatibility of values and interests. Islam and the West are seen as incompatible in terms of moral values and are locked in a zero-sum struggle for power and control. At the global level there is a clash of civilisations and at local levels Muslims and non-Muslims cannot live and work harmoniously and constructively together, other than in relatively superficial ways. Muslims subvert local democracy: in Britain's northern cities, for example, through manipulating *biraderi* kinship networks. They are misogynist and homophobic, use repressive educational methods in their mosques and madrasahs, and are opposed to all things Western.

Lack of Muslim leadership. Religious leaders such as imams, and secular leaders such as office-holders in Muslim organisations, are said to be out of touch with the people they are supposed to guide and represent, particularly young people. They are insufficiently vocal and proactive in condemning extremism and in encouraging integration into mainstream society. Some even glorify extremism and terrorism. All or most are in denial about the presence and growth of extremism in their communities and do not see that theirs is the principal responsibility for removing it. The few who might be inclined to speak out on these issues are in fact frightened to do so, because of the opposition they would encounter from most other Muslims.

Corroborating evidence from overseas. The perceptions listed above are about Muslims *within* Europe. They gain additional persuasiveness and plausibility, however, from how Muslims *outside* Europe are described as behaving – their hatred of the West, abuse of human rights, use of barbaric punishments, intolerance of debate and disagreement, glorification of martyrdom, antisemitism, plans to create a worldwide caliphate, obscurantist religion, and support for terrorism and insurgency. These features of Muslim societies and cultures combine with beliefs that they are culturally and morally superior to the West, which they see as corrupt, shallow, and in need of being converted to, and reshaped in accordance with, Islam.

Weak national governments. The threats posed by Muslims, outlined above, are made even more serious by the failures of successive European governments, and by metropolitan intelligentsias, particularly in London. In the 1950s and 1960s governments did not foresee the dangers of permitting immigration from cultures so different from their own. More recently, governments have consistently failed to police and protect their borders effectively and do not appreciate the severe dangers posed by Islam in general and Islamism in particular. They have also failed to insist on full assimilation and integration, while promoting multiculturalism, political correctness, cultural relativism and the nanny state. Some of these failures have been exacerbated by the human rights legislation that governments have introduced against the interests of

Europe's majority populations. The overall effect has been to appease Muslims rather than to oppose and control them.

How widespread are these perceptions and allegations among non-Muslims? And in which social classes and socio-economic circumstances are they most prevalent, and by what other views are they typically accompanied? Professionally conducted opinion polls provide a useful guide to, though not a definitive and quantified description of, the climate of opinion in a society at any one time. There are inevitable sampling errors, and the ways in which questions are phrased, and the circumstances in which they are asked, can make the results difficult to interpret. A further problem is that respondents may be inclined to give what they consider to be the 'right' answer rather than to say what they really think. Despite these and similar practical problems, however, opinion polls yield a valuable broad overview. A range of key findings is reviewed below.

Most recently, at the time of writing, the annual survey of British social attitudes shows widespread hostility towards Islam in Britain (National Centre for Social Research, 2010). 'Social class, sex and race may be objectively more important,' it concludes, 'but religion – and particularly Islam – now appears to provoke more anxiety than these other traditional distinctions'. Specific findings included:

A large proportion of the country believes that the multicultural experiment has failed, with 52 per cent considering that Britain is deeply divided along religious lines and 45 per cent saying that religious diversity has had a negative impact.

Only a quarter of Britons feel positive towards Muslims, while more than a third report feeling 'cool' towards them.

People are becoming intolerant towards all religions because of the degree to which Islam is perceived as a threat to social cohesion.

This apparent threat to national identity (or even, some fear, to security) reduces the willingness to accommodate free expression.

Respondents with no qualifications were twice as likely to have negative attitudes towards Muslims as those who had degrees.

There is a high level of unease regarding the UK's Muslim population, estimated at around two million, with many people considering that it poses a threat to the nation's identity.

While 55 per cent say that they would be 'bothered' by the construction of a large mosque in their community, only fifteen per cent
would be similarly concerned by a large church.

A study of 104 separate public opinion polls in the UK conducted
between 1998 and 2006 came to the following conclusions (Field,
2007):

Although people in the UK are still far from seeing all or most Muslims
as terrorists or terrorist sympathisers, the proportion inclining to
this position appears to have doubled since July 2005, standing in
2006 at around one in five. Muslims' dual loyalties to Britain and
to Islam are perceived by many as increasingly in potential conflict,
those holding this view having doubled from 2001 to reach forty-
one per cent in 2006. The proportion perceiving Islam to be a
threat to Western liberal democracy has also climbed steeply, from
thirty-two per cent in 2001 to fifty-three per cent in 2006.

Taking a cross-section of attitudinal measures, somewhere between
one in five and one in four Britons now exhibit a strong dislike
of, and prejudice against, Islam and Muslims.

Certain demographic groups have been consistently prone to demonstrate more negative views towards Islam and Muslims than
others. This has been particularly true of men as distinct from
women, the DE social class, the oldest age cohort (not least pen-
sioners) and Conservative voters. The most positive have been
women, the AB social group, the youngest age cohort (under 30)
and Liberal Democrats.

For all segments of the population negative or positive views cor-
relate strongly with the amount of knowledge of Islam and of direct
contact that people have with Muslims: the greater the knowledge
and familiarity, the lower the level of prejudice, and vice versa.

This was also one of the findings of a large-scale study of young people in Sweden (Bevelander and Otterbeck, 2008). It is relevant in this regard to note that a study of 150 local authorities in England in 2009 showed that support for the British National Party (BNP), which campaigns not only against immigration in general but against the 'Islamification' of Britain in particular, was highest in areas where there are below-average numbers of recent immigrants. The research did not look at attitudes towards Muslims in particular, but its findings and conclusions are almost certainly relevant in the current context:

> Our findings suggest that areas that have higher levels of recent immigration than others are not more likely to vote for the BNP. In fact, the more immigration an area has experienced, the lower its support for the far right. It seems that direct contact with migrants dissuades people from supporting the BNP … The evidence points to political and socio-economic exclusion as drivers of BNP support. In particular, areas with low average levels of [educational] qualifications (which can mean people struggle in today's flexible, knowledge-based economy), low levels of social cohesion, and low levels of voter turnout (indicating political disenchantment) are the ones that show more BNP support.
>
> (Institute for Public Policy Research, 2010: 2)

The form of narratives – open and closed ways of thinking and relating

The dominant narratives outlined earlier in this chapter were described with regard to their content. But their form also needs attention – the way views are formulated, presented and argued. The journalist Peregrine Worsthorne once claimed that Islam was 'once a great civilisation worthy of being argued with' but now 'has degenerated into a primitive enemy fit only to be sensitively subjugated' (*Sunday Telegraph*, 3 February 1991). He made two distinctions in this claim, the one to do with content ('great civilisation'/ 'primitive enemy') and the other with regard to forms of thinking and relating ('argued with'/'subjugated'). To see an individual or a group or a civilisation as 'worthy of being argued with' is necessarily to be open-minded towards them. The hallmarks of open-mindedness include:

readiness to change one's views, both of others and of oneself, in the light of new facts and evidence;

not deliberately distorting, or recklessly over-simplifying, incontestable facts;

not caricaturing the views of people with whom one disagrees;

not over-generalising;

not being abusive when arguing, for example not claiming that one's opponents are evil or insane or sub-human;

not using double standards when comparing and contrasting others with oneself;

seeing difference and disagreement as a resource for understanding more about oneself, not as a threat;

seeking to understand other people's views and standpoints in their own terms, and where they are coming from – the narratives and stories with which they interpret events;

not claiming greater certainty than is warranted;

seeking consensus or, at least, a *modus vivendi* which keeps channels of communication open and permits all to maintain dignity.

Milton Rokeach's (1960) distinction between the open and the closed mind was concerned with developing attitudes and inclinations such as those listed above. His open/closed distinction was used by the Commission on British Muslims and Islamophobia (1997) in its discussion of views on 'the West' and 'Islam', and subsequently revised by the Commission on the Future of Multi-Ethnic Britain (2000) to evaluate all representations of self and other. The key issues include:

whether the other is seen as monolithic, static and authoritarian, or as diverse and dynamic with substantial internal debates;

whether the other is divided into two broad categories, good and bad, moderate and extreme, or whether multi-faceted complexity, both in the present and the past, is recognised and attended to;

whether the other is seen as totally separate from the self, or as both similar and interdependent, sharing a common humanity and history, and a common space;

whether the other is seen as an aggressive and devious enemy to be feared, opposed and defeated, or as a cooperative partner with whom to work on shared problems, locally, nationally and internationally;

whether the other's criticisms of the self are rejected out of hand or whether they are considered and debated;

whether double standards are applied in descriptions and criticisms of the other and the self, or whether criticisms are even-handed.

At an admittedly high level of abstraction, these are key questions for consideration of all media portrayals of the 'Muslim world' and 'the West' and, more especially, of relationships between them.

Concluding note

'There is a difference', wrote Edward Said in the 2003 Preface to his magisterial *Orientalism*, first published in 1978:

> between knowledge of other peoples and other times that is the result of understanding, compassion, careful study and analysis for their own sakes, and on the other hand knowledge – if that is what it is – that is part of an overall campaign of self-affirmation, belligerency and outright war. There is, after all, a profound difference between the will to understand for purposes of co-existence and humanistic enlargement of horizons, and the will to dominate for the purposes of control and external domination.

(2003: xiv)

The difference to which he referred corresponds to the distinction outlined here between open and closed ways of relating and engaging. He continued by urging 'that the terrible reductive conflicts that herd people under falsely unifying rubrics like "America", "The West" or "Islam" and invent collective identities for large numbers of individuals who are actually quite diverse, cannot remain as potent as they are, and must be opposed, their murderous effectiveness vastly reduced in influence and mobilising power.'

He concluded with words that are particularly relevant to the role and responsibility of the media in modern societies, and to analysis of the narratives, histories and stories which they tell, and the big pictures and daily details which they set forth:

> Rather than the manufactured clash of civilisations, we need to concentrate on the slow working together of cultures that overlap, borrow from each other, and live together in far more interesting ways than any abridged or inauthentic mode of understanding can allow. But for that kind of wider perception we need time and patient and sceptical inquiry, supported by communities of interpretation that are difficult to sustain in a world demanding instant action and reaction.

3

Images of Islam in the UK

The Representation of British Muslims in the National Press, 2000–8

Justin Lewis, Paul Mason and Kerry Moore[1]

Edward Said's well-known work on 'orientalism' explored the portrayal of Islam and the Arab world in Western culture, and found a deeply embedded set of negative stereotypes that invariably positioned Islam as antagonistic – symbolically or literally – towards the West. Islam thereby comes to be understood as intrinsically threatening:

> The idea that Islam is medieval and dangerous, as well as hostile and threatening to 'us', for example, has acquired a place both in the culture and in the polity that is very well defined … Such an idea furnishes a kind of *a priori* touchstone to be taken account of by anyone wishing to discuss or say something about Islam.

> (1997: 157)

Since the publication of *Orientalism*, a number of academic studies have focused on more contemporary representations of Islam and of

Muslims in the news media. This research generally echoes Said, suggesting that the kinds of stories told about Muslims – and that seem to 'ring true' or to 'make sense' *as news* – are limited, negative and stereotypical (Macdonald, 2003; Said, 1997).

The volume of news coverage featuring Muslims has increased dramatically since the terrorist attacks of 2001 (Whitaker, 2002). More recent scholarship has suggested that the news media tend to position Islam as a threat to security, to 'our way of life', and to reproduce 'common sense' ideas which position the religious and cultural values of Muslims and those of 'mainstream' British society in a relation of conflict (Commission on British Muslims and Islamophobia, 1997; Insted, 2007; Poole, 2002, 2006; Richardson, 2004). Poole (2002, 2006) found that the majority of coverage featuring Muslims in the British press focuses upon global events – for example in relation to the Taliban in Afghanistan, the conflict in the Middle East or the 2003 war in Iraq – which tends to entail a regular association of Muslims with situations of conflict and violence.

When coverage of Muslims is domestically orientated, studies have indicated that the 'framework of reporting' has also usually led to an emphasis upon violence and conflict (Insted, 2007; Richardson, 2004). Poole's study of the print news media in 2003, for example, found that the main topics associated with Muslims were 'terrorism', 'politics' and 'reactions to the war in Iraq' (2006). News media coverage, these studies suggested, has focused upon social tensions, raised questions about the 'loyalty' and 'belonging' of Muslims living in Britain, and emphasised concepts such as 'integration' and 'social cohesion' as pressing political issues.

A growing body of evidence suggests that Muslims themselves consider the news media to 'misrepresent' or to represent them unfairly and to be an important factor contributing to discrimination and/or a lack of understanding between communities (Ahmed, 1992; Ameli et al., 2007; Fekete, 2006; Weller et al., 2001). At the same time, evidence from the Home Office and independent research suggests that violence and discrimination towards Muslims, already significant before 11 September 2001, has indeed palpably increased since that date (Allen and Nielsen, 2002; Fekete, 2006; Weller et al., 2001). However, while the news media are often cited as a likely contributor to the tensions and hostilities that Muslims experience, it is very difficult to establish the extent to which it is directly responsible for constructing them.

As Said demonstrated, menacing images of Islam run throughout the culture, and the news media are just one site of representation that constructs ideas about Muslims in Britain. We would nonetheless contend that it is an important one. Journalism specifically seeks to persuade its audience that a particular version of events is the most meaningful or 'true' one, including expressions of opinion which are 'embedded in argumentation that makes them more or less defensible, reasonable, justifiable or legitimate as conclusions' (van Dijk quoted in Richardson, 2004: 227). Print journalism in particular has an important determining role in the circulation of news, contributing to broadcast news agenda-setting practices (Gross et al., 2007). Furthermore, newspapers serve as a forum for communication between political and other elites in ways that potentially influence the political and policy agenda (Davis, 2003). However, journalists and the news media do not operate in a cultural and political vacuum. Like the rest of us, they function within and make sense of the world through existing frameworks of understanding. Journalists may have more influence than ordinary people upon a dominant public discourse which continues to articulate Muslims as potentially threatening and 'other' to mainstream British society, but they nonetheless remain constrained by it, as well as by the professional and institutional structures within which they work.

In this chapter we examine print media representations of British Muslims and Islam in Britain. Since discussions about representation can often get bogged down in claims – and counter-claims – about context or typicality, we have tried to apply aspects of a more discursive analysis to a large sample, based on a systematic analysis of national print media content in Britain between 2000 and 2008. We are mindful that previous research in the field exploring 'orientalist' portrayals provides an important context for our study, but we have approached the research with minds open to the prospect that our findings may or may not corroborate the prevailing view among scholars that media coverage of Islam is negative and stereotypical. Moreover, since this research was commissioned to inform a Channel 4 television documentary,[2] we are also conscious that the research undertaken for this chapter not only analyses press coverage of Muslims in Britain but also contributes to the production of further media coverage in this area. We hope that our research and its dissemination in this forum will help to highlight some important and challenging issues regarding print media representations of Islam, and contribute to an informed debate about the role of the media in general in constructing ideas about Muslims in Britain.

Methodology

The sample for the analysis was gathered from the Nexis database of British newspapers. The use of the Nexis database has limits – keyword searches are indicative rather than comprehensive – and thus most of our analysis is based on a more detailed study of a sample of news articles (although we begin our analysis with a brief report on the results of our initial data gathering). We began by searching for all stories about British Muslims from 2000 to the end of May 2008, using various strings of keywords that connected Muslims or Islam to the UK or to parts of the UK.[3] We tested various keywords and, while the list can never be entirely comprehensive, we are confident that our search captured most stories about British Muslims during this period. This search yielded around 23,000 stories (broken down over time in Figure 1 below). We used this corpus to construct a sample of just under 1000 articles, focusing on five alternate years from 2000 to 2008. To create our sample, we selected one in every twenty stories in 2000, 2002, 2004, 2006 and 2008, eliminating those that referred to British Muslims only in passing. We also eliminated the few articles turned up by the keyword search that did not refer to British Muslims at all, but nonetheless used the relevant keywords. This gave us a sample of 974 stories across our five selected years.

The use of even years between 2000 and 2008 allowed us to avoid what we anticipated as the two *most* newsworthy relevant events in the period – the terrorist attacks in September 2001 in the US and July 2005 in Britain – while capturing the longer-term aftermath of those events (as well as terrorist attacks in Bali in 2002 and Madrid in 2004). Our aim here was to focus on routine, everyday coverage of British Muslims. It also allowed us to refine the sample, eliminating stories that were not relevant to the analysis.

Nonetheless, we wanted to reflect the overall ebbs and flows in the coverage, so our samples from each year were commensurate with the volume of coverage in that year. So, for example, our sample from 2006 – when there was a greater volume of coverage of British Muslims – was proportionately larger than our sample from 2002. After a pilot coding exercise, all these stories were then coded in order to capture the discursive character of the coverage. While we wanted to go beyond the more simplistic forms of counting often associated with content analysis, we were careful to avoid more interpretative judgments – classifying stories as 'positive' or 'negative' for example. Our aim was to construct quantitative data that, in certain key ways, *described* the nature of the coverage.

In order to complement our text-based content analysis, we conducted an analysis of the images used in the British press in articles about British Muslims. Our sample was based on a seven-month period from 1 November 2007 through to 25 May 2008. We began with the Nexis search used in the content analysis, and moved to hard copies of the newspapers (based on our library collection, which holds the most recent year of UK newspapers) to see if images accompanied stories. We found that approximately one in four articles used accompanying images, which we then categorised. An examination of approximately 1800 articles therefore gave us a sample of 451 articles with images. Where articles involved multiple images or actors doing different things, these were coded individually, giving us in some cases over 700 units of analysis. Since images tend to be less precise than text, the verifiable forms of information contained in those images are less detailed than in our content analysis.

The volume of coverage of British Muslims

Our analysis of the Nexis database suggests that the coverage of British Muslims in the British press increased dramatically after 11 September 2001 (with seventy-four per cent of the coverage in 2001 falling in the months of September, October and November). This was the starting point of an increased focus on British Muslims, and, although coverage in 2002 fell back a little, coverage in 2002 appears to be nearly five times higher than in 2000. From 2002, we see a steady increase in coverage year on year until 2006 (see Figure 1). What is notable about this increase is that it appears to have its own momentum (rather than simply being a response to terrorist attacks).

As we might expect, we see another significant increase in 2005 (the year of the 7 July attacks) although, again, the momentum of coverage appears to be independent of that event, as coverage continued to increase further in 2006, reaching a level twelve times

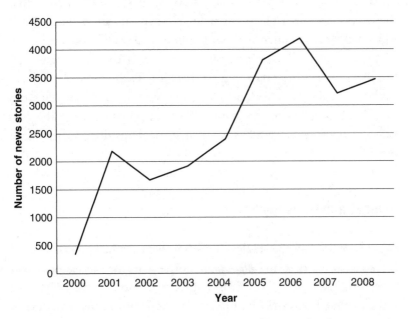

Figure 1 Stories about British Muslims over time (all UK national newspapers)

higher than in 2000. Although coverage appears to level off a little in 2007 and 2008, it remained higher in those two years than in any year before 2005. This suggests that while the increase in coverage of British Muslims from 2000 to 2008 is clearly related to the terrorist attacks in 2001 and 2005, it has also developed a momentum of its own, lasting well beyond these highly newsworthy events.

This gives the first indication that while the 'War on Terror' is the main lens through which British Muslims are reported in recent years, as others have suggested (Commission on British Muslims and Islamophobia, 1997; Poole, 2002, 2006; Richardson, 2004), we have also seen the growth of other related topics that do not depend upon acts of terrorism – notably cultural differences between Muslims and non-Muslims in Britain. The rest of our analysis is based on our sample of 974 news articles from 2000 to 2008.

Finally, we note that the increasing coverage given to terrorism after 2001 does not necessarily reflect levels of risk. Up until 2004, the US State Department's figures on the global level of terrorist incidents suggests – perhaps surprisingly, given the source – that there was no verifiable increase in terrorist incidents after 2001. Indeed, their data puncture the prevailing wisdom that the attacks on 11 September 2001 were a turning point when 'the world changed'. On the contrary, their data suggest that, despite the heavy number of casualties in the New York attacks, there were, in fact, more fatalities as a result of terrorist attacks in 1988 than in 2001, while the two years *after* 2001 recorded fewer terrorist incidents than in any of the previous twenty years (see Lewis, 2005).

Context and news hooks

We categorised all the stories in our sample by what we call a 'news hook'. This refers to the *main focus* of the story or the element that makes it newsworthy. We found three common 'news hooks' for stories about British Muslims, accounting for more than two-thirds of stories overall (Figure 2). These could be categorised under the

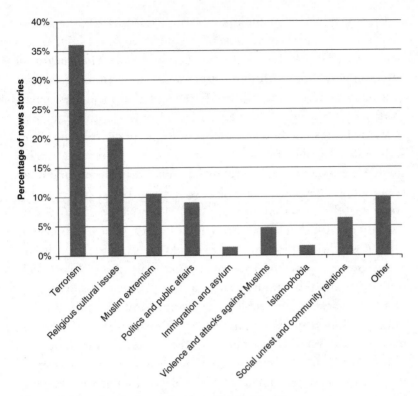

Figure 2 News hooks for stories about British Muslims
Note: Number of stories in sample = 974.

headings 'terrorism, or the war on terror', 'religious and cultural issues' and 'Muslim extremism'. As we might expect from previous research, 'terrorism, or the war on terror' was the most conspicuous news hook, accounting for 36 per cent of stories overall. This involved stories about terrorism trials, the 'war on terror' and hostage-taking, although most of the stories in this category were about terrorism more generally rather than a specific terrorist event (for example, statements or reports about terrorism by politicians or police chiefs).

The second most common news hook, 'religious and cultural issues', accounted for 22 per cent of stories overall. This included discussions of Sharia law, debates about the wearing of veils, dress codes, forced marriages, the role of Islam in Britain, and the Danish cartoons story. These stories generally highlighted cultural differences between British Muslims and other British people. The third most common news hook, 'Muslim extremism', accounted for eleven per cent of all stories. Stories about Abu Hamza, the single most newsworthy British Muslim, were especially prominent in this category.

It may be possible to tell a number of stories under these headings, and some of the literature on texts and audiences in recent years has stressed the possibility of interpretation rather than closure and fixity of meaning. This would, nonetheless, seem to be a case when the concept of the 'preferred meaning' (Hall, 1980; Morley, 1980) is particularly germane.[4] It seems plausible to say that, while there may be other possibilities, these three news hooks are *likely* to cast Muslims as the source of problems or in opposition to traditional British culture. By contrast, we found that only five per cent of stories were based on attacks on or problems *for* British Muslims. Perhaps ironically, the notion of Islamophobia (which many see as the consequence of this kind of coverage) scarcely features as a news topic.

If we look at the prominence of these issues over time, we can see that various news hooks have increased in prominence (Table 1). Terrorism remains consistently high, although as a proportion of coverage it reaches its peak in 2002 and then declines. This is not because there are fewer terrorism-related stories after 2002 (as we have indicated, coverage of British Muslims overall generally increases over time), but simply because that *after that date other kinds of stories about British Muslims become more significant* (the figures for 2000 should be treated with caution, as the numbers here are low across the board).

Most striking is the increase in the coverage of religious and cultural issues, which increased steadily as a proportion of stories, from eight per cent in 2002 to 32 per cent by 2008. Indeed, by 2008 it overtakes terrorism as the most common news hook for stories about British Muslims. Stories about Muslim extremism also increase in prominence between 2000 and 2004 and remain high in 2006 and 2008. By contrast, the potential downside of this prominence – the increase in attacks on British Muslims – is not reflected in

Table 1 Prominence of news hooks over time from 2000 to 2008

	2000	2002	2004	2006	2008
Terrorism	28%	51%	34%	34%	27%
Religious cultural issues	20%	8%	12%	27%	32%
Muslim extremism	3%	8%	14%	11%	10%
Politics and public affairs	10%	8%	8%	10%	8%
Immigration and asylum	0%	3%	1%	1%	2%
Violence and attacks against Muslims	10%	5%	9%	3%	1%
Islamophobia	0%	1%	4%	1%	1%
Social unrest and community relations	13%	6%	7%	7%	2%
Other	18%	10%	12%	7%	16%
Totals	100%	100%	100%	100%	100%

Note: Number of stories in sample = 974.

the coverage. On the contrary, while stories about anti-Muslim racism and attacks on British Muslims constitute ten per cent and nine per cent of stories in 2000 and 2004, this drops to three per cent in 2006 and one per cent in 2008.

If we break down coverage between tabloid and broadsheet newspapers, we can see that while there may be differences in emphasis and style, patterns of coverage are, on the whole, fairly consistent across the British press (Figure 3). Nonetheless, some differences do emerge. In particular, we found a greater proportion of stories about Muslim extremism in the tabloids. This manifests itself in the volume of coverage given to Abu Hamza, who has become a popular hate figure in the tabloids, with stories related to him becoming a sub-genre in their own right. By contrast, the tabloids were less concerned with stories about social unrest among Muslim communities or community relations generally. Although terrorism stories and religious/cultural issues dominated broadsheet coverage, we found a wider range of stories about British Muslims in the broadsheets, with

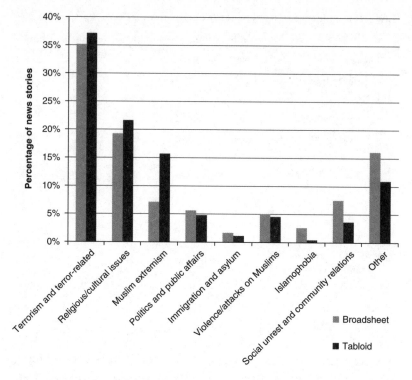

Figure 3 Broadsheet vs. tabloid news hooks

Muslim extremism, social unrest and attacks on/treatment of Muslims all receiving comparable levels of coverage. We also found more broadsheet stories about British Muslims that did not come under any of these headings (these were generally stories in which Muslims appear in more conventional settings, like business news).

Thus far, our data would seem to confirm that the news value attributed to certain kinds of stories – in which Muslims are likely to be positioned as threatening or antagonistic – make the use of orientalist representations either likely or inevitable. However, before we proceed to look in more detail at the discursive character of these stories, we want to stress the extent to which these portrayals involve more than simple racial stereotypes.

The comparison of Islam to other religions

The coverage of terrorism in Northern Ireland tended to see divisions between the Catholic and Protestant communities as sectarian rather than religious. Although one of the key figures in the troubles – Ian Paisley – might well have been described as a 'radical cleric', the nature of the doctrinal difference between Catholics and Protestants was rarely highlighted. By contrast, roughly one in five stories about British Muslims in our sample (nineteen per cent) made specific comparisons between Islam and other religions. This demonstrates the degree to which the focus of coverage is on *religious* differences between Muslims and other British people, rather than on political issues that are significant among many Muslim communities (the war in Iraq, Israel and the Palestinians and so on).

As we might expect, Islam was most commonly compared to Christianity (thirteen per cent of news articles did so), around twice as often as it was compared to other religions (such as Judaism or Hinduism). Just under half of these comparisons (47.8 per cent) avoided being explicitly judgemental, drawing out differences rather than making *overt* value judgements. Slightly more articles did make comparisons, however, and these tended to be negative: unfavourable comparisons (42.5 per cent) outnumbered those that compared Islam favourably (9.5 per cent) by more than four to one.

Although broadsheets and tabloids were equally unlikely to compare Islam *favourably* to other religions, broadsheets tended to be more even-handed than the tabloids. We found that fifty-seven per cent of broadsheet comparisons could be described as broadly neutral, with around a third being explicitly negative. The tabloids were, perhaps predictably, less equivocal: only thirty-six per cent of tabloid comparisons could be termed even-handed, while over half the tabloid stories compared Islam unfavourably to Christianity or other religions.

Many of these comparisons informed stories about religious and cultural issues, and illuminate the extent to which Islam – and those who practise it – are represented as 'a problem'. This becomes clearer when we look at the discourses used in these stories about British Muslims.

The dominant discourses about British Muslims

To a great extent, the impression created about British Muslims is likely to come from the context in which they appear: thus the fact that the stories tend to be about terrorism, cultural differences or extremism (especially in the tabloids) is likely to create associations in people's minds between Islam and these issues. (On the role of repeated associations in news coverage see Kitzinger, 2000; Lewis, 2005). In order to explore this issue in more detail, we looked for specific kinds of statements or ideas – or discourses – used repeatedly in the coverage of British Muslims. While it may be possible to subsequently cluster discourses under headings like 'positive' or 'negative', this more discursive approach allows us to be much clearer about what such descriptions entail.

We are aware that this discursive approach takes us beyond the simple categories generally associated with content analysis. Coding therefore required a fairly high level of interpretative skill and, more specifically, frequent discussions among the coding team about the nature, limits and features of particular discourses. Inevitably, the slippery nature of discourse meant that the decisions we made were, at times, pragmatic. However, read alongside our more specific look at the adjectives and nouns used to describe British Muslims, they allow us to portray the character of the coverage in a way that brings some of the richness of discourse analysis to representative samples.

In our sample of 974 stories, we found 1412 instances of particular discourses being used. As these figures suggest, many stories contained more than one of these discourses: so, for example, an article might propose, on the one hand, that most moderate Muslims oppose the use of terrorism, while at the same time suggesting that a growing minority are falling into the hands of terrorist extremists. This article would be seen as containing two discourses: one suggesting that Muslims support dominant moral values and one linking Muslims to terrorism.

The most commonly used discourses about British Muslims are illustrated in Figure 4. The two most common discourses are clearly linked (symbolically if not explicitly): first a discourse in which British Muslims are linked to the threat of terrorism, followed by a discourse

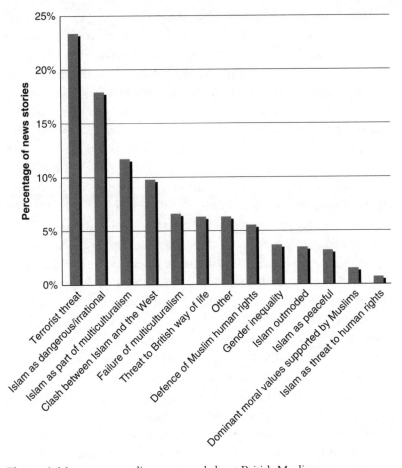

Figure 4 Most common discourses used about British Muslims
Note: Number of discourses used = 1412 (from the sample of 974 stories).

in which Islam or Muslims in the UK are seen as dangerous or irrational. The third most common discourse is less pejorative (although it may be, depending on its articulation), and involves a discussion of British Muslims in relation to British multiculturalism. The next three most common discourses are more clearly orientalist in character: the 'clash of civilisations' between Islam and the West, the problematic nature of Islam demonstrating the failure of British multiculturalism, and Islam portrayed as a threat to British values and traditions.

Again, we cannot assume that these discourses are necessarily explicitly positive or negative, nor that they contain overt positive or negative assertions. What we can say, however, is that four of the five most common discourses about Muslims in Britain in the British press *associate* Islam/Muslims with threats or problems or opposition to dominant British values. By contrast, only two per cent of stories contained the proposition that Muslims supported what might be called dominant or mainstream moral values. Most of these discourses are consistently prominent from 2000 to 2008, although we do see some shifts. So, for example, discourses in defence of Muslim human rights have, on the whole, become *less* prominent, while the idea that Islam is dangerous or irrational has become more commonplace.

If we compare the discourses used in tabloid and broadsheet newspapers, we see, once again, that the similarities are more striking than the differences. Nonetheless, some of the more overtly negative discourses appear to be more prominent in the tabloids. Thus we found that the two most common discourses, 'Muslims linked to the threat of terrorism' and 'Islam as dangerous, backward or irrational' are both more common to tabloid newspapers (although we should note that these are also the most common discourses in the broadsheets, albeit by a smaller margin). The broadsheets are, accordingly, more likely to feature some of the less pejorative discourses, such as 'defence of Muslim human rights' and 'Islam as part of multiculturalism' (although they are also more likely to discuss the failure of multiculturalism). The idea of the 'clash of civilisations' – with its more negative connotations – also tends to be a broadsheet rather than a tabloid discourse, placing Muslims in opposition to Western values in a more internationalist framework.

We took this discursive analysis further by examining the descriptive nouns and adjectives used directly in conjunction with British Muslims. We found 796 instances where descriptive nouns were used in relation to Islam or Muslims (as in 'Muslim preacher' or 'Islamic zealot'). By far the most common nouns used were 'terrorist', used in twenty-two per cent of stories, and 'extremist', used in eighteen per cent of stories. The other nouns frequently used are shown in Figure 5.

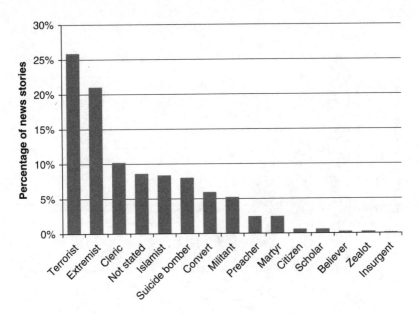

Figure 5 Most common nouns used in conjunction with British Muslims

Apart from 'cleric' and 'convert', it is fair to say that all the most commonly used nouns – 'terrorist', 'extremist', 'Islamist', 'suicide bomber' and 'militant' – have overtly negative connotations. We found very few nouns used that might, on their own at least, be seen as positive (such as 'scholar', used in only 0.5 per cent of stories). As our other findings suggest, if British Muslims are most likely to feature in news about terrorism, extremism or religious and cultural differences, then it is not surprising if the nouns used reflect these topics. What these findings do indicate, however, is the extent to which the dominant news hooks have implications for the way British Muslims are generally described. Or, to provide further evidence to inform a long-running debate, they show the extent to which news values are neither innocent nor impartial.

We conducted the same analysis with adjectives, with very similar results. We found 287 adjectives used in relation to Islam or Muslims (as in 'moderate Muslims' or 'militant Muslims'). The most common adjectives are shown in Figure 6. We found few instances of apparently more positive adjectives – such as 'respected' – used in the British press.

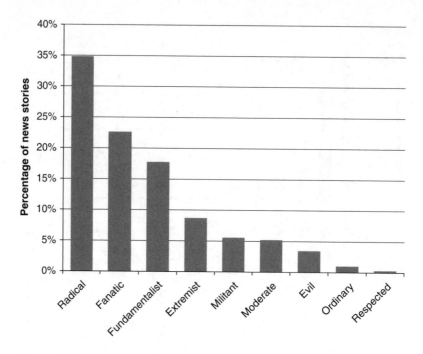

Figure 6 Most common adjectives in conjunction with British Muslims

Although words like 'evil' are fairly unambiguous, some of these adjectives might be seen as positive in some contexts. How we see the word 'radical', for example, depends on point of view and the context in which it is being used. The use of these terms should be seen in the context of our more discursive analysis – a series of contexts in which terms like 'radical' are negatively nuanced.

What is striking is that the five most common adjectives used – 'radical', 'fanatical', 'fundamentalist', 'extremist' and 'militant' – might all be found under the same heading in a thesaurus, all being in marked contrast to the less used adjective 'moderate'. In short, we see far more references to a radical, fanatical, fundamentalist, extremist and militant Islam than to a moderate Islam. Indeed, references to radical Muslims outnumber references to moderate Muslims by seventeen to one.

If we break down these data by newspaper type, we see a remarkable level of consistency, suggesting that these words are not simply
part of a more colourful tabloid vocabulary. The differences that do
emerge suggest an almost quaint – and distinctly class-related – form
of lexical preference. So, for example, the broadsheets favour the
word 'Islamist' in a way that the tabloids do not. Broadsheets favour
the word 'cleric' to describe religious figures, while the tabloids prefer
'preacher' (despite the latter being the slightly longer of the two
words). There was very little variation at all in the adjectives used
across the British press, with even the most pejorative – 'fanatical' and
'evil' – being used by broadsheets and tabloids in equal measure.

Who speaks about British Muslims?

One of the most conventional measures used in our analysis is also, in
some ways, the least revealing, although it does add some detail to our
more discursive analysis. We found that, of the 1250 sources quoted
across our sample, the dominant source for stories about British
Muslims is politicians (generally white, British politicians), who comprise nearly a quarter of all sources. This figure indicates the degree to
which the Muslim community has been a subject of political debate,
as well as the willingness of some politicians to be quoted on the
dominant issues in which British Muslims make the news (terrorism,
cultural values and extremism). Members of the public are also widely
used – often to add colour to a story in the 'vox pop' tradition. This is
common to most kinds of story: Lewis et al. (2005) have documented
the degree to which the 'vox pop' is used in contemporary news, their
findings suggesting that there are more than twenty 'vox pops' for
every one opinion poll.

There was also widespread use of criminal justice professionals,
such as police chiefs and judges, who comprise eleven per cent of all
sources used. Again, this reflects the focus of many of the stories –
in this instance terrorism-related stories. By far the most dominant
Muslim voice is the Muslim Council of Britain (MCB). While they

Table 2 Sources quoted in articles

Source	Number	%
Politicians	286	23%
Public (other)	160	13%
Criminal justice professionals	134	11%
Campaign groups	108	9%
Muslim Council of Britain	105	8%
Victims	58	4%
Radical Islamic group	56	4%
Religious leader (Christian)	55	4%
Religious leader (Muslim)	34	3%
Academic	34	3%
Statistics/surveys	28	2%
Celebrity	24	2%
Defendant/perpetrator	20	2%
Education (other)	18	1%
UK military	16	1%
Community group	15	1%
BNP	9	1%
International military	8	1%
Terrorist organisation	6	0%
Religious leader (other)	5	0%
Not stated (other)	71	6%
Totals	**1250**	**99.00%**★

★ Numbers are rounded up/down, hence the total is not 100 per cent.

are sometimes used as a 'moderate' Muslim voice, they are also portrayed to suggest the degree to which Muslims leaders are out of touch with mainstream British opinion.[5] More radical Islamic groups are also widely quoted. Interestingly, more Christian religious leaders were quoted in articles about British Muslims than were Muslim religious leaders. Although the 'British Muslim community' is often the subject of discussion (a point stressed by our visual analysis), community groups are rarely used as sources.

As the case studies will suggest, we cannot assume that being quoted means that the newspaper is giving voice to a certain group or providing balance. In particular, radical Islamic voices (or voices portrayed as radical) are often used as a way of provoking disquiet or outrage.

Images of Islam

As we might expect, most of the images we found accompanying articles – sixty-nine per cent – were photographs taken by journalists, agencies or other photojournalism sources (Figure 7). What is striking, however, is that the next most significant category by some distance – comprising eleven per cent of all images used – involved police mugshots. The explanation for this is fairly straightforward: a high number of stories about British Muslims are terrorism-related and

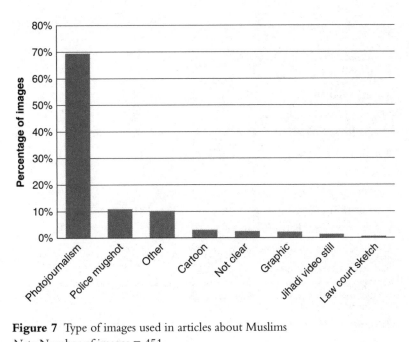

Figure 7 Type of images used in articles about Muslims
Note: Number of images = 451.

may therefore involve Muslims who are in the criminal justice system. It is worth commenting, however, that the regularity of such images is significant: the police mugshot is an image that comes encoded with a number of negative associations.

Around half the images of 'actors' in articles about British Muslims *were* of British Muslims (Table 3). By far the most dominant image is of a single Muslim male. As our content analysis and case studies suggest, these images tend to be of people – terrorist suspects or 'extremist' figures such as Abu Hamza – who are the subject of the article rather than those defining its terms. The fact that a third of those quoted in news articles are politicians or criminal justice professionals shows who is more likely to define the terms a story.

Although most pictures of Muslims show individual men or women, a fairly high proportion – twenty-nine per cent – show men or women

Table 3 Pictures of British Muslims, anonymous or identified

	Number	%
Muslim male	**189**	**60%**
Identified Muslim male	176	56%
Unidentified Muslim male	13	4%
Muslim female	**35**	**11%**
Identified Muslim female	30	9.5%
Unidentified Muslim female	5	1.5%
Muslim male group	**47**	**15%**
Identified Muslim male group	16	5%
Unidentified Muslim male group	31	10%
Muslim female group	**21**	**7%**
Identified Muslim female group	11	3.5%
Unidentified Muslim female group	10	3.5%
Muslim mixed group	**23**	**7%**
Identified Muslim mixed group	14	4%
Unidentified Muslim mixed group	9	3%
Totals	315	100%

Note: Number of images = 315.

in groups. While individuals tend to be identified (it is unusual to show a picture of an individual without naming them), Muslims shown in groups are often *not* identified. This is especially the case with groups of Muslim men, who are approximately twice as likely to be shown in an unnamed group as in an identified group. This suggests two points. First, that Muslim men are often represented as an anonymous group – the *object* of rather than the *source* of statements, and, second, that a group of unidentified Muslim men is seen as an image that 'speaks for itself', thus requiring no further specificity. This speaks, perhaps, to the embedded nature of orientalist imagery.

We also noted that while the individual Muslims we see are over-whelmingly male – by a ratio of more than five to one – the ratio of individual men and women in non-Muslim photos is much closer, men outnumbering women by less than two to one. Muslims are more than twice as likely to be pictured in groups: twenty-nine per cent of Muslims are pictured in groups, compared to only thirteen per cent of non-Muslims. Furthermore, Muslims are also twice as likely to be unidentified – twenty-two per cent were unidentified, as opposed to eleven per cent of non-Muslims. Although this is, in part, because they are more likely to be pictured in groups, we found more unidentified Muslims in all categories.

While most pictures we examined (seventy-nine per cent) did not show specific types of location, if we look at those that did, we find that one of the most popular locations for photographs of British Muslims is outside a police station or a law court (Figure 8): twelve per cent of the images in our sample were in this setting. This, once again, expresses the link between terrorism and Muslims, and these stories were nearly always about terrorism-related stories rather than more conventional crime reports.

While many images – police mugshots or close-ups, for example – do not show people actively doing something, we also looked at those that did in order to gain a sense of what we were most likely to see British Muslims – and non-Muslims – actually doing in news-paper images. The largest category involved people at work in some way (for example in a classroom, making a speech and so on).

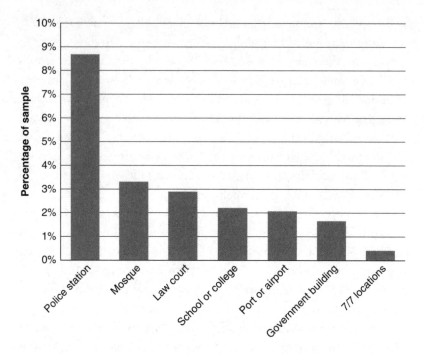

Figure 8 Locations in which British Muslims were represented

What is striking, however, is the high proportion of images of people protesting or demonstrating. Other studies suggest that protests are the *least* common form of citizen representation in news: for instance Lewis et al. (2005) found that of all the ways in which citizens were represented or invoked in the British media, on only 1.5 per cent of occasions were they shown protesting or demonstrating.

Our analysis confirms that the image of a group of Muslims in protest has become a familiar archetype. If we break this down to compare images of Muslims with non-Muslims, a number of points emerge. Although we found that Christian religious figures were used as sources more often than Muslim religious figures, Muslims are more likely to be seen in prayer and much more likely (by a factor of more than ten to one) to be seen preaching. By contrast, non-Muslims are much more likely to be seen in work-related roles (such as government minister or police chief).

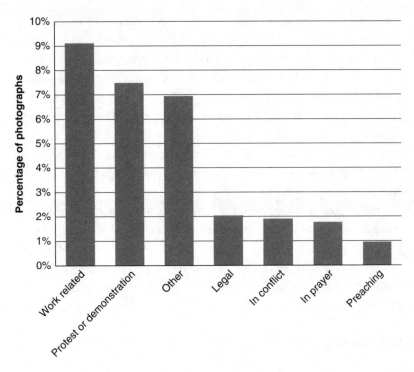

Figure 9 What people in photographs are seen doing

The findings of our image analysis are rather less clear than our discursive analysis. This is, in large part, because of the ambiguity of images, as well as the widespread use of conventional images of individuals. While we did find some evidence of stereotypical images, such as groups of Muslim male protesters, the quantitative nature of the analysis does not pick up the nuances of these images. So, for example, it is difficult to code for the pantomime quality of some of the pictures of Abu Hamza (which often go to great lengths to include his hooked hand in a head and shoulder shot), while a quantitative analysis tells us little about the more egregious use of stereotypes – such as the mocked-up picture of Britney Spears in a burka, following a story that her boyfriend came from a Muslim background. Nonetheless, we do see a number of indications that the visual representation of Muslims reflects the portrayals described in the content analysis. The widespread use of mugshots and images of Muslims outside police stations and law courts is very much in keeping with the high proportion of terrorism-related stories about British Muslims.

Similarly, we see some indications of the focus on cultural/religious differences, with Muslims seen engaged in religious practice in a way that non-Muslims rarely are, and Muslim men being far more visible than Muslim women. There are also suggestions in these data that Muslims are identified simply *as* Muslims rather than as individuals or particular groups with distinct identities. So, for example, Muslims are much less likely than non-Muslims to be identified in terms of their job or profession, while the greater use of unnamed or unidentified images of Muslims (especially in groups) suggests a degree of stereotyping in which images are deemed to speak for themselves.

Conclusions

Overall, then, our findings point to two main conclusions. First, while portrayals of Muslims have a long history, their presence in news coverage has increased significantly over the last decade. British Muslims are a now a familiar part of everyday news reporting. Second, while we found some careful and considered stories about British Muslims, as well as some reporting of some of the difficulties they face – and even a few in which Muslim identity is viewed as entirely unproblematic – the most frequent portrayals tend to fit within an orientalist framework. Like most forms of orientalism, this stresses certain forms of difference and portrays Muslims as a problem or a threat.

This is not to suggest that representations are static or fixed. In particular, the cultural has now eclipsed the criminal, with stories about Islamic cultural values overtaking the number of stories about 'Islamic terrorism' in 2008. But the development of these representations does appear to be constrained by an orientalist ideology. We have, in that sense, moved from a simple set of associations between

Muslims and terrorism to a more developed narrative in which we are offered both explanation and context. Terrorism remains the focal point of this narrative, but coverage has moved from an avoidance of the articulation of motives – in which terrorists are simply 'bad people' – towards locating and detailing Islamic beliefs as the source of the problem. Thus we have a growing genre of stories that focus on the incompatibility between Islamic and British values – a 'clash of civilisations' writ small.

We found a number of instances where the link – between the perceived problematic nature of Islam and terrorism – is made explicitly. As one commentator in the *Sun*, 13 October 2007, put it: 'I don't recall Jews carrying out suicide bombings or calling for their own form of law in Germany' – a phrase that links Islamic legal traditions with terrorism and underpins both with a comparison with a less 'problematic' religion. But the fact that this can be done with one simple sentence suggests that the discursive ground within which these links 'make sense' has already been well covered.

So, while many of the stories we found are, on the surface, about culture rather than terror, a sense of threat and danger lurks unspoken (because it does not *need* to be spoken) in the background. More than this, their news value is enhanced by the hint of menace that the constant stream of terrorism stories provides.

4

'Political Correctness Gone Mad'

Hugh Muir, Julian Petley and Laura Smith

'**B**ritishness is being destroyed,' declared a leader headed 'Corrosive PC nonsense is destroying our way of life' in the *Daily Express* on 2 November 2005, 'in a misplaced bid to kowtow to other ethnic sensitivities. This pathetic attempt to appease everyone all the time is pleasing no one. It is just turning everything that is best about British life into something of which we are supposed to feel ashamed. And it is disgraceful.' In the context of a front-page splash in the *Daily Express* on the same day, it was totally clear that the alleged kowtowing and appeasing of which the paper disapproved was in relation to Muslims. Fear of 'political correctness' in Western countries precedes anxieties about Muslims, and is associated with issues such as policing, 'the nanny state', human rights legislation, gender equality, adjustments for people with disabilities and so forth, and not only with issues to do with what the *Daily Express* called 'ethnic sensitivities'. But increasingly in recent years, anxiety about political correctness has been combined with anxieties to do with Britishness and multiculturalism.

This chapter mainly concerns four stories. Each was relatively trivial in itself. But each was portrayed in the media as illustrating the claim that 'common sense' is under attack from 'the PC brigade'. In two of the four instances, the attack on 'political correctness' was combined quite explicitly with an attack on Muslims. The third implicitly concerned Muslims, though the underlying principle had to do with all non-Christian religions. In the fourth, the attack was primarily directed against the police and the Crown Prosecution Service (CPS); however, the bullying against which they had taken action had had an anti-Muslim dimension and it is for this reason that it is included here. All four stories, in addition, had in common that the media coverage involved serious factual inaccuracies and distortions. Each original story is reproduced here as it first appeared. There then follows a consideration of how the story was commented on in leader columns, op-ed pieces and readers' letters. Finally, the actual truth behind the story is revealed, based on interviews with, and statements by, people who were directly involved in it. Three of the interviews have not previously been published. The fourth was published, to the paper's credit, in the *Mail on Sunday*. The chapter closes with a discussion of the concept of 'political correctness'.

Council chiefs ban Christmas

This story was a front-page splash with a huge headline 'Christmas is banned: it offends Muslims'. The full text of the story, which appeared in the *Daily Express* on 2 November 2005, is shown in Box 1.

Box 1 Christmas is Banned: It Offends Muslims

Council is 'ashamed' to be Christian

Britain's proud heritage suffered a devastating blow yesterday after council chiefs banned Christmas. Critics immediately accused a politically correct local authority of being ashamed to be Christian.

The council ordered Christmas lights in its town centres to be called 'winter' or even 'celebrity' lights to avoid upsetting other faiths. The astonishing diktat is one of a string of decisions by town hall bureaucrats which have undermined many age-old traditions. Their obsession has already seen crucifixes removed for being too Christian, Bibles taken out of some hospitals and even teachers told they can no longer 'fail' children.

Last night there was widespread condemnation of the ruling with residents, MPs and leaders from all faiths joining forces to condemn the outrageous move. Steve Jenkins, spokesman for the Church of England, said the move by Lambeth in south London left him 'speechless'. 'I thought we were over all this stuff. I thought people had stopped this', he said. 'The way for everybody to recognise everybody in their community is to recognise each other's festivals in the way we saw recently with the Diwali celebrations. We would not call Diwali lights celebrity lights would we? Christmas is Christmas, Diwali is Diwali and Ramadan is Ramadan.'

The Muslim Council of Britain agreed, saying the decision beggared belief. Lambeth, which has earned a reputation as one of the worst-run councils, is home to the official residence of the Archbishop of Canterbury. The council, which includes Brixton and Clapham, has now replaced the word 'Christmas' in its advertising material for the various switch-ons of lights over the festive season. In three districts it will now be the 'winter lights' while, in a fourth area, locals will be invited to enjoy the 'celebrity lights'.

The council's latest attack on the symbols of the festival celebrating the birth of Christ provoked widespread outrage. Culture secretary and local MP Tessa Jowell branded the order 'ridiculous', adding: 'It is a completely misguided way to recognise and respect Lambeth's diversity. Children right across my constituency get excited about Christmas and what it means.'

Inayat Bunglawala, of the Muslim Council of Britain, said: 'It beggars belief that people think naming them Christmas lights would be offensive. Being sensitive does not entail being dismissive of the festivals of other people and faiths. Christmas is a festival enjoyed by many other faiths who also look forward to Christmas time. It is actions like this that can actually contribute to creating tensions.'

IT consultant Shabbir Aslam said: 'I am not a Christian and I don't find the term Christmas lights offensive. I don't understand how anyone could find Christmas in any way upsetting. Britain is a predominantly Christian country after all. Even though we are Muslims my family celebrate Christmas.' Halal butcher Ahmad Rezai added: 'I know what Christmas is and it does not upset me, why should it?' Mr Rezai, who is originally from north Africa, added: 'I like Christmas even though I am a Muslim.'

Local Vauxhall MP and former minister Kate Hoey said: 'This is absolutely stupid and puts the council into a position of ridicule. It is typical of many local authorities acting out of sync with what local people want. I have yet to meet a single constituent from whatever faith or background who does not enjoy the Christmas lights.'

Lambeth Tory councillor Bernard Gentry said it was 'political correctness gone mad'. He added: 'It makes us look stupid. We should not be too scared to acknowledge the Christian festival of Christmas in the same way as we mark the Hindu festival of Diwali, the Muslim month of Ramadan and the Jewish Yom Kippur.'

Metropolitan WPC Gemma Clemson, 25, said: 'It's terrible that we have got to the situation that we have to accept everyone else's culture and beliefs but we are not allowed to celebrate our own. It's a sad state of affairs.'

TV company assistant Caroline Drummey, 27, said: 'I don't think this should be an issue at all. The Muslim month of

Ramadan is celebrated and that doesn't upset anybody so why should Christmas? I think the council is going completely overboard.' A spokesman for the council, which calls guide dogs 'enabling dogs', said: 'The term winter lights simply reflects the fact that a number of religious festivals take place over the winter period when the lights are switched on.'

Last week some high street banks revealed that they were banning 'piggy banks' in case they offended Muslim customers. Earlier in the month the Chief Inspector of Prisons, Anne Owers, said prison officers should not wear St George Cross tie pins in case inmates found them offensive.

The word 'fail' is also set to be erased from schools and replaced with 'deferred success'. On the religious front, a crucifix was removed from a Devon crematorium because it was not multifaith enough. It was only returned after a public outcry led by *Daily Express* readers.

How the story developed

There was actually nothing at all in the news item itself to substantiate the headline that Christmas offends Muslims, or even that anyone has ever thought that it offends Muslims. Nevertheless the story was recycled in other papers and on the BBC. 'A decision to call Christmas lights "Winter Lights" in south London', said the BBC, 'has been condemned as showing a "total lack of respect" for Christians. Advertisements for the switch-on of the lights in multi-cultural Lambeth have renamed them, apparently for fear of offending other faiths' (BBC Online, 2 November 2005). It was repeated also by *Voice of Freedom*, the British National Party magazine, which combined it with a story on the same theme from a town in Waveney:

A council is to stop paying for Christmas lights because they are not politically correct. Waveney District Council in Suffolk says the festive illuminations do not fit in with its core values of equality and diversity. The decision followed just days after Lambeth Council in south London re-branded their Christmas lights as 'Winter Lights' so as not to upset the borough's ethnic minorities.

What actually happened

The story first appeared on 1 November 2005 in the *South London Press*, under the heading 'Do they know it's Christmas any more?' Such stories often get into the national press through a local stringer or politician. When two of the authors of this chapter contacted Lambeth council to ascertain whether there was any truth in this story, a spokesperson explained:

> The important point in all this is that it was NEVER council policy to rename the Christmas lights switch-on events, or to change the name to winter lights. The naming decisions were made at a local level and this inconsistency in naming should have been picked up before council literature went to print, but it wasn't spotted until it was too late.

What started out as a joke in the *South London Press* (a cartoon with the headline 'Christmas is cancelled'), turned into a full-blown media assault with the *Daily Express* carrying the headline 'Christmas is banned: It offends Muslims' on its front page, turning it into a religious statement. It should be noted that the *Daily Express* did not once contact Lambeth council press office to find out the truth of the matter before printing their cover story.

From that point on the 'story' about Lambeth pandering to certain communities at the expense of British/Christian culture and tradition, was picked up by the rest of the nation's media and blown out of all proportion. Our response to the story was that it was absurd. Christmas was going on as usual, the Christmas tree was up in the town hall, the usual Christmas carols were being sung, the lights were up. The different names really were born out of inconsistency, they were never the official council policy, yet it escalated into this huge story.

Indeed, the council issued a press release on the same day as the *Daily Express* coverage cited above, but no national newspaper used it. The release stated that 'the suggestion Christmas has been banned is absolutely ridiculous. The usual Christmas tree will be up in the town hall, the usual Christmas carols will be sung and we're looking forward to the Christmas lights being switched on.' Subsequently the council issued details about six Christmas events that had been planned. 'Town centres in Lambeth are all a-glow', it said, 'as they prepare to flick the switch for our biggest and best ever Christmas lights. The borough's high streets have benefited from a £200,000 boost from the Lambeth Opportunities Fund this year, which has been spent on extending and improving Christmas light decorations.' All six shopping centres had Christmas trees and all the ceremonies included carol singing. Indeed, the lights in north Lambeth were switched on by the Archbishop of Canterbury himself. But absolutely none of this was reported in the national press, which did, however, report that Father Christmas had been banned by Havant Borough Council in Hampshire. 'Yes, it's hard to believe, but now Santa Claus AND Christmas lights have been banned', said the *Daily Express* on 16 November, though the 'story' rested on the fact that a charity organising Santa's grotto had moved the venue. The *Daily Mail*, on the same day, under the heading 'Is this the most miserable town in Britain?', said that 'the decision to drop Christmas lights was greeted with amazement in a borough where 99.1 per cent of residents are white', the clear implication being that 'white' and 'Christian' are synonymous.

Piggy banks to be sacrificed

This story, like the one above about 'banning Christmas', explicitly referred to Muslims. And like the one about Christmas it was a front-page splash. It appeared in the *Daily Express* on 24 October 2005. The principal word, in capitals, was Hogwash. The explanatory sub-title was 'Now the PC brigade bans piggy banks in case they upset Muslims.' The full story is shown in Box 2.

Box 2 Hogwash

Now the PC brigade bans piggy banks in case they upset Muslims

Piggy banks are being banned in case they offend Muslim customers, it emerged last night. The decision by high street banks was condemned as 'barmy' and 'bonkers' by critics. They warned that such moves would only fuel inter-community tensions. Branch bosses imposed the ban because they fear the time-honoured symbol for thriftiness could upset ethnic customers.

All promotional material bearing the figure has now been scrapped because the Koran forbids Muslims from eating pork and pigs are considered by them to be unclean. Muslim leaders in East Lancashire, where there is a large immigrant community and the first bans were imposed, applauded the action by the Halifax and NatWest.

But the move was condemned by critics headed by a leading Church of England clergyman. The Dean of Blackburn, the Very Reverend Christopher Armstrong, said: 'This is petty and political correctness gone mad. The next thing we will be banning Christmas trees and cribs and the logical result of that process is a bland uniformity. We should learn to celebrate our differences, not be fearful of them.'

He was supported by Andrew Rosindell, Tory MP for Romford, who said: 'Those responsible for this decision are making themselves look extremely foolish. It is quite absurd. In no way can piggy banks be termed offensive. I cannot believe the majority of Muslims genuinely object to seeing a picture of a piggy bank on a wall or in a leaflet. This is the sort of political

---

correctness that makes normal-thinking people very angry. It's barmy.' Mike Penning, Tory MP for Hemel Hempstead, described the decision as 'bonkers'. He said: 'I have never met a single Muslim, and I know many, who would be offended by the image of a piggy bank. It is sheer stupidity.' But the plan was backed by Salim Mulla, secretary of the Lancashire Council of Mosques, who said: 'Within our faith there are strict rules about not consuming pork or coming into contact with pigs. This is a sensitive issue and I think the banks are simply being courteous to their customers.' The Halifax will base future promotions around Howard Brown, the customer services adviser who fronts their 'Who gives you extra?' TV ads.

A spokesman said: 'We no longer have any advertising that features piggy banks or is piggy bank related.' NatWest admitted that piggy banks had been removed from branches in the area but insisted there had been no direction from head office. 'The decision has been taken at local branch level', said a spokesman.

'So', commented the *Express* in a leader:

Our piggy banks are to be sacrificed – not because we have become a nation that has forgotten how to save (which we have) but because they may be offensive to people whose religion forbids the eating of pork. This is nonsense, piffling nonsense but dangerous nonsense, too. It is unhealthy to indulge in the sort of political correctness that makes us trim our popular culture in ludicrous ways. It is important and correct that Britain has become more sensitive about language and symbols that are truly offensive to ethnic minorities and that decent Britons will no longer use. But piggy banks and Winnie the Pooh's Piglet do not fall into that category. Removing them for bogus reasons is an insult to our intelligence and that of Muslim bank customers, too.

Readers' reactions included the following:

> What a sad state of affairs when we have to think all the time about what may offend some sections of society. I am convinced that the vast majority of Muslims have more important things to think about than whether or not we use the term 'piggy bank'. What next? Can we still give our children a 'piggyback'? If not, what do we call it? Are we allowed to use the term 'pig in the middle'? What are we to call a pigtail? It beggars belief that we are concerned with such trivial matters – or am I being pig-headed?

> What a country we live in when, after a weekend of celebrating the life of one of the greatest Englishmen in history – Lord Horatio Nelson – we are now told that piggy banks are off limits for fear of offending Muslims.

> Hogwash indeed! If I remember rightly a similar fate befell the harmless little golliwog. This is England. We are rightly proud of our heritage and yet we kowtow to the insane demands of people who want to live in our country but are not prepared to accept our ways. If they don't like who we are and what we stand for, why do they stay? Could the benefits and free healthcare have anything to do with it? I for one am tired of increasingly feeling like a foreigner in my own country. I suspect I am not alone.

What actually happened

When two of the authors of this chapter contacted NatWest Bank in May 2006 they explained:

> This started with a local paper in the North. They rang us and we gave them a verbal statement which it appears they completely misinterpreted. From there it ended up in the *Star* and

75

the *Express*, neither of which checked it with us. The story was nonsense.

In September last year, piggy banks featured on posters in our branches as part of a nationwide savings campaign. When that campaign finished at the end of September, these posters were taken down to be replaced by new posters supporting the October branch campaign on personal loans. At this time we were contacted by a local paper asking if the decision to remove them was based on the posters causing offence. This, of course, was absolute nonsense and without any foundation whatsoever. The posters were removed simply to make way for the new posters supporting the next scheduled campaign. This happens with all campaigns throughout the year at NatWest. In fact, we have again had the piggy bank posters in all our branches throughout April this year in support of an April savings campaign and again taken down when that campaign finished at the end of April.

How that was misinterpreted by the local paper that broke the story is still a mystery to us. It was then picked up by some national newspapers who, regrettably, did not contact us and give us the opportunity to respond before going to print.

'Now Christ is banned'

Again, this was a front-page splash, in the *Daily Express* on 4 November 2005; it is reproduced in Box 3. Although neither the headline nor the text referred explicitly to Muslims, the context included the two stories described above, and the headline, in capitals, 'Now Christ is banned', was a clear follow-up to the splash about Christmas that had appeared only two days earlier in the same paper. Thus most readers would have undoubtedly interpreted it as being about not offending or upsetting Muslims, even though the point was not made explicitly.

Box 3 Now Christ is Banned

BC (Before Christ) is out ... it has to be BP (Before Present)

Museum bosses are trying to erase Jesus Christ from the pages of history. In the latest ludicrous attempt to tear down traditions, curators have banned the phrase BC – Before Christ – and insist on using BP – Before Present – to avoid offending other faiths. The astonishing decision caused national outrage last night.

Church of England spokesman Steve Jenkins said: 'I always thought BP was where you go to fill up with petrol. I just can't understand the point of introducing other initials and I'm sure no one else can. It's unnecessary and incredibly silly.' Historian Dr David Starkey dubbed it 'infantile'. He added: 'I am not a Christian, indeed I am anti-Christian, but BC is an essential feature of our history and to dispense with it in such a frivolous way is very foolish.'

The term BC is used for dates leading up to the birth of Christ to help place the timing of eras throughout history and is internationally accepted. But officials at the Cheddar Caves museum in Cheddar Gorge, Somerset – one of Britain's most popular tourist attractions – say that is not politically correct and have changed all exhibit dates to BP. Catholic academic Dwight Longenecker said the museum's decision was a desperate attempt to please everyone. 'BP is confusing because it sounds like "before today", which makes no sense at all in terms of timescale', he said. 'It sounds like a totally unnecessary thing to have done.'

Massoud Shadjareh, chairman of the Islamic Human Rights Commission, said people of all faiths were now 'getting really annoyed' with the political correctness sweeping the country. 'The reality is there is nothing wrong with calling something what it is', he said. 'Muslims and other faiths have no problem in celebrating Christmas or using the term BC, especially when there are many more major concerns that society is not addressing such as Islamophobia. This level of sensitivity is silly and stupid.'

The outcry over the attempt to write Jesus out of history comes soon after council bosses and the taxman were accused of banning Christmas. Earlier this week Lambeth Council climbed down in the face of condemnation after renaming its festive decorations 'winter lights' and restored the word Christmas. And it emerged yesterday that Inland Revenue bosses have stopped staff from taking part in a Christmas charity collection in case it offends other religions.

Cheddar Caves museum curator Bob Smart was unrepentant last night, however.

He acknowledged that the BP signs were politically correct but claimed they were a more accurate form of measuring dates. 'The only criticism of BP is that it is annoying to Christians', he said. 'It is politically correct but different religions have different dating systems, such as Muslims using before and after Mohammed. BP at least has the merit of applying to the whole world. We have had complaints about BP but we would have had complaints about whatever system we used.'

The museum is home to Britain's oldest complete skeleton – the Cheddar Man. Hugh Cornwall, director of the current exhibition 'Cheddar Man and the Cannibal', said many people misunderstood what BC meant but that he had not wanted to change it. 'I was dragged kicking and screaming into using BP. I share the view that it is politically correct. When I wrote the displays I wanted to use BC and AD but I was told that all the academics have used BP since the 1980s. The dates are all very vague anyway. Prehistory is an inexact science.' Dr Starkey, a firm supporter of BC, said the internationally accepted phrase was not BP but Common Era or CE. 'Not only is this silly but they can't even get it right.' A spokesman for the British Museum in London said it only ever used BC and was unaware of any other museums using the term BP.

Several day-trippers have written in the visitors' book at the Cheddar Man exhibition to complain. A guide said: 'We get people saying, "Where's God and Christ in all of this?" but the museum takes the view that God is only in our minds.' Accountants Rosemary and Mark Yule, both 45, were shocked to see the BP signs when they visited the museum with their sons Greg, eight, and Robbie, seven. Rosemary said: 'These signs are all over the walls and every date says BP instead of BC. It is political correctness gone mad. They have decided you can't refer to the word Christ because it might offend people so they've tried to re-write all the dates throughout history.' Rosemary, of Witherley, Leics, added: 'The whole point of BC is that it's a specific point in time that never moves and everyone knows what it means. But BP has no meaning and if it means the present day then it's always moving. It really is a completely nutty idea.'

A leader in the same day's *Daily Express* commanded: 'Stop PC brigade before it destroys all we hold dear.' It continued:

Fanatics of political correctness seem to be in overdrive this week … Few people give a thought to the meaning of BC and if they do it is extremely unlikely to cause offence to non-Christians. Yet someone in the Cheddar Caves exhibition in Somerset has found time to worry about such a thing and to order a change to the exhibition charts. Surely he has better things to do. Yet, like so many others, he is eroding the very foundations of British culture by trying to appease everyone when absolutely no one has taken offence. This political correctness must be brought under control.

'Instead of trying to second-guess what every ethnic minority might feel', continued the leader, 'we need to be proud of British culture and traditions. Or else we will wake up to find that everything we hold dear has been toned down to bland uniformity or destroyed altogether.'

What actually happened

The director of the Cheddar Caves and Gorge Museum issued a statement on 5 November correcting many of the alleged 'facts' in the *Daily Express* story. He began, in response to the opening word of the headline ('Now Christ is banned') and the claim in the leader cited above that the term BP had been introduced only within the last few days, by clarifying that the exhibition in question had opened on 23 March, some seven months earlier. Even if it was remotely true that the museum had 'banned Christ' this certainly was not something that had only just happened. The director stated that he would like to apologise to everyone who had been upset by the newspaper report and acknowledged that, 'from the telephone calls and numerous emails that I have received, there are a large number of individuals who have been deeply upset by the assertion, and understandably so, were the assertion well founded'. However, he continued, 'my use of BP does not signify a denial of Christ, a denial of my own Christian upbringing, the denial of our collective Western European cultural heritage which dates back to the Greeks and Romans, or even some lapse into vapid and irritating "political correctness" '. The Cheddar Museum, he stressed, is a museum of prehistory or 'before history'. It is not a museum of history or even of ancient history (Romans, Greeks, Persians, Egyptians, Sumerians). Its subject-matter pre-dates ancient civilisations by hundreds of thousands of years, tracing the origins of humankind back six million years to when humans shared a common ancestor with the great apes. Historical events can be precisely located, using recorded corroborative evidence, on an historical time line from the birth of Jesus Christ – *Anno Domini* (AD) meaning 'in the year of the Lord' – and working forwards using AD or backwards using BC. So there is a high degree of certainty and agreement that, for example, the Battle of Waterloo was fought on 18 June 1815 and that the earliest recorded 'historical' battle took place in 1282 BC, between the Egyptian Pharaoh Ramses II and the Hittites.

However, the director also pointed out, such certainties do not apply to events that took place in prehistory, which is defined as the time before historical records began; here the dating techniques are relatively inaccurate and 'finds' are relatively few and far between. He mentioned that radiocarbon dating can date organic material back 40,000 years, but only to an accuracy of plus or minus 500 years, and discussed technical matters relating to uranium series dating. He also mentioned, to give a further sense of the context in which his museum uses the abbreviation BP, that the oldest anatomically 'modern' humans, whose remains were found in Ethiopia in 1967, were originally believed to have lived 130,000 years ago; this was subsequently re-dated as 160,000 years ago and then again in 2005 to 195,000 years ago – plus or minus 5000 years.

Popular books dealing with prehistoric events invariably use the term 'years ago'. In academic texts, however, the shorthand abbreviation BP has been used since 1950. This was the benchmark year in which calibration curves for carbon-14 dating were established. The reason for using BP in the Cheddar Museum, rather than 'years ago', is for the sake of brevity in interpretative scripts which, for presentational purposes, have to be kept to a maximum length. The concept of BP is clearly explained in a panel at the start of the exhibition.

When two of the authors of this chapter contacted the Museum Manager, Bob Smart, he further explained that:

A couple of freelance journalists came to see us about the Cheddar Man and the Cannibals Museum. Journalists come to see us all the time and we thought that was all right. Whether they came with a secret agenda is another issue. The discussion was about the museum and one of the points was that we used the BP dating system, which is what scientists tend to use. I mentioned in passing in the course of the discussion that some people find the use of AD and BC offensive but said that was not the reason we did it.

What happened next took us completely by surprise. We only realised what had happened when a local radio network rang and asked if we had seen the front page of the *Daily Express*. I was taken aback. It was a deliberate piece of sensationalism. Various other papers picked it up, although most of the local papers took our point of view. We received a lot of very rabid hate mail and some death threats. I was very displeased by the death threats. The story ran for about two weeks in various papers and on the Internet. One religious fundamentalist used it as a reason why creationism should be taught. The idea that it was all PC is laughable. We were talking about the world's first museum of cannibalism – nothing about that is PC!

We didn't complain to the *Daily Express*. It would have been a waste of time. They would have seen that as a success. It was the sort of thing they like to print and they were given that opportunity. Sensational news stories allow people to believe what they want to believe.

'Have you had enough of the PC brigade?'

A few days after the above story was published, on 9 November, the Archbishop of Canterbury was reported in the *Daily Mail* to have expressed concern, in answer to a question, about the dropping of traditional Christian festive symbols from public life. 'Archbishop attacks PC brigade ban on Christian symbols', read the headline. In connection with this story, the *Daily Mail* asked its readers if they had 'had enough of the PC brigade'. Extracts from their responses are printed below and show the kinds of fears, assumptions and desires that the discourse of so-called 'political correctness' both reflects and stirs up. References to Islam were mixed in with criticisms of immigration, demands that immigrants should assimilate to a particular notion of British culture, anxieties about national identity and a sense of threat from the political left. Underlying references to specific threats there is a pervasive sense of immanent malaise and uncertainty:

> The PC brigade are the ones who are making life in the UK difficult – they are deciding you cannot do this or that for fear of upsetting others. Why on earth has this country allowed itself to be dictated to? ... Time the PC brigade realised people have choices, come and stay in this country and accept the way of life or don't come! Simple! Our country should be one where people want to live here but not at the cost of changing it to suit them, take us the way we are or don't come!

> Political correctness is the new cancer. It erodes rather than builds; divides rather than unites.

> For all their pronouncements the PC brigade remains nameless and faceless.

> I thought we lived in a Christian country? If I lived in a Muslim country would they rename Ramadan for fear of offending me? I'm sure most of this renaming of Christmas is caused by geeky left wing twits who have nothing better to do.

> I am heartily sick of the PC brigade and all the claptrap they spout. I want my country to stay British and Christian and for all to see this. I want to see Union Jack flags, Christmas decorations, Easter eggs and hear English spoken as I walk down the street.

> It's about time these political correctness twits were put in their place. This is a Christian Country, not a Communist State.

Though it would appear at times that it is being run as such through the back door, by loony left Town Councils. Christians should take note of this fact the next time their local elections come round.

Can somebody please enlighten me as to where (and when) the pc brigade came from? I like many others are thoroughly sick of the way they are changing everything we have grown up with in this country and it is time they were held to account.

If you think this looks bad, imagine how bad it looks to someone who has fought for our freedoms in Britain. Did I see my friends perish just so that Tony's Cronies could give away our sovereignty to the PC brigade?

We know that there are certain things in our history that must not be mentioned and this is sensible, but to start renaming Christmas is just left wing lunacy!

This really is madness on a vast scale. I'm starting to think that what with the (failed) push to detain anyone who looks like a terrorist for 90 days, and all this erasing of Christian symbolism, Blair and his party really are trying to turn Britain into a 21st Century version of Stalin's Russia.

'Only a cliché will do'

This story broke in the national press on Friday 7 April 2006. Much the same words and details appeared in several different papers and it is probable therefore that there was a common source in one of the agencies, itself perhaps based on a text filed by a local reporter who had been in Salford Magistrates Court on the previous day. Opposite, in Box 4, is the story as it appeared in the *Daily Telegraph* on 7 April 2006.

Box 4 CPS 'Is Crazy' to Take Playtime Insults to Court

A JUDGE lambasted the police and Crown Prosecution Service yesterday for taking a 10-year-old boy to court over a playground spat. District Judge Jonathan Finestein said the decision to prosecute the youngster – accused of calling a fellow pupil a 'Paki' and a 'nigger' – was 'political correctness gone mad'. He attacked the police for not 'bothering' to prosecute more serious crime such as car theft but readily picking on a 'silly' incident. He added that he used to be called fat at school and said that in the old days the headmaster would have given the children 'a good clouting' and sent them on their way.

Judge Finestein spoke out when the boy, from Irlam, Greater Manchester, appeared at Salford youth court accused of racially abusing a fellow pupil. He called an 11-year-old boy 'Paki', allegedly referred to him as 'bin Laden' and chanted: 'He's on the run, pull the trigger and shoot the nigger.' He is said to have made the comments in the school playground between July 1 last year and Jan 30 this year.

The 10-year-old denied the racially aggravated public order offence and said he was now friends with the boy. He admitted calling him a 'Paki' but said he did not use any other racist terms and claimed the complainant had called him 'white trash'.

Judge Finestein said he thought prosecuting the youngster was 'crazy' and urged the Crown Prosecution Service to reverse its decision. He said: 'Have we really got to the stage where we are prosecuting 10-year-old boys because of political correctness? I was repeatedly called fat at school. Does this amount to a criminal offence? This is political correctness gone mad. It's crazy. Nobody is more against racist abuse than me but these are boys in a playground. This is nonsense.' He did not condone what was supposedly said but doubted the defendant understood bin Laden or al-Qa'eda and said there 'must be other ways of dealing with this apart from criminal prosecution'.

He added: 'In the old days the headmaster would have given them a good clouting.' It was wrong for children to have racist views, he said, but he was 'anxious to avoid the criminal conviction of somebody so young'.

Addressing the boy's parents, he said: 'I'm not blaming you, kids hear these things, but to refer to people as Pakis or refer to their race or religion is wrong.' He told the court: 'This is how stupid the system is getting. There are major crimes out there and the police don't bother to prosecute. If you get your car stolen it doesn't matter, but you get two kids falling out because of racist comments – this is nonsense.'

Judge Finestein adjourned the case so the Crown Prosecution Service could decide whether it was in the public interest to proceed with the prosecution.

A spokesman for Greater Manchester Police said it took all reports of crime seriously and remained totally opposed to racism in any form.

The Crown Prosecution Service said that because proceedings were ongoing it would not comment.

How the story developed

The Muslim dimension of the affair was clearly indicated by the terms 'Bin Laden' and 'Paki' in the abuse, and by the judge's comments on these. It was indicated also in the *Daily Mail*, 8 April, by the use of a quotation from Tahir Alam, chairman of the Muslim Council of Britain's education committee, who had said: 'We need to be sensible in relation to 10-year-old children. The issue of racism is, of course, very serious but we should educate them, not take them to court.' The *Daily Mail* commented that: 'To its credit, the Muslim Council of Britain sees this affair for what it is and says the case should never have come to court.' It contrasted this with 'the bovine, brainwashed, politically-correct mindset of the liberal establishment'.

'The only good news in this sorry story,' said Minette Marrin in *The Sunday Times*, on 9 April, in a lengthy article entitled 'Up on a charge for being a typical child', 'is that the Muslim Council of Britain has taken a wise and adult line, sensitive though Muslims are to racism. It has supported the judge in his comments.' In her view, however, 'this entire episode has a faint whiff of the Soviet show trials or the Salem witch-hunts about it, a kind of public hysteria. Whom the gods wish to destroy, they first make mad.'

There was substantial comment on the story in op-ed pieces and leader columns throughout the national press. 'Common sense at last', said the *Daily Express*, on 7 April, and commended Judge Finestein for 'slamming' police and crown lawyers. 'Law enforcement', it continued, 'has been turned upside down in this country. Hardened criminals are allowed to roam free to commit crime, while children who should have been given a sharp talking to are prosecuted.' The same line was taken by the *Daily Telegraph*, on 8 April, which quoted the judge at length and argued that 'every word uttered by Jonathan Finestein … rang with common sense'. Referring to his remark about 'political correctness gone mad', it stated that 'there are times when only a cliché will do to describe the sheer crassness of modern British bureaucracy'. Branding the decision of the CPS to prosecute as 'breathtaking' and 'idiotic', it also expressed incredulity at the fact that:

> So many people have sought to defend it. We understand why the police in Greater Manchester have refused to acknowledge how stupidly they have behaved. It is much less trouble for them, after all, to pursue schoolchildren for calling each other names in the playground than to catch proper criminals. But it is harder to understand why the teachers' unions are supporting the CPS and attacking the judge. They really ought to think harder about where the true interests of children lie. Judge Finestein and the two schoolfriends whose playground spat provoked all this nonsense have a great deal to teach the police, the CPS and the unions about growing up.

The *Daily Mail*, on 8 April, similarly argued that racist name-calling in school playgrounds is basically of trivial importance, merely 'a playground spat':

> It happens all the time. Schoolchildren squabble. There may be tears. They call each other utterly unacceptable names. Their teacher calls them over and tells them not to be so offensive and learn to respect each other. So children learn to become responsible adults. Not this time. Now a playground quarrel engages the full majesty of the law, with a police investigation, a file prepared for the Crown Prosecution Service, an appearance in court ... This is political correctness gone mad. How sad that a country once known for its common sense should come to such a sorry pass.

Meanwhile in the *Daily Telegraph*, on 8 April, Simon Heffer wrote:

> Since neither the CPS nor the police have anything better to do, perhaps I could suggest an extension of this policy, starting with abandoning the minimum age of criminality. It is obvious that all primary schools and, indeed, nurseries should be regularly inspected for signs of racist tots, with exemplary prosecutions where necessary. And don't forget maternity wards – you can't catch them too young, and heaven knows what harm is being done to our nation by bigoted babies.

And in the *Daily Express*, on 12 April, in an article headed 'Don't take playground tiffs into the courtroom', Ann Widdecombe reflected that 'the country is well nigh paralysed by political correctness, fear of giving offence and the compensation culture. It is a pity the head could not apply the slipper, as the judge acknowledged.'

Particularly in the light of the final section of this chapter, it is highly instructive to compare much of the press comment on this case with statements put out by the BNP on 7 April. These included:

[Finestein's] common sense statements have drawn criticism by the real bully boys and girls; the hate filled Marxists of the National Union of Teachers. While the taunts are unpleasant, name calling in school playgrounds is an every day fact and has been going on long before Windrush arrived at Tilbury Docks. It is a straightforward issue that can be tackled by teachers and parents themselves, however it seems that some self-loathing white advocates of multiculturalism are happy to indulge in persecuting primary school kids using taxpayers' hard earned money.

The short lived experiment of multiculturalism has failed and the days of the general public bowing meekly to the forces of political correctness are over. The average voters, namely the vast majority outwith the ranks of the Labour Party, the broadcasting editing suites and the union headquarters are sick and tired of this PC nonsense and episodes like this regarding a young lad who is still learning about life shows just how far removed from normality these preachers of political correctness have gone.

What actually happened

To its great credit, the *Mail on Sunday*, on 9 April, carried a lengthy and detailed article by Andrew Chapman and Louisa Pritchard which revealed the true facts of this particular case. In brief, the incident was in no sense a playground spat, tiff or squabble but was part of a pattern of persistent bullying and physical attacks taking place over several months. It had not been a single child doing the bullying, but three. The police and the CPS had not taken the case to court on a whim, but had first attempted to use restorative justice approaches to try to persuade the three perpetrators to accept reprimands or warnings; they had been successful with two them but not with the third, which was precisely why he had been brought before the court. Nor was it true that the two boys had ever been friends.

The *Mail on Sunday* article was substantial and was based largely on an interview with the mother of the boy who had been at the receiving end of the bullying. She stated that:

> I was disgusted by the judge's remarks that seemed to belittle my son's ordeal even further. The judge is wrong. He may have been fat at school and he may have been called names. But my son can never change the colour of his skin and that's the difference here. I just wish the judge had seen the tears streaming down my son's face when he finally broke down and told me all about what had happened to him. How dare the judge match being called fat in the same vein as the racist abuse my son has had to suffer? I was angered by his comments. This has not just been a one-off name-calling session, this has amounted to several months of systematic taunting and bullying which has left my child withdrawn and miserable. Some of the names he has been called would make your hair curl.

Recalling the first signs of bullying the previous July she said:

> My son complained to his teacher about the things they were saying to him. All parties were brought in to school – parents and kids – to discuss the problem individually. There were class talks with the children en masse about how wrong it is to say racist things, but the taunting just went on and on. It got to the stage where the school was left with no option but to bring in the police. There was nothing else for it as nothing was getting any better. My son even had an incident book to write down the things they were saying to him, that's how bad it was. Racist taunts and songs, sometimes even in the classroom. He was in a terrible state – withdrawn-sulky and upset. It was very cruel and humiliating. He'd never encountered anything like this before. The school was magnificent throughout and tried to deal with what was happening through normal disciplinary channels.

The article also quoted from a statement by the CPS, which explained that:

> We originally decided the case did not need to be brought before the courts, and an official reprimand by the police was offered to the three boys. In one case a reprimand was accepted and given, in another a final warning was given because he already had a reprimand for another matter but the third boy, although he admitted some of the offence, would not accept the reprimand after his parents took legal advice.

The point that needs to be borne in mind here is that a reprimand or warning is seen as an admission of guilt and can be given only if a child's parent or guardian will accept it. Thus the case ended up in court only because the parents of one of the alleged bullies effectively left the police and CPS with no other option than to expose their child to the full force of the law. Showing an understanding of the situation entirely absent from most of the British press, not to mention a remarkable degree of forbearance towards one of her son's tormentors, his mother revealed that: 'The daft thing is that I even feel sorry for him. He wasn't even the worst perpetrator but he has ended up in court. If his parents had brought him to apologise to my boy before the school was forced to bring in the police, this court case need never have happened. It is all very unfortunate.'

In due course, before the case came back to court, the third accused did accept a warning and the case was dropped. The Chief Crown Prosecutor for Greater Manchester, John Holt, stated that:

> Mr Finestein made remarks about the decision to prosecute which were highly critical of the CPS. He was not aware of the full history of the matter, in particular the prior disposal of the allegations against the other two boys. He has accepted that he may well have been less forthright in his comments if he had been aware. In my review I have taken into account the fact the other two boys, who had a greater involvement, have

accepted a reprimand and a final warning over their behaviour. As the third boy has now been given the warning about his conduct, we feel that this matter is now closed.

Greater Manchester Police revealed that Chief Constable Michael Todd had received a letter from Mr Finestein expressing 'regret' about his criticisms of the police in court (BBC Online, 26 April 2006). Needless to say, no such regrets were forthcoming from the newspapers which had so vociferously amplified his claims without bothering to check the facts of the case.

'Political correctness' as ideological shorthand

The widespread use of the term 'political correctness' in its current pejorative sense dates back to the beginnings of the 1990s in the United States. On 24 December 1990 a *Newsweek* cover warned readers to 'Watch what you say' and splashed the words 'Thought police' across the middle of the cover in large block letters. In May 1991 President Bush at the University of Michigan claimed that 'political correctness' (PC) 'replaces old prejudices with new ones. It declares certain topics off-limits, certain expressions off-limits, even certain gestures off-limits. What began as a cause for civility has soured into a cause of conflict and even censorship … In their own Orwellian way, crusades that demand correct behaviour crush diversity in the name of diversity' (Wilson, 1995: 8).

Bush's speech gave the nascent anti-PC campaign a tremendous boost, and in the ensuing years the notion of PC enabled conservatives to unify into a single conspiracy issues such as multiculturalism, affirmative action and speech codes, and gender and sexual politics. The term 'PC' became a form of ideological shorthand, brought into play to decry, as Valerie Scatamburlo argues, 'any position that challenges the virtuosity of capitalism, the nobility of right-wing cultural values, or the notion that oppressive relations of racism and sexism are still pervasive in America'(1998: 27). It provided a way of

92

dismissing criticism, quelling dissent and stifling critical discourse, all the while claiming to fight a conspiracy to destroy freedom of speech.

The phrase quickly crossed the Atlantic and the anti-PC campaign became an extension of the sustained governmental and press attack that had taken place on the alleged antics of 'Loony Left' London councils in the second half of the 1980s. (For a detailed discussion of this campaign, its antecedents and aftermath, see Curran et al., 2005.) Thus, for example, the research director at Conservative Central Office recalled the populist strategies employed by his party in the 1992 general election: 'Immigration, an issue which we raised successfully in 1992 and again in the 1994 Euro-elections campaign, played particularly well in the tabloids and has more potential to hurt. Then there is the "loony left" and political correctness. Voters can't define it, but they don't like it and Labour councils are the arch exponents' (quoted in Parekh, 2000: 226).

'PC' thus came to refer to any Labour policy deemed overly liberal and in due course was applied even to the notion of human rights. The classic anti-PC narrative is exemplified by Anthony Browne's *The Retreat of Reason* in which he alleges that 'by the early twenty-first century, political correctness had completed its long march through the institutions of Britain' (2006: xii) and that 'the long march of PC through every nook and cranny of national life, was helped by the fact that there is little competing ideology' (2006: 34). (For a critique of this thesis see Petley, 2006a.) In the present context, what is particularly significant is the way in which Browne links 'political correctness' to the treatment of Britain's Muslim population (along with other minority populations), in which instance it acts as part of a grand strategy 'to redistribute power from the powerful to the powerless. It automatically and unquestioningly supports those who it deems victims, irrespective of whether they merit it, and opposes the powerful, irrespective of whether they are malign or benign' (2006: xiii). He continues: 'Since the Holocaust, Jews have often been portrayed as the ultimate victims, and anti-Semitism as the ultimate bigotry. But in the early 2000s, partly as a result of the intifada – where the Jews are seen as oppressors rather than the oppressed – and partly as a result of rising concerns about Islam after September 11th, Muslims became the ultimate victim group, and Islamophobia the greatest bigotry' (2006: 12).

Browne further develops his 'victimhood' thesis thus:

> Since victims are supported not because they are right but because they are vulnerable, critically questioning them is seen as attacking them, and those who do so are vilified as oppressors. In the world of PC, victims can say anything or ask for anything, not because they are right or deserve it, but because they are safe from public scrutiny or objection. The most overt racism, sexism and homophobia in Britain is now among the weakest groups, in ethnic minority communities, because their views are rarely challenged, as challenging them equates to oppressing them.

> (2006: 13)

Indeed, according to Browne, there is so much to be gained from achieving victim status that individuals and groups actively seek it out: 'Few things are more powerful in a public debate than publicly acknowledged victim status, and the rewards for public victimhood are so great that there is a large incentive for people to try to portray themselves as victims' (2006: 13–14). With specific reference to Muslim 'victims' in Britain, Browne claims that:

> One of the most successful campaigns for victim status has been by Muslim groups in Britain, notably the Muslim Association of Britain, which increases its clout by inflating the number of Muslims in Britain by a million more than the official census, and by accusing anyone who tackles its extremist Islamist agenda of 'Islamophobia'. Although it has a thoroughly oppressive agenda (supporting terrorism against innocent civilians, promoting the rights of husbands to beat their wives and the execution of gays), the MAB passes itself

off as oppressed so convincingly that it has fooled the PC establishment, notably the *Guardian, Independent* and BBC, into promoting it unquestioningly.

(2006: 43)

Much the same 'argument' is advanced by Melanie Phillips in her book *Londonistan* (2008 [2006]). The victim culture, in her view, is a form of 'moral inversion' which holds that 'since minorities are oppressed by the majority they cannot be held responsible for what happens to them. As a result, a climate of intimidation developed in which minorities could demand special treatment and denounce anyone who objected as a bigot. Minority wrongdoing was thus excused and the blame shifted instead onto the majority' (2008 [2006]: 26). Furthermore, not only are those doing wrong excused if they belong to a 'victim' group but 'those at the receiving end are blamed simply because they belong to the "oppressive" majority … There is a tendency to equate and then invert the behaviour of the perpetrators of violence and that of their victims, so that self-defence is misrepresented as aggression while the original violence is viewed sympathetically as understandable and even justified' (2008 [2006]: 126). Turning specifically to British Muslims, Phillips argues that they 'consider themselves to be pre-eminently victims of Western culture' and that they have managed to 'turn reason and justice on their heads by blaming any wrongdoing of Muslims on others' (2008 [2006]: 26). In this vision of things, 'since Muslims regard Western values as an assault on Islamic principles, they routinely present their own aggression as legitimate self-defence. This moral inversion has been internalised so completely that the more Islamic terrorism there is, the more hysterically British Muslims insist that they are under attack by "Islamophobes" and a hostile West' (2008 [2006]: 26).

More generally, according to Phillips: 'Britain has become a decadent society, weakened by alarming tendencies towards social and cultural suicide. Turning upon itself, it has progressively attacked or undermined the values, laws and traditions that make it a nation, creating a space that in turn has been exploited by radical Islam' (2008 [2006]: 22). Britain, the diatribe continues, 'has effectively allowed itself to be taken hostage by militant gays, feminists or "anti-racists" who used weapons such as public vilification, moral black-mail and threats to people's livelihoods to force the majority to give in to their demands' (2008 [2006]: 28).

Interestingly, when *Guardian* journalist Jackie Ashley politely suggested that in her book she might be 'going a little over the top', Phillips characteristically reprimanded her thus:

> If the response to the kind of things I'm saying is to pretend that it's not happening, and worse, to characterise people like me as paranoid, hysterical, mad, this is first of all nasty stuff, it's vicious, but it is aimed at shutting down discussion of this completely. It's the tactics used by Stalin to call political opponents mad. But it does have echoes of the 1930s because the Jews then tried to draw attention to what was going on in Germany, and they too were told they were hysterical and paranoid.

> (*Guardian* 16 June 2006)

'Political correctness' and political consequences

The facts elucidated and the arguments put forward elsewhere in this book clearly demonstrate a vast, indeed unbridgeable, gulf between the perspectives of the authors of its various chapters and those of Browne and Phillips. Our purpose in this chapter, however, is not specifically to take issue with their views (the whole book does this, albeit mainly implicitly), but simply to demonstrate how remarkably closely their notion of 'political correctness' is mirrored by views routinely expressed in a large and influential section of Britain's national press. Take, for example, the following articles, all of which appeared in the *Daily Mail* during 2005 and 2006 (in which year both *Londonistan* and *The Retreat of Reason* were first published):

On 3 May 2006, an article headed 'A shameful failure to enforce the law' argued that the failure to deport Abu Hamza was because 'Britain's all-powerful Liberal-Left censors have, by promoting an obsessive political correctness, so cowed the nation that everyone from the Met under Sir Ian Blair to the CPS and the BBC suspends their normal value judgments, common sense and even the concept of justice when dealing with anything to do with race.'

On 1 February 2006 the paper turned its attention to the Incitement to Religious Hatred Bill in a piece headed 'Why this Bill is so insulting'. This was written by a young Muslim woman, Munira Mirza, who stated that many young Muslims 'see such legal "protection" as signalling that they are a downtrodden, vulnerable group. This is not how they see themselves and they will not thank the Government for its concern. What is particularly alarming is that a preoccupation with political correctness when dealing with Muslims may eventually haunt those it is supposed to protect. The country is far less racist than we are led to suppose. The true danger is this Government has risked inadvertently provoking an anti-Muslim backlash. Already you can detect resentment in the "host community" over seemingly endless concessions not wanted by most of us.' However, as this chapter has demonstrated, many of these alleged 'concessions' actually have no basis whatsoever in fact.

A long article about Bradford, 'Inside the ghetto', by Ann Leslie on 24 September 2005, claimed that 'the only group that cannot compete for taxpayers' funds in the "multicultural orthodoxy" – the working-class, secular, inner-city whites – complains that it is being discriminated against, that it is being made to forget its own culture in the cause of political correctness. "I mean, I'm not a racist", one white Bradfordian told me, "but why do these Asians say we got to celebrate their festivals, but that we're being 'insensitive' for celebrating ours?" '

The question of apparent double standards was raised in a comment piece on 23 August 2005, which contrasted the charging under the Public Order Act of Alan Buchan, the editor of a Scottish newspaper, for writing what even the *Daily Mail* admits was 'a savage diatribe against the possibility of a refugee camp being built in his area', with the non-prosecution of Dr Yaqub Zaki, deputy leader of the Muslim Parliament, who had said that he would be 'very happy' if Downing Street was bombed, and of Inayat Bunglawala of the Muslim Council of Britain, who had (before 9/11, it should be pointed out, although the *Daily Mail* failed to do so) called Osama bin Laden a 'holy warrior' and 'defended suicide bomb attacks against Israeli troops'. The *Daily Mail* stated that: 'This paper carries no torch for Mr Buchan and his wildly over-the-top views but doesn't his treatment compared to that of Messrs Zaki and Bunglawala tell you all you need to know about the way political correctness and a fear of offending Muslim sensibilities have tied this country up in knots?'

A case similar to that of Abu Hamza's was brought up by the *Daily Mail* on 10 August 2005. This was that of Omar Bakri Mohammed, whom the paper described as 'the most poisonous of the extremist clerics and a lightning rod of hatred for a whole generation of impressionable young Muslims', who had just left the country to visit the Lebanon. The *Daily Mail* argued that he should not be allowed to return, and indeed should have been deported long ago. However, 'a lethal cocktail of political correctness and inertia stayed the hand of the authorities and allowed this loathsome individual to continue spouting his incendiary message unhindered'.

An endless stream of such stories emanating from most national newspapers has political consequences. For example, in the run-up to the May 2005 election, Tory MP Philip Davies accused mainstream politicians of failing to debate asylum and immigration sufficiently, thus making voters feel that their concerns on this issue were being ignored and so turning to the far right. He was quoted in the *Observer*, 23 April, as saying:

People feel nobody is standing up and talking about [asylum and immigration] issues. The whole thing about political correctness is a key driver of that. They feel the only way they've got now to express their opinions is to put a cross in a secret ballot for the BNP. The fear is if you are white and you say something that may be considered derogatory by somebody about an ethnic minority, you are going to be sacked or locked up.

This may have been simply a ploy to try to get his party to become tougher on these issues, but it is nonetheless the case that the BNP has indeed played the PC card for all it's worth. For example, its 2005 general election manifesto argued that 'our dearly-bought birthright of freedom is under mortal threat once more. The political elite are nearing the end of a process which will outlaw any expression of opinions deemed to be politically incorrect', and promised that 'all laws against traditional free speech rights will be repealed, starting with the vague, politicised, and hypocritically enforced laws pertaining to race and religion, which are virtually never enforced against foreigners attacking the racial and religious groups indigenous to Britain'. British Conservative newspapers which habitually lament the rise of the BNP should seriously consider the role which the paranoid and divisive myths which they have created about 'political correctness' have played in this process. And while Anthony Browne (now an aide of London mayor Boris Johnson) cannot of course choose his admirers, he should nonetheless find it disturbing that *The Retreat of Reason* is lauded on a number of far-right blogs and sold on the website on Excalibur, the merchandising arm of the BNP, as 'a devastating expose of the effects of Political Correctness and its poisonous effect on public debate in modern Britain. The author shows how the media and government even resort to employing misleading statistical evidence to support their PC objectives. A far reaching book which has the left squealing in horror.'[1] It is also strongly recommended by Richard Barnbrook, the sole BNP member of the Greater London Assembly and the deputy head of the BNP grouping on Barking and Dagenham council, who eulogises 'the thoughts and ideas of a man that is both feared and despised by the politically correct fantasists and other assorted anti-British vermin that currently take their living from our torment'.[2]

5

'A Question of Leadership'
Who Speaks for British Muslims?
Julian Petley

Part I: Setting the Scene

On 21 August 2005, the BBC broadcast an episode of *Panorama* entitled 'A Question of Leadership'. This is how the programme was presented on the BBC News website:

> In this Sunday's *Panorama Special*, John Ware examines questions raised by senior members of the Muslim community themselves: Questions about the direction and role of the Muslim Council of Britain and the influences on the leadership of the organisation and its affiliates.

> After 7/7 the Commissioner of the Metropolitan Police said the Muslim community in Britain is 'fairly close to denial about the extent of extremism in its midst'.

> The Muslim Council of Britain (MCB) is generally regarded as the community's main representative body. After meeting

the Prime Minister at Downing Street, the Secretary General, Sir Iqbal Sacranie, promised that 'the community is determined to deal with this issue head on'.

Several prominent Muslims explain to *Panorama* why they believe the MCB is unlikely to meet this challenge at the moment. Indeed one of the founding members of the MCB tells us that 'It is my personal belief ... that they are in a state of denial.'

Panorama examines the extent of Islamist ideology which some of the affiliates which make up the MCB have brought to Britain from Pakistan and the Middle East over the past forty years.

We show that beyond Iraq, even within some of the mainstream, there exists sectarianism, anti–Semitism, and a powerful conviction that Christians and Jews are conspiring to undermine Islam. Some MCB affiliates also promote the belief that Islam is a superior ideology to secular Britain.

In a wide-ranging interview with Sir Iqbal the discussion ranged from his views on the efforts to deal with extremism in some young British Muslims, to the Regent's Park mosque declaration on suicide bombings, to the rhetoric of some MCB affiliates, the relationship between religion and politics, as well as dealing with direct questions about suicide attacks and Sir Iqbal's views on the targeting of civilians around the world, including in Israel.

Despite some critical comments to the contrary, it is certainly not the case that nearly all the questioning of Sir Iqbal Sacranie was about Israel.[1]

As the final sentence suggests, the programme had become embroiled in controversy, for reasons that will be examined below, even before it was aired. The broadcast itself only increased the controversy, the

Muslim Council of Britain (MCB) writing to the BBC to say that: 'We are saddened and shocked at what we see as a grossly unfair presentation of both our community and our organisation.' The Council accused the programme of being 'dishonestly presented, mischievously edited and clearly aimed at maligning the Muslim Council of Britain and its major affiliates including the Muslim Association of Britain, the Islamic Foundation, Markazi Jamiat Ahl-e-Hadith and the Leeds Grand Mosque, without regard for the facts'. They also criticised it for being presented in a 'sensationalist style' which was 'completely irresponsible'. Worse still, in their view, 'John Ware clearly entered the debate with a preconceived idea of how Muslims should behave, and then sought out individuals, who have very little grassroots support, to try and support his conclusions'. They criticised the programme as 'maliciously motivated' and called upon the BBC to apologise to the MCB and all British Muslims for a 'shoddy and Islamophobic piece of work which will contribute to furthering distrust and divisions in our society'.

The BBC responded that this was a film which:

Reflected the debate within the Muslim community in Britain about the leadership that the MCB offers. The questions in the programme about the MCB's leadership came from members of the Muslim community, and from very many Muslims who did not appear in the final film but who were spoken to during the course of our research.

The letter concluded:

The programme's purpose was to reflect, inform and generate debate in the Muslim community and the wider population, about the nature and direction of the leadership of British Muslims. In the light of the London bombings this is a debate which many Muslims, to whom we spoke, believe is long overdue. They raised important questions about all the issues to which we drew attention. As this debate goes forward I very much hope that you will desist from unwarranted and wildly inaccurate attacks on the honesty of our journalism and the good faith of the *Panorama* team.[2]

On 23 August, the BBC website carried a piece on the controversy. Among other things, this stated that:

Audience reaction to the show has been mixed. More than 640 people have contacted the BBC to complain that the programme portrayed Muslims and the Islamic faith in a negative light. However, nearly 100 people have been in touch to say the programme was excellent and NewsWatch has received emails praising the show.[3]

So what was all the fuss about?

A little history

Before this question can be answered adequately, it is necessary to know something of the history of the MCB.

As Ehsan Masood (2005) pointed out: 'There is a war being fought out at the heart of British Islam', which has been waged since the mid 1970s when the first British Muslim institutions were established. One of the sites around which this war has been waged is the Muslim Council of Britain which was launched in 1998 and now has around 500 affiliates. It owed its initial emergence to a demand in March 1994 from the then Home Secretary Michael Howard for a single representative Muslim body with which the government could deal. This was seized upon by a group of Muslims who had first come to prominence during the *Satanic Verses* affair. According to Jonathan Birt (2005: 99–100), this group was comprised of:

Middle-class Islamic activists, intellectuals and businessmen broadly inspired by the South Asian Islamic reform movements,

103

the Jamaat-i-Islami and, to a lesser extent, the Deobandis, although the Council cannot be defined by the ideologies of these movements, as subsequent political praxis has been much more constitutive of its outlook. Informed by a commitment to faith-based political activism and a suspicion of the compromises inherent in party politics, the subsequent actions of the MCB are in practice only explicable as a balancing act between affiliate expectations and the maintenance of favoured access to if not influence with government.

The MCB aimed to establish control of political patronage for British Muslims and tended to marginalise rival activist Muslim groups operating in Whitehall and Westminster. It was also given a role in recommending appointments from the Muslim community to government advisory committees. However, it is important to note that it has never received core funding from government, only funding for specific projects, and, for reasons that will become clear below, nothing since 2004.

At first, the MCB, for the most part, enjoyed quite a close association with New Labour, and, in the wake of 11 September 2001, played a key role in the government's attempts to make a clear distinction between Islam and terrorism, thus trying to defuse anti-Muslim sentiment at home, stressing that the 'War on Terror' was not a war on Islam, and isolating the more radical elements within the Muslim population. In the days following the bombing, MCB representatives met Jack Straw, David Blunkett and Tessa Jowell, and the government's spin machine was used to influence the press, resulting in, *inter alia*, a centre-spread in the *Sun*, 13 September, headed 'Islam is not an evil religion'. However, once the bombing of Afghanistan began in November, the idea that the 'War on Terror' was not a war on Islam was increasingly questioned by many Muslims, and the MCB declared its public opposition to the action, much to Blair's fury. However, it did stick to the line that the Afghan war was not part of a more general war against Muslims and Islam. According to the only professional poll of Muslim opinion conducted (by ICM) during the war, eighty per cent of Muslims opposed the bombing, and fifty-seven per cent believed this was a war against Islam. Thus, as Birt (2005: 104) puts it, in the wake of 9/11 the MCB 'struggled to retain its credibility with British Muslim opinion while attempting to keep channels of communication open with the government'.

Disappointed with the MCB, Labour looked to support for the war from Muslim MPs, members of the Lords and local councillors, but without much success. By the end of the year, and particularly in the light of a series of official reports into various disturbances involving Asian Muslims in northern towns during the summer of 2001, 'the MCB and, by extension, all other Muslim leaders, were effectively accused of having exacerbated religious separatism and inadvertently laid the grounds for a further youthful radicalisation that they neither condoned nor could control' (2005: 99).

Birt concluded that: 'Having groomed and promoted a unified Muslim lobby for nearly a decade, the British government depicted it as part of the problem when it proved insufficiently compliant' (2005: 105).

Altogether unsurprisingly, there were those Muslims who thoroughly resented the MCB's closeness to government, as well as the government's tendency to treat it as a proxy for mainstream Muslim opinion in general. However, it is actually very doubtful whether such a thing actually exists, as is emphasised by the fact that some Muslims found it too 'political' (citing, for example, its links to organisations such as the Muslim Brotherhood and Jamaat-i-Islami, and its one-time refusal to attend Holocaust Memorial Day), while for others, particularly certain young Muslims, it was nothing like radical enough. Meanwhile, secular Muslim groups have complained about the MCB's failure to engage with the modernisation of Islam, and have taken issue with the former leader of the MCB, Sir Iqbal Sacranie, calling homosexuality 'not acceptable' and same-sex civil partnerships 'harmful'. Yet others felt that it was overly dominated by Muslims of Pakistani origin (who, according to the 2001 census, account for forty-three per cent of the Muslim population, thus making them the largest individual group). A further (and related complaint) is that many Muslims in Britain belong to the Sufi tradition (which now has its own representative organisation, the Sufi Muslim Council) while MCB members come largely from outside that tradition.

There are thus two important points to bear in mind at this stage. First, the MCB is not exactly short of critics among the Muslim population. And, second, although according to the 2001 census, sixty-eight per cent of the Muslim population of Britain may be of South Asian origin, the population as a whole is very far from being homogeneous in any sense. As Ceri Peach (2005: 25) points out:

> Although South Asian groups represent Islam in Britain, there is a danger in essentialising Islam and arguing that South Asian characteristics are fully representative of Islam itself. Pakistanis and Bangladeshis may be almost entirely Muslim, but Islam is pan-Ethnic and there are Muslims in Britain of Arab, Albanian, Bosnian, Iranian, Nigerian, Somali, Turkish and many other groups of origin whose characteristics and socio-economic profiles are very different from those of the South Asian groups. There are huge differences between Sunni Barelwi Pakistanis and East African Ismailis. What is true of the Pakistani and Bangladeshi populations as a whole is not necessarily true of individuals drawn from those populations.

And, regarding what one might call the Muslim public sphere, Mirza and colleagues argue:

> It is important to recognise that British Muslim groups are far from uniform in outlook. Apart from the historic theological differences between Sunnis and Shias, Muslims espouse a range of political and religious views, often in contradiction to each other ... Despite claims about the 'Muslim community', Muslim organisations are deeply split over the appropriate way to pursue Muslim ends.

(2007: 30)

Thus some groups are avowedly political (such as Hizb ut-Tahreer) while others are more culturally and religiously oriented. There are also secular Muslim organisations too, as noted earlier, such as Muslims for Secular Democracy. The more radical political groups generally renounce the machinery of democratic politics (as radical groups of all kinds are wont to do) while the Muslim Public Affairs Committee totally rejects the idea that voting is un-Islamic, and on its website quotes the European Council for Research and Fatwa to the effect that: 'Muslim participation in elections is a national duty; it falls under co-operation on that which is good and righteous for the society and warding off harms from it.'[4]

It is in these various contexts that the following narrative needs to be understood.

Setting the agenda

On 14 July 2005, John Ware was interviewed on the Radio 4 *Today* programme about a forthcoming *Panorama* programme. The presenter Carolyn Quinn introduced the item thus:

> All but a tiny fringe of Muslim organisations in the UK have condemned the London suicide bombings. But are those organisations condemning in London what they are failing to condemn abroad? *Panorama* reporter John Ware is examining the role of the country's main Muslim organisation, the Muslim Council of Britain.

In response to light questioning by Quinn, Ware explained that Sir Iqbal Sacranie had condemned the bombings, and had also said that the loss of both Israeli and Palestinian lives in a suicide bombing in Israel by two British citizens could not be condoned. However, he continued, Sacranie had nevertheless attended a memorial service at the Central Mosque in London after Sheikh Yassin had been assassinated by the Israelis and had described him as 'the renowned Islamic scholar', while Ware described him as 'the chief ideologist of an organisation [Hamas] which seeks the destruction of Israel' and which 'has conducted a fair number of the 160 or so suicide bombings since the second intifada'. Ware also pointed out that Dr Yusuf Qaradawi – 'the man who the mayor of London, Ken Livingstone, welcomed to City Hall last year and described as "moderate" ' – similarly condemned the London bombings, but, when it came to suicide bombings in Israel, stated that: 'We must all realise that the Israeli society is a military society – men and women. We cannot describe the society as civilian … they are not civilians or innocent.' Ware went on to suggest that Qaradawi's remarks on Iraq 'would imply support for attacks on British soldiers as well as American obviously', and pointed out that the MCB had described him as 'a distinguished Muslim scholar … a voice of reason and understanding'. Finally, the interview turned to the subject of Dr Azzam Tamimi, a senior member of the Muslim Association of Britain, which is affiliated to the MCB. Ware pointed out that he too had condemned the London bombings but had also said that, if given the chance in Israel, 'I would sacrifice myself, it's the straight way to pleasing my God.'

Quinn then asked Inayat Bunglawala of the MCB for his thoughts on 'the rather serious charges John Ware is making, alleging the Muslim Council of Britain never expressly condemns all suicide bombings'. Bunglawala replied:

Well let me make clear then, once and for all, we condemn the killing of all innocent people, wherever they are. Human lives everywhere are of equal value, whether they are British, American, Iraqi or Palestinian. Jewish lives are not worth more than Palestinian lives. All are worth equal and it's been quite nauseating over the past week to see how Israel and its highly placed supporters in the media have been trying to make political capital out of last week's atrocities against Londoners. It is shameful on them and shameful on those who are trying to help Israel improve its PR image after the brutalities it commits against the Palestinian people … We always condemn the taking of innocent life anywhere. But can I just make it clear here, it's quite misleading to compare the situation here in the UK with that in Israel. The 1.6 million Muslims in the UK live in peace. They are free to practise their faith and they are free to go about their daily lives without let or hindrance. The Palestinians, by contrast, live under a very brutal occupation, a very repressive Israeli military occupation, seeing their land every day being gobbled up by illegal Jewish settlements.

The interview with Bunglawala was considerably more challenging than that with Ware. For example, sparked off by Quinn's remark that 'that still can't be justification for suicide bombing', the following exchange took place:

Bunglawala: No it cannot. But many of our own columnists, even Members of Parliament, have said that if they were Palestinians, if they were living under those conditions, if they were seeing their children humiliated in the way the Israelis humiliate their children, if they saw their children being blown to pieces, they would consider doing what the Palestinians do. Our own parliamentarians have said that. If they can say that, then of course Muslims will feel a greater affinity for the Palestinians.

Quinn: But you are now saying you must not, you should not, do that. That the Qur'an does not say that that's an acceptable practice.

Bunglawala: Absolutely. The Qur'an says you cannot take innocent life. But, again, to explain is not to justify. When we try and explain why the Palestinians are being driven to what they are doing it is not to justify it. It's trying to explain why they are doing what they are doing. Even our own parliamentarians have tried to do the same.

Questioned about Sheikh Yassin, Bunglawala repeated the point that he was indeed a renowned Islamic scholar, and added that he was assassinated by Israel in defiance of international law. Pressed by Quinn about Tamimi, he responded that the MCB has over 400 affiliates and that 'if he makes that comment he should answer for that'.

Bunglawala's remarks were the subject of criticism by Charles Moore in the *Daily Telegraph*, 16 July. Moore noted that Bunglawala condemned the killing of all innocent people, which, he said, 'sounds fine, but leaves room for dispute about who is innocent and allows you to get in your pitch about other killings'. 'Translating' what he called Bunglawala's 'muddy language', he concluded:

> The murder of British citizens is seen as an occasion to criticise Israel. Support for suicide bombers, though regrettable, is in effect defended; and one leader of the bombers, it is said, should be respected in death, because he was a Muslim scholar. What is happening to a religion when its scholars are telling people to kill others and themselves? The BBC is notoriously shy of using the word 'terrorist' about people who plant bombs: would 'renowned Muslim scholar' be a useful substitute?

Writing in the *Sunday Mirror*, 17 July, Carole Malone complained that:

> In the past week there has been less time spent talking about the victims of London's 9/11 and more on what this atrocity means to British Muslims. To make matters worse the head of the Muslim Council, Iqbal Sacranie, has been screaming about how we keep referring to the terrorists who killed 54 people and injured 700 more as Muslim extremists: 'Why not just call them criminals?' he demanded. And that's precisely the kind of idiocy that gives root to the political correctness that has allowed this country to become the world headquarters for Islamic terrorism.

A few days later, in the *Daily Express*, 23 July, Richard Madeley, writing in the regular 'Richard and Judy' column, revealed that, the previous week, a member of their TV programme team had phoned the office of the MCB, which 'claims to be, and is regarded as, the acceptable face of Islam in the UK', for a quote about a Muslim guest on the show, Irshad Manji. According to Madeley, a spokesman for the MCB had said that she couldn't represent Islam because she was a lesbian, and, when questioned about possible links between the London bombings and Iraq, had responded that he would rather Iraqis were governed by 'a bastard and a dictator' because 'at least he is an Arab'. Madeley commented: 'Remember, this is the official "moderate" voice of British Muslims. And it echoes with homophobic, pro-totalitarian, intolerant stupidity; the kind of language that a member of the British National Party would be comfortable with.'

From a very different perspective there then came attacks on the MCB by Ziauddin Sardar in *The Times*, 25 July, and Salman Rushdie in the same paper on 11 August. For Sardar, in an article entitled 'It is time for a new generation to wrest the leadership away from ageing traditionalists', the main problem was that bodies such as the MCB are old-fashioned and out of touch with younger Muslims. As he put it:

> Traditional Muslim organisations – whether mosques, community or political groups – are run by obscurantist leaders. These people came to the fore in the 1960s and 1970s; many have been made 'life presidents'. The archaic language of tradition and authority they speak is quite incomprehensible to the young. Even the so-called 'democratic' Muslim bodies, such as the Muslim Council of Britain, are run by ageing cliques, working behind the scenes.

Meanwhile, Rushdie focused more squarely on the MCB and its leader Sir Iqbal Sacranie. Reminding his readers that Sacranie had supported the fatwa against him over *The Satanic Verses*, was currently supporting the Religious Hatred Bill and had not attended the commemoration of the sixtieth anniversary of the liberation of Auschwitz, Rushdie argued that:

> The Sacranie case illustrates the weakness of the Government's strategy of relying on traditional, but essentially orthodox, Muslims

to help to eradicate Islamist radicalism. Traditional Islam is a broad church that certainly includes millions of tolerant, civilised men and women, but also encompasses many whose views on women's rights are antediluvian, who think of homosexuality as ungodly, who have little time for real freedom of expression, who routinely express anti-Semitic views, and who, in the case of the Muslim diaspora, are – it has to be said – in many ways at odds with the (Christian, Hindu, non-believing or Jewish) cultures among which they live. In Leeds, from which several of the London bombers came, many traditional Muslims lead lives apart, inward-turned lives of near-segregation from the wider population. From such defensive, separated worlds some youngsters have indefensibly stepped across a moral line and taken up their lethal rucksacks. The deeper alienations that lead to terrorism may have their roots in these young men's objections to events in Iraq or elsewhere, but the closed communities of some traditional Western Muslims are places in which young men's alienations can easily deepen. What is needed is a move beyond tradition – nothing less than a reform movement to bring the core concepts of Islam into the modern age, a Muslim Reformation to combat not only the jihadi ideologues but also the dusty, stifling seminaries of the traditionalists, throwing open the windows of the closed communities to let in much-needed fresh air.

A number of articles critical of the MCB also appeared in the *Observer*, August 14. For example, in his regular column, Nick Cohen pointed out that Muslims have the highest male unemployment rates in Britain. And yet, he continued:

Although Muslims are suffering disproportionately, the Muslim Council of Britain's website has nothing to say about poverty and joblessness. Its campaigns in the past two years have been sectarian, occasionally repellently so. Many are about extending religious privilege, most notably the drive to ban the incitement of religious hatred. A recent anti-semitic entry heightens the sectarian mood by denouncing a forthcoming *Panorama* investigation into the legitimacy of unelected 'community leaders' as a Jewish conspiracy: the *Panorama* team is furthering a 'pro-Israeli agenda', a charge which isn't levelled at the BBC too often.

An article by the paper's then political editor Martin Bright claimed that:

> Far from being moderate, the Muslim Council of Britain has its origins in the extreme orthodox politics in Pakistan. And as its influence increases through Whitehall, many within the Muslim community are growing concerned that this self-appointed organisation is crowding out other, generally moderate, voices of Muslim Britain. Far from representing the more progressive or spiritual traditions within Islam, the leadership of the Muslim Council of Britain and some of its affiliates sympathise with and have links to conservative Islamist movements in the Muslim world and in particular Pakistan's Jamaat-i-Islami, a radical party committed to the establishment of an Islamic state in Pakistan ruled by sharia law.

The article then went on to detail, in terms remarkably similar to *Panorama's*, the history of the MCB and the links of certain of its affiliates, such as the Birmingham based Jamiat Ahl-e-Hadith, with Jamaat-i-Islami. It also alleged that the MCB had used its influence in Whitehall to gain a place on the board of trustees of the forthcoming Festival of Muslim Cultures, but that the organisers feared that they would lose political backing if the festival included material that the MCB deemed 'un-Islamic'. The article quoted Sacranie to the effect that: 'If any activities are seen to contradict the teachings of Islam, then we will oppose them. If you organise a festival in the name of Islam then it must be Islamic. We will advise them accordingly.' Bright concluded that: 'There are those in Britain struggling to transform the austere image Islam has in this country, including the organisers of the Festival of Muslim Cultures, who will not find his words reassuring.'

A further article revealed that the *Observer* had seen the 'extraordinary' letter of complaint that the BBC had received from the MCB, in which it accused the *Panorama* programme of having a 'pro-Israel agenda' and predicting that it will create mistrust and undermine community relations. In turn, the *Observer* asserted that the letter 'will be used by critics of the MCB as evidence that it is out of touch amid growing concern that it does not represent moderate Muslims', and quoted a BBC spokeswoman to the effect that: 'The BBC rejects completely any allegation of institutional or programme bias and is confident the *Panorama* programme will be fair and impartial.' The article reprised a number of the above points about Jamaat-i-Islami and quoted from critics of the MCB such as Rushdie and *Q-News* editor Abdul-Rehman Malik; however, it also gave space to Sacranie, who stated that:

> We are concerned that the test of whether we are doing good work in the UK is whether we pass the Israel test. We have a clear position: we oppose the Israeli occupation. But our prime concern is with the Muslim community in this country.

He also voiced the opinion that, since 7 July, the MCB had been subjected to a 'campaign orchestrated by the pro-Israel lobby'.

Finally, an editorial in the *Observer* entitled 'Muslims deserve better leaders', argued that:

> There is a tendency whenever there is an incident or an issue which could conceivably be viewed through a prism of ethnic or religious identity for the media or politicians to seek out 'community leaders'. In the rush to talk, few stop to think how representative these people might be. But we should. Everyone agrees that many British Muslims feel alienated and disenfranchised. Their voices, 1.5 million of them, need to be heard. It is not right that the Muslim Council of Britain, a group that boycotts a ceremony to honour the multi-faith victims of the Holocaust

and often supports hardline views that are far from universally accepted by all Muslims, should monopolise that function.

It was thus perhaps unsurprising that Yasmin Alibhai-Brown noted in the *Independent*, 15 August, in an article headed 'Britain's Black and Asian communities have squandered the unity that gave us strength', that: 'Suddenly, and unexpectedly, Sir Iqbal Sacranie's Muslim Council for [sic] Britain has found itself under media scrutiny. Perhaps it was inevitable. There is little we can do to stop iniquitous inquisitors, for whom all Muslims are treacherous suspects.' On the other hand, she too added to one of the strands of criticism of the MCB, arguing that:

> Equally we must accept that Muslim organisations have got to be accountable. Although Sacranie is a perfectly decent chap, I believe his MCB should be interrogated more thoroughly than it has been up to now. Recently knighted, Sacranie has been too closely connected with the British establishment, regularly sipping tea in fine china cups at 10 Downing Street; he has crowned himself spokesman for all British Muslims, a position both fanciful and arrogant. The MCB cannot proclaim itself representative of British Muslims when none of its members have ever been elected by the million-plus Muslims in Britain. And many of us resent this presumption.

That day's *Independent* also carried a sympathetic piece about Sacranie, which noted that the MCB 'has set up an investigation into mosques, women's organisations and Islamic youth centres across the country to root out extremism'. In an interview, Sacranie dismissed the allegations of the MCB's links with extremism as 'absolute nonsense' and stated that the efforts to discredit the organisation were born of an 'Islamophobic agenda'. Of the Jamaat-i-Islami party and its founder Sayyid Mawdudi, Sacranie stated: 'We agree with many of his views and disagree with some. The Jamaat-i-Islami party happens to be a perfectly legitimate and democratic party, which through an alliance with other parties, is in power in the North-west Frontier province of Pakistan.' He also defended Jamiat Ahl-e-Hadith, noting that they 'are respected among British Muslims for their educational and outreach programmes. It is absolute nonsense to describe them as separatist. They are not an extremist sect but a national body.'

On the same day, one of Alibhai-Brown's 'iniquitous inquisitors' was in full flood in the *Daily Express*. This was Leo McKinstry in his 'Monday column' entitled 'Let's stop pretending Muslim hardliners are a tiny minority'. McKinstry cited the forthcoming *Panorama* programme as evidence that: 'Far from existing only on the lunatic fringes, the hardliners are part of the Muslim mainstream.' Arguing that the programme highlights 'the extremism at the heart of the Muslim Council of Britain, the most important Islamic organisation in the country', he continued:

> The response of the Muslim Council to the *Panorama* investigation is revealing. Instead of disputing the facts, it accuses the BBC of promoting a 'pro-Israel' agenda and warns that the programme could inflame mistrust towards Muslim communities. Such hysteria has been characteristic of Muslim leaders since 9/11. Rather than challenging their co-religionist zealots, they turn on western societies, moaning about Islamophobia and sliding into anti-semitic rhetoric dressed up as criticism of Israel.

McKinstry attacked Sir Iqbal Sacranie for his 'sinister past' (the Rushdie affair) and concluded that:

> In truth, Sir Iqbal is part of a much wider pattern, with the concept of Muslim moderation being exposed as a sham … The sorry fact is that the extremists are not a tiny minority but a sizeable section of Muslim opinion. According to an ICM poll, 13 per cent of Muslims in this country actually support terrorism. Given that estimates put the Muslim population in Britain at 1.6 million, that is a terrifying figure. And it is reflected in the fact that more than 3,000 men from this country are thought to have volunteered to fight for the Taliban in the war in Afghanistan.

(No source is given for the final statistic)

On the day of the programme itself, 21 August, Joan Smith in the *Independent on Sunday*, in a piece entitled 'Lord Tebbit didn't go far enough', argued that 'the alienation of some young Muslims in this country has its roots in a vicious, separatist theology', and cited one of *Panorama*'s examples of alleged double standards to illustrate this theology:

> Last year the East London Mosque, whose chairman Dr Muhammad Abdul Bari is also deputy general secretary of the Muslim Council of Britain, invited a prominent Saudi cleric to be guest of honour at the opening of a £10m Islamic centre. Sheikh Abdur-Rahman al-Sudais came to London and talked about tolerance but on other occasions he has denounced the 'enemies of Islam', a predictable list of Jews, Christians and secularists, as 'monkeys, pigs and rats'.

The same day's *Sunday Telegraph* turned its attention to the MCB's Inayat Bunglawala, stating that:

> A Muslim accused of anti-Semitism is to be appointed to a government role in charge of rooting out extremism in the wake of last month's suicide bombings in London. Inayat Bunglawala, 36, the media secretary for the Muslim Council of Britain, is understood to have been selected as one of seven 'conveners' for a Home Office task force with responsibilities for tackling extremism among young Muslims, despite a history of anti-Semitic statements. Mr Bunglawala's past comments include the allegation that the British media was 'Zionist-controlled' ... In January 1993, Mr Bunglawala wrote a letter to *Private Eye*, the satirical magazine, in which he called the blind Sheikh Omar Abdul Rahman 'courageous' – just a month before he bombed the World Trade Center in New York. After Rahman's arrest in July that year, Mr Bunglawala said that it was probably only because of his 'calling on Muslims to fulfil their duty to Allah and to fight against oppression and oppressors everywhere'. Five months

before 9/11, Mr Bunglawala also circulated writings of Osama bin Laden, who he regarded as a 'freedom fighter', to hundreds of Muslims in Britain.

Bunglawala himself was not given the opportunity to comment on any of these allegations (most of which are extremely elderly), and the article went on to summarise a number of the points made in the *Panorama* programme itself. There was also a short piece about Bunglawala to the same effect in the *Sunday Mirror*, while the *Sunday Express*, in an article headed 'Muslim leaders are accused of failing to root out extremists', contented itself with reprising some of the programme's main claims. Finally, the *News of the World* summed up the programme thus: 'British Muslim leaders refuse to denounce Islamic extremists who call for the death of Christians and Jews, according to tonight's BBC *Panorama* documentary. The Muslim Council of Britain also fail to admit how widespread radical Islam is – and are blasted by moderates as in a "state of denial".'

But again it was the *Observer* which devoted the most space to the issue. To a certain extent, this balanced the previous week's articles, as Sir Iqbal Sacranie was granted a right of reply, and a range of comments culled from a 'huge response' from readers was printed. Another piece by Martin Bright reported on the ongoing feud between the BBC and the MCB, quoting a 'senior source close to the programme' to the effect that: 'The BBC is aware that the MCB have been making unorthodox approaches to a number of contributors, putting pressure on them to withdraw.' The article glossed a number of points made by the programme, but also quoted Sacranie as saying that:

It is unfortunate that just when Britain's 1.6 million Muslims are beginning to make progress in terms of their political participation in the mainstream, there are those who are trying to sabotage that process.

What this section has attempted to demonstrate is that in the weeks leading up to the broadcasting of the *Panorama* episode

'A Question of Leadership', a very great deal of interest was expressed by the press in the issues that it raised, which, for the most part, were dealt with uncritically and on the programme's own terms. Presumably a good deal of this was inspired by briefings from the BBC press office and by the *Panorama* team itself, and it is of course quite unexceptionable that the BBC should have tried to gain press coverage for the programme in advance of its transmission, especially in today's hyper-competitive television environment. It is notable, however, that the vast majority of the reports presented the programme's findings in supportive terms, although overt comment took very different forms, from McKinstry on the one hand to Sardar and Rushdie on the other. Interestingly, however, it was a liberal newspaper, the *Observer*, which devoted the greatest amount of space to the issue. Interesting because the *Observer*, like Britain's only other liberal newspapers the *Guardian* and the *Independent*, has generally adopted a far less critical and hostile attitude towards Britain's ethnic communities and their representative organisations than the rest of Britain's press. The *Observer*'s coverage of the issue is relatively balanced but, taken as a whole, it clearly comes down on the side of the MCB's critics. However, unlike McKinstry and Malone, for example, it is concerned less with demonising the MCB (although there is an element of this) than with arguing, as in the leader of 14 August, that Britain's Muslims are diverse and thus require heterogeneous organisations in order to represent their various interests, needs and points of view. In this respect, then, the paper's coverage of this issue was not seriously at odds with its generally liberal agenda on matters concerning Britain's ethnic communities.

Part II: *Panorama*, 'A Question of Leadership', 21 August 2005

According to John Ware in a letter to the *Guardian*, 23 August, the purpose of the programme was to 'highlight how the MCB is either

in denial of, or tolerates, racism and sectarianism in some of its affiliates'. And in his introduction to the programme itself he stated:

> Extremism feeds off a conviction that Islam is a superior faith
> and culture which Christians and Jews in the West are conspir-
> ing to undermine. My journey through Muslim communities
> since the London bombings suggests their leaders have not
> acknowledged the extent to which these views are held in
> Britain. Muslim leaders have condemned utterly the bombings.
> And yet this murderous rage grew from within their communi-
> ties. Some Muslims believe that the time for a full and frank
> debate about where Islam is going here is long overdue.[5]

Central to the programme's arguments is what Ware refers to as
'Islamism', which he defines as 'the fusion of politics and faith', an
ideology which, he claims, 'burst into the British arena' with the
Rushdie affair. Via the Shabina Begum case (see below), Ware argues
that the MCB is firmly identified with this fusion. However, as Ware
points out (and as noted above), most British Muslims are Sufis,
which, in his view, means that 'they do not politicise their faith;
theirs is personal and spiritual'. This leads on to a double charge
against the MCB. First, that it does not effectively represent the views
of the majority Muslim population. And second, that it is 'playing
politics in a secular country'.

The case for the MCB being 'in denial' and politicising the faith
is presented by Dr Ghayasuddin Siddiqui of the Muslim Institute;
Mehboob Kantharia, a founding member of the MCB; Professor
Neal Robinson of the University of Louvain, Belgium; Dr Taj Hargey,
Chairman of the Muslim Council, Oxford; Sheikh Musa Admani,
Imam at London Metropolitan University; and Nicholas Mehdi
Lock, Teacher at Nottingham Islamia School. The case against is put
by Dr Muhammad Abdul Bari, Chairman of the East London
Mosque and Deputy General Secretary of the MCB; Sir Iqbal
Sacranie, Secretary General of the MCB; Professor Kurshid Ahmad,
Chairman and Rector of the Islamic Foundation, and Vice President

of Jamaat-i-Islami; and Dr Azzam Tamimi, introduced as 'a Palestinian who often acts as a senior spokesman for the MCB'.

Clearly, the programme raises a large number of extremely complex issues, and, as noted at the start of this chapter, has been the subject of considerable comment and controversy. In the circumstances, perhaps the best way to undertake an analysis of the controversy is through a number of specific points raised by the programme's critics, and then move on to consider the rather more general ones.

Selective quotation

One of the main criticisms that has been made of the programme is that it engaged in selective and out-of-context quotation. Let's examine a particular example.

In a section of the programme devoted to the Islamic Foundation, it is stated that its online book sales 'promote the ideology' of Sayyid Mawdudi, who is described as 'the ideologue and founder of the Jamaa'at Islami [sic]', a party which, we are told, 'wants Pakistan to become an Islamic state governed by Sharia holy law'. Ware goes on to state that: 'In Mawdudi's ideal Islamic state, private and public life would be inseparable. In this respect it would bear "a kind of resemblance to the fascist and communist states".' The quotation itself is not only spoken on the soundtrack but flashed up on screen as well. (The actual manner in which the programme presents quotations will be discussed below.)

In its letter to the BBC, the MCB complained that the programme had quoted Mawdudi's words out of context, and quoted a fuller version of the passage concerned, which is taken from Mawdudi's book *Islamic Law and Constitution*:

Considered from this aspect the Islamic State bears a kind of resemblance to the Fascist and Communist states. But you will find later on that, despite its all-inclusiveness, it is something vastly and basically different from the totalitarian and authoritarian

121

states. Individual liberty is not suppressed under it nor is there any trace of dictatorship in it. It presents the middle course and embodies the best that the human society has ever evolved.

The BBC's response was to produce a yet fuller version of the disputed passage:

A state of this sort cannot evidently restrict the scope of its activities. Its approach is universal and all-embracing. Its sphere of activity is coextensive with the whole of human life. It seeks to mould every aspect of life and activity in consonance with its moral norms and programmes of social reform. In such a state, no one can regard any field of his affairs as personal and private. Considered from this perspective the Islamic State bears a kind of resemblance to the Fascist and Communist states. But you will find later on that, despite its all inclusiveness it is something vastly and basically different from the totalitarian and authoritarian states. Individual liberty is not suppressed under it nor is there any trace of dictatorship in it. It presents the middle course and embodies the best that the human society has ever evolved. The excellent balance and moderation that characterise the Islamic system of government and the precise distinctions made in it between right and wrong elicit from all men of honesty and intelligence the admiration and the admission that such a balanced system could not have been framed by anyone but the Omniscient and All-Wise God.

According to the BBC:

Given that Mawdudi writes that the Islamic state 'seeks to mould every aspect of life and activity in consonance with its moral norms and programmes of social reform', the applicability of the reference to 'a kind of resemblance to Fascist and Communist states' is clear. The commentary in the film limited the application of this Mawdudi quote to precisely the same limits as he did in writing the above paragraph, namely: in respect of making private and public life inseparable.

However, this response not only fails to meet the original criticism, it actually strengthens it. It is abundantly clear from the full quotation that Mawdudi's comparison of an Islamic state with a fascist or communist one is meant only in an extremely limited sense, a sense that is not in the least adequately communicated by Ware's parenthetical 'in this respect', particularly given the manner in which the words 'a kind of resemblance to the fascist and communist states' are intoned on the soundtrack and presented on screen (see below), and particularly given the tone and stance of the programme *as a whole*. Nor is it acceptable to claim, as the BBC seems to imply, that the programme ignored the passage about a Muslim state being 'something vastly and basically different from the totalitarian and authoritarian states. Individual liberty is not suppressed under it nor is there any trace of dictatorship in it' because 'the claim was one that the production team and I considered as flying in the face of known facts about Mawdudi's own values'. If this really is the case, then the passage should have been quoted and then challenged; instead the programme team simply formed their own judgement on the matter and effectively denied viewers the opportunity to do likewise.

Shabina Begum and 'fundamentalism'

Let us now consider the programme's presentation of the case of Shabina Begum who in 2002 told her school, Denbigh High in Luton, that she wished to wear a *jilbab* (an ankle-length gown) rather than the *shalwar kameez* (trousers and tunic) worn by the school's other Muslim pupils. The school said that she could not attend lessons except in an approved uniform, so she worked at home, and then went to another school where the *jilbab* was allowed, while taking her case for re-instatement through the courts. Eventually she lost.

There appear to be two reasons why this case is included in the programme. First, according to Ware: 'The Muslim Council of Britain has recently helped politicise the issue [of the *jilbab*] in state schools.' However, from the programme itself it is completely impossible to deduce the manner in which the MCB has allegedly helped to 'politicise' either the *jilbab* issue in general or the Begum case in particular. Nor have I found evidence for this view from other sources. Indeed, all that the BBC News website shows is that, at the time of the case, Sir Iqbal Sacranie stated that: 'Those that choose to wear the *jilbab* and consider it to be part of their faith requirement for modest attire should be respected.'[6]

Furthermore, the BBC's reply to the MCB's letter of complaint offers something of a hostage to fortune by quoting from the transcripts of the court case thus:

> On 30 September Mr Shahid Akmal, Chairman of the Comparative Religion Centre in Harrow wrote to Mr Moore [assistant headteacher of Denbigh High], enclosing advice from the Muslim Council of Britain setting out the dress code for women in Islam. This included:
>
> (i) there is no recommended style
> (ii) modesty needs to be observed at all times
> (iii) trousers with long tops/shirts for school wear are absolutely fine
> (iv) a Muslim school girl's uniform does not have to be flowing or of such length that there will be a risk of tripping over and causing an accident. Mr Akmal wrote: 'In summary, the dress code prescribed by your school for Muslim females as per your "School Uniform Requirements" leaflet is in accordance with the tenets of Islam.'

From this, the BBC concludes, perfectly correctly, that: 'It seems that the MCB has considered the uniform requirements at Denbigh High School to be sufficient to meet the requirements of modesty mentioned in the Qur'an.' In which case, then, it is quite impossible to understand how the MCB can be accused of 'playing politics' with the *jilbab* issue, either in general or in the specific case of Shabina Begum.

However, there is yet more to this issue. According to Ware: 'Ms Begum appeared to be following a fundamentalist agenda' and was 'advised by the women's section of the radical Hizb ut-Tahreer group, which the government is planning to ban.' This manages to push a number of negative buttons simultaneously. First of all, it's worth pointing out that the government has repeatedly failed to ban Hizb ut-Tahreer, who have denied that they advised Begum, stating in the *Guardian*, 4 March 2005, that: 'We were not involved in her case in any way, but we were there for her in terms of explaining Islamic values as we are for the Muslim community in general.' Nor is the sense in which Begum is a 'fundamentalist' (a word which, given its immensely negative connotations in such a context, should be used only with the greatest of care) explained in any way. A clip of Begum shows her merely stating that she acted 'out of my faith and belief in Islam' while, outside the context of the programme, in an interview in the *Guardian*, 3 March 2005, she said that: 'Today's decision is a victory for all Muslims who wish to preserve their identity and values despite prejudice and bigotry.' In her view, the school's decision had been 'a consequence of an atmosphere that has been created in western societies post-9/11, an atmosphere in which Islam has been made a target for vilification in the name of the "war on terror" '. She also told the *Guardian*:

> I hope in years to come policy-makers will take note of a growing number of young Muslims who, like me, have turned back to our faith after years of being taught that we needed to be liberated from it. Our belief in our faith is the one thing that makes sense of a world gone mad, a world where Muslim women, from Uzbekistan to Turkey, are feeling the brunt of policies guided by western governments.

It would be interesting to know in what sense the BBC believes that such views constitute 'fundamentalism'.

Before leaving this topic, we might also note that the MCB pointed out in its letter of complaint that:

> Many other schools do allow the wearing of the *jilbab* by Muslim schoolgirls without it causing any problems whatsoever, yet Ware, once again, did not mention this. This omission would have left the unsuspecting viewer to believe that it was Shabina who was behaving intransigently, instead of Denbigh High School, which made the headlines precisely because it refused to allow Shabina Begum to exercise her rights.

The point is well taken.

A secular country

Ware makes the point on three separate occasions that the UK is a secular country and, on the third occasion, in an interview with Sir Iqbal Sacranie, repeatedly accuses the MCB of 'playing politics with religion in a secular country'. Maintaining a hard and fast opposition between the secular and the non-secular is absolutely central to the programme's strategy, but such a distinction is in fact nothing like as clear-cut in the case of the UK as the programme implies. For example the Queen is head of both the state and of the established Church, Christian clergy sit in the Lords, and the country is governed by Christian values in a broad sense. In response to the MCB's complaint on this topic, the BBC replied:

> I think you are missing the broad point that was being made. The programme examined whether the MCB was failing to acknowledge the extent to which British society separates religion and politics, and operate with an accepted and fundamental recognition of the distinction between sacred and secular. The production team considered that Britain's modern political culture is a secular one – it does not elevate religious

126

beliefs to the level of a party or group manifesto, nor does it accept that religious demands have the status of political imperatives. This political culture sits within a broadly secular culture in 21st century Britain.

Broadly speaking, this is true. But it is quite impossible to discuss the beliefs of Muslims in Britain without rapidly running up against the issue of Israel in particular and the Middle East in general, and, of course, of Britain's position on these issues, as the *Panorama* programme amply demonstrates. Among the non-Jewish population of the UK, this is not a religious issue. But for many in the USA (particularly members of the Bush administration, which was in power at this time), including many in the current administration, it most certainly is. As the BBC's own religious affairs correspondent Robert Piggott put it in a particularly strong edition of the BBC series *Heaven and Earth*, 23 July 2006, largely devoted to the Middle East crisis:

America's steadfast support [for Israel] is strategic and political, but it seems to have another, religious, source. The abiding support for Israel among American law-makers isn't based just on strategic concerns or on the relatively small number of Jews living in America – it's also fed by an influential Christian lobby whose Bible-based, evangelical views mean that they see the Jewish people as central to the history of Christianity and to its ultimate destiny. Its most powerful expression comes in something loosely known as end-times theology, which is based largely on Old Testament prophecies. One version has it that Jews must be gathered in the land of Israel before the battle of Armageddon can occur and Jesus return to rule over a re-made Earth.

Piggott estimated that the US contains 17 million evangelicals who hold these or similar views. He also interviewed Kevin Phillips, a former Republican party strategist, whose book *American Theocracy* (2006) is a key text on this subject. Phillips argues that about half of those making up the Republican coalition ruling the country believe in the literal account of the second coming set out by end-times theology, and that it is these people, rather than simply the Jewish lobby, who drive American policy in the Middle East. A non-evangelical Christian also points out that neo-conservatives, who are not necessarily evangelicals, or even Christian, deliberately exploit end-times theology in order to push the pro-Israel agenda. Piggott concludes that: 'The nation faces terrorism, a resurgent Iran with nuclear weapons and an unstable Middle East, and it does so with an administration that sees the world as a battle between good and evil. They're circumstances that seem to come uncomfortably close to setting up the Armageddon that many in America expect', and at the end of the item, the programme's co-presenter David Grant calls end-times theology a 'very potent mixture, some would say incendiary mixture, of fundamentalist religion and politics'.

The point here is a simple one. If American policy towards Israel is to some extent religiously motivated, then the opposition on which the programme turns between the modern, rational West versus the backward, theocratic East starts to look distinctly shaky. Furthermore, even though Britain's support for Israel is not based on religious grounds, it is, in its support for US policy on Israel in particular and the Middle East in general, backing a policy that is to some extent religiously motivated.

'Islamism'

As already noted, central to the programme's arguments is what Ware refers to as 'Islamism', which he defines as 'the fusion of politics and faith' and which he argues is a distinguishing feature of the MCB and some of its affiliates. Here it is extremely important to understand that, although Ware characteristically fails to mention it, 'Islamism' is actually a highly controversial term, and very far from value-free.

An excellent discussion of the term's history and usage is provided by Martin Kramer, who points out that, in the 1980s, the word 'Islamism' came into play to denote the political manifestation of the religion of Islam and also as an attempt to displace the term 'Islamic fundamentalism', with all its negative and pejorative connotations. However, what happened in the 1990s was that:

> As Islamism gained currency, it too became associated with benighted extremism, from the Taliban to the Algerian Armed Islamic Group, culminating in the mega-terror of Usama bin Ladin. Critics of Islamism found it easy to add Islamism to the list of dangerous twentieth century 'isms' that had defied the liberal West and gone down to defeat.

(2003: 73–4)

Hence, for example, the typically moderate and conciliatory piece in the *Guardian*, 12 February 2002, by Margaret Thatcher headed 'Islamism is the new Bolshevism'. Meanwhile in the Islamic world itself, the word is also controversial. For example, it is used in a positive sense by some Muslims who argue that Islam is not only a religion but a political system, and that the Qur'an lays down the basis for an Islamic form of government. For others, however, it has unwelcome connotations of radicalism and extremism. Meanwhile there are those who deny that there is any difference between Islam and Islamism. For example, an editorial by Abid Uallah Jan on 27 February 2006 on the Al-Jazeera website asked: 'If Islam is a way of life, how can we say that those who want to live by its principles in legal, social, political, economic, and political spheres of life are not Muslims, but Islamists and believe in Islamism, not Islam?', while Kramer notes that when the French academic François Burgat published his book *L'Islamisme au Maghreb* in 1988, Abassi Madani, the leader of the Algerian Islamic Salvation Front, told him: 'In your book, you must first of all change the title! Why "Islamism"? It is Islam that is at work in Algeria, nothing but Islam. We are Muslims!' (2003: 74).

The personal and the political

Ware also states that most British Muslims are Sufis, which, in his view, means that 'they do not politicise their faith; theirs is personal and spiritual'. Taken in the context of the programme as a whole, this effectively sets up a binary opposition between 'non-political' Sufis and the 'political' MCB. However, Sufism in Britain is nothing like as homogeneous as Ware implies, and in particular, as the MCB pointed out in its letter of complaint, by no means all Sufis can be considered 'non-political':

> Muslims who follow the 'Sufi way' as well as others are both in the same Muttahida Majlis Amal (MMA) coalition party as the Jamaat-i-Islami in Pakistan. This is the same Jamaat-i-Islami that Ware attempts to portray as extremists. The primary anti-colonial jihadist movements of the 19th century were all Sufi-inspired. For example, Imam Shamil in Daghestan belonged to the famous Naqshbandi order, Umar al-Mukhtar in Libya to the Sanusi order, Amir Abdul Qadir in Algeria to the Qadiri order and so on.

A similar point was made by Abdullah al-Kateb (2005) who argued that:

> Those who do follow a Sufi *tariqa* (path) are not necessarily apolitical. Some medieval Sufis, such as Abu-Hamid al-Ghazali (1058–1111), wrote tracts on the political issues of their day. The late Syrian *sheikh* and modern Sufi, Abdul Fattah Abu-Ghuddah, was one of the main leaders of the Muslim Brotherhood in Syria. Others, such as Imam Shamil (1797–1871), led a long war of resistance against the Russian occupation of the Caucasus.

Unfortunately for the MCB, it misquoted Ware in its letter, which served to cloud the issue. However, in its response the BBC stated that: 'Nothing in our report precludes the idea that followers of Sufi teachings, or indeed any other Muslims motivated by the values of their faith, might be strongly involved in political processes either today or in the colonial past', thus setting up an extremely fine, and some might say extremely tenuous, distinction between Muslims who 'politicise their faith' and Muslims 'strongly involved in political processes'. It is also impossible to grasp how this sentence can, logically, be reconciled with Ware's contention that: 'They [Sufis] do not politicise their faith; theirs is personal and spiritual.'

In this context, it's also important to note that Abdullah al-Kateb (2005) also contested the distinction between Sufi and non-Sufi Islam, even going so far as to claim that 'there is no such thing as "Sufi Islam"'. While agreeing that there are most certainly differences among various Muslim groups in Britain, he also claimed that: 'Most of these theological issues are decades (and sometimes centuries) old; they arose long before the modern phenomenon of terrorism.' He also argued that one of the main problems with the *Panorama* programme is that it did not address these differences and issues 'in the context of scripture and theology', adding that:

> Some differences relate to theology, others to law; some groups that differ with each other on one point may find common ground on another. The process of understanding sects and groups can be painstaking, and many journalists are unable or unwilling to undergo it. John Ware's *Panorama* is illuminating in this respect.

Not without reason, al-Kateb thus enquired: 'Why are such issues being hashed together as if they were directly related to the London attacks?'

The question of the personal and the political in Islam was also taken up, from a different perspective, by Abidullah Ansari in *Q-News*, November 2005. As might be expected from a magazine that speaks for Sufis and is a trenchant critic of the MCB, the article welcomed many of the programme's revelations about some of the MCB's affiliates, but it was also extremely critical of Ware's simplistic distinction between the 'political' and 'non-political' in Islam:

The problem of Islamist control of key organisations was explained in terms of 'political religion', not of mistakes in interpreting shariah and *aqeedah*. Clearly, any attempt to depoliticise Islam is foolish, given the religion's origins and its historic achievements. The presenter suggested that 'It's a battle of ideas – between those for whom Islam is personal – and those who also wish to pursue Islam as a political ideology.' Here he spilled his secularist beans. Mainstream orthodox Islam is not, and never has been, apolitical. Leaders such as the former Bosnian president Izetbegovic saw their struggle against Christian oppression in Islamic terms. This is where the programme failed totally, since it presented the struggle between the Muslim community and the Islamists as a fight between apolitical and political religion, when no one on either side sees it like this. Properly understood it is a fight between orthodox Islam, full of mercy and wisdom, and the British extrusion of Middle Eastern and Pakistani Islamism, popular only among some middle-class technocrats with a weak Islamic education. The programme claimed to range the apolitical against the politicised; but what we really saw was scholars ranged against Islamists. Few in the British establishment seem to comprehend that British Islam should be represented by scholars, rather than by medics and accountants who have read Mawdudi.

Guilt by association

As should now be evident, one of the programme's central strategies is repeatedly to suggest guilt by association. Here, from many possible examples, are three particularly clear ones.

This is how John Ware introduced the Islamic Foundation:

I'm on my way to the organisation that mobilised the Rushdie protests. It too is an important affiliate of the MCB. It was once

132

described as the most influential outpost of militant Islamist ideology in the West – it's based in Leicester. The Islamic Foundation was set up in 1974 by leading figures in an Islamist opposition party from Pakistan. The Jamma'at Islami [sic] wants Pakistan to become an Islamic state governed by Sharia holy law.

But what exactly is being suggested or implied here? That the MCB wants Britain to become an Islamic state governed by Sharia law?

Ware also informs us that when Sir Iqbal Sacranie went to Leeds in the wake of the London bombings, he prayed at the Grand Mosque there. Ware notes that this is where Abdullah Jamal, one of the bombers, spent a good deal of time, and adds: 'It too is an affiliate of the Muslim Council of Britain – and the only mosque in Leeds that follows a political version of Islam.' But, again, what exactly is being suggested or implied here? That Sacranie and the rest of the MCB also want to bomb London?

Over shots of a demonstration in Trafalgar Square against the invasion and occupation of Iraq, Ware states:

> The joint-organisers of this demonstration see themselves as the conscience of the Muslim Council of Britain. The Muslim Association of Britain is a major affiliate of the MCB and rallies young Muslims to the cause of their brothers and sisters in Palestine and Iraq. These placards equating Zionism with Nazi Germany were displayed on MAB's website. They've appeared regularly at MAB organised rallies.

But as it is hardly news that some people equate Zionism and Nazism, what exactly is the point that Ware is trying to make by linking the MAB to the MCB in this particular context?

In actual fact, these passages conspicuously fail to make any concrete or substantive points whatsoever, and are simply examples of smear journalism, an odious form of journalism that either lacks the proof for the points it wishes to make, or the courage to say what it means and face the legal consequences, or both. This is exactly the kind of journalism that one expects from the tabloid press (for which Ware, entirely unsurprisingly, once worked), but to find it in full flower on what is supposed to be the BBC's flagship current affairs programme is surely quite unacceptable.

The grand inquisitor

As noted earlier, the programme marshals six interviewees in support of its thesis, and four who oppose it. In terms of the screen time allotted to both sides the programme is fairly well balanced. However, the *manner* in which the representatives of the two sides are interviewed is noticeably, indeed dramatically, different, Ware adopting the stance of friendly interlocutor with the supporters, and prosecuting counsel or grand inquisitor with the opponents. Even his body language varies startlingly according to whom he is speaking, sitting back and nodding at the supporters, peering accusingly over his spectacles at the opponents and burrowing in his files to produce the supposedly killer quotes which apparently reveal their affiliates to be extremists of one kind or another. When all else fails he resorts simply to badgering and browbeating them. (In this respect it's not surprising that the Muslim Council's concerns about the programme pre-dated its transmission – the manner in which Ware had interviewed those involved with it had obviously alerted them to what was coming.) The spectacle is not only unedifying, it is also completely un-illuminating (other than of Ware's journalistic methods). Let's look at three examples.

The case against Dr Abdul Bari, Chairman of the East London Mosque and Deputy General Secretary of the MCB is that he invited Sheikh Abdur-Rahman Al-Sudais, an Imam from Saudi Arabia, to the opening of a new Islamic Centre in the East End. There the Sheikh spoke of the history of Islam being a testament to how different communities can live together in peace and harmony, but in Saudi Arabia he had attacked 'aggressive Jews and oppressive Zionists', as well as Christians and Hindus. This is another case of guilt by association, but it does seem extraordinary that a journalist as experienced as Ware should apparently find it so shocking that a speaker has said one thing to one audience and something else to another – politicians do this all the time. And it is surely particularly unsurprising that speakers should adopt a different tone when speaking in a region as strife-torn as the Middle East from that used when speaking in the peaceful UK.

The case against Dr Azzam Tamimi, introduced as 'a Palestinian who often acts as a senior spokesman for the MCB' and who 'on behalf of the MAB ... has avowedly promoted Islam as a political ideology', is that 'he supports suicide bombings in Israel and the resistance in Iraq'. This is an extremely complicated and controversial issue, but Ware is concerned simply with accusing Tamimi of breaking the law by allegedly 'glorifying terrorism' and of being an 'apologist for terrorism'. Thus:

John Ware: Following the London bombings, to stop more young British Muslims being drawn into terrorism the government says it will prosecute anyone who glorifies terrorism – wherever it happens.

Dr Azzam Tamimi: I don't glorify killing anybody. I explain, I ... my job is to explain. I explain why people resort to certain tactics in certain contexts.

John Ware: So when you said for example: 'For us Muslims, martyrdom is not the end of things but the beginning of the most wonderful of things.' That's more than explanation, that's glorification, isn't it. Glorification?

Dr Azzam Tamimi: Martyrdom is an Islamic concept. You cannot rule it out of Islam. If people abuse it, or use it in the wrong place, or kill innocent people and call it martyrdom, that's something else. But martyrdom is definitely an Islamic concept.

John Ware: 'The blood of martyrs provides nourishment and sustenance for those who continue this struggle.' That's more than explanation, isn't it, that's glorification – isn't it?

Dr Azzam Tamimi: Well if you … if you occupy other people's lands, people have to …

John Ware: No, I'm sorry, just answer the question. You said all you do is explain, you don't glorify it, and I'm saying that what you've said goes further than that, I think it does glorify.

Dr Azzam Tamimi: So what?

John Ware: Well does it or doesn't it?

Dr Azzam Tamimi: It has to be attached to a context. What are we talking about? About the concept of martyrdom in general which means offering yourself for the sake of defending your homeland, for the sake of defending your community, then that has to be glorified of course.

John Ware: You said that martyrdom in Israel is quotes: 'divine bliss'. That's glorifying, that is glorifying the tactics in another country irrespective of the rights and wrongs of the Israeli government, that is glorifying a terrorist tactic, the same tactic that was used in London. You, Mr Tamimi, are an apologist for terrorism, aren't you?

Dr Azzam Tamimi: If you want to consider me so that's up to you.

The real problem here is that Ware is so keen to press his prosecution of Tamimi that the latter is quite unable to explain what is actually meant by martyrdom in this context. It is thus perhaps hardly surprising that Tamimi's attitude towards Ware becomes increasingly contemptuous and dismissive. Martyrdom in an Islamic context is an extremely complex subject, and in the context of suicide bombing a highly controversial one too, but this confrontation throws not the slightest light on either topic. As Humayan Ansari (2005: 150) puts it: 'Martyrdom for a Muslim can be a choice – between accepting "disgraceful death of a humbled people" and a "desired death when confronted with the destruction of one's freedoms and rights". For most Muslims, as the programme does in fact make clear, suicide bombing is entirely *haram* (forbidden), but among Palestinian Muslims there is, nonetheless, a different view, as Faisal Bodi explained in the *Guardian*, 28 August 2001:

> Faiths don't operate in a vacuum and the dominant context in the West Bank and Gaza has been the Israeli occupation. Consequently, resurgent Islam has expressed itself in the language of resistance. Nearly 1400 years before it entered international conventions, the right of resistance was etched into Muslim tradition by Mohammed.

> Islam taught the feuding Arabian tribes the sanctity of human life, as well as faith, property and dignity. An obvious corollary of placing such a high value on these sanctities was that they should be defended when threatened. And so came about the idea of jihad, or sacred struggle.

> Islamic eschatology extols the one who puts his life on the line for a greater cause. It raises him in the sight of God – the ultimate goal for all believers. To those who fall in battle it grants the highest station in paradise.

> Such is the value of martyrdom that Islamic history is replete with romanticised accounts of the juvenile, elderly and infirm feigning battle-readiness to avoid missing out on the chance to die in God's way. This is the mental and spiritual state of the human-bomber. Faith has driven him to seek salvation in an act of supreme selflessness.

> In the Muslim world, then, we celebrate what we call the martyr-bombers. To us they are heroes defending the things we hold sacred. Polls in the Middle East show 75% of people in favour of martyr-bombings.

They also carry the weight of religious authority. The world's most quoted independent Islamic jurist, Sheikh Yusuf al-Qaradawi, calls the bombs 'commendable' and 'among the greatest form of holy struggle against oppression'.

It does need to be stressed that such views are rare in the Muslim world, at least outside the Middle East, but they do exist, and indeed are increasing in strength. Having brought up the topic of martyrdom in the context of suicide bombing, the programme surely owed it to its audience to explain what this actually means, as opposed to using it to stage a macho, and frankly, given the context, extremely tasteless, gladiatorial confrontation.

Finally, let's turn to the case against Sir Iqbal Sacranie. This can be divided into four parts.

The first charge is that an affiliate of the MCB, Ahl-e-Hadith is 'inspired by puritanical Saudi ideology', that its website makes negative comments about Jews and Christians, and that it propagates a 'them and us culture'. Sacranie replies: 'I don't subscribe to that. I'm not a member of Ahl-e-Hadith but it's a membership that we have, it's diversity that exists in the community, having different views on life.' Ware responds: 'Isn't it a form of diversity that you should disown?' Sacranie replies:

Well we must accept the reality on the ground that the diversity that we have with the Muslim Community in the UK, and as long as they subscribe to our constitution, which is very clear, which is on the website and it's totally transparent in terms of its activities of a work which is through the teachings of the Qur'an and upholding the principles of Islam; then what they do outside the Council, there is no control that we have on them.

This, of course, is yet another example of guilt by association, but it also, like many of Ware's other charges, completely misunderstands the nature of the MCB,[7] as Sacranie clearly points out again later in the programme:

Our job is not to go and monitor what every single Imam in this country is delivering at the Friday Khutbah. This is perhaps an over-estimation of what we as a community organisation can do. We have representatives from across the country, organisations that take our view, it's such a diverse group of membership that we can only agree upon the common denominator, the lowest common denominator.

The umbrella-like nature of the MCB, as well as the radical heterogeneity of Muslim views and organisations in the UK has been touched upon earlier in this chapter, and Madeleine Bunting in the *Guardian*, 22 August, took up these points with specific reference to the above exchange, in which, she claimed:

Ware revealed his lack of comprehension of the Muslim community. Sacranie only has as much power as the MCB affiliate organisations allow him – the idea of him putting an imam right is ridiculous. The tiny, volunteer-run MCB doesn't have the power to police the views of its disparate membership. Sacranie and the MCB have a tightrope to walk. On the one hand, the government and non–Muslim Britain are piling on the pressure that they deliver a law–abiding, loyal ethnic minority. On the other, an increasingly restless younger generation of Muslims criticise the MCB as far too moderate, a sell-out establishment stooge cosying up to Tony Blair.

The second charge is that, after the London bombings, Sacranie went to Leeds, where three of the bombers had lived. Ware notes that: 'At this impromptu press conference Sir Iqbal Sacranie focused on the conduct of the police' and a clip then shows Sacranie saying:

Immediately when the raids were carried out, there's hardly any communication with the community leaders. We've had cases where the pressures on some of the family members while not directly involved with the people who had committed the crime, have been under immense pressure, and their personal material has been removed and been displayed in the national press.

However, as there is a great deal of reliable evidence to suggest that oppressive and not infrequently racist behaviour by the police has been a major factor in inflaming Muslim opinion in Britain over the years, and especially since the 'War on Terror', it seems utterly extraordinary for Ware implicitly to criticise Sacranie for speaking thus.

Third, and as already noted, Ware accuses Sacranie – three times – of 'playing politics with religion'. This comes about because of Sacranie's refusal to distance himself from the notion that the 'War on Terror' is a 'war on Islam', and the interviewer's refusal to accept the validity of such a point of view, even though this is exactly what many Muslims in Britain and across the world do indeed believe. Given our earlier discussion of end-times theology, as well as the thesis expressed in Samuel Huntington's *The Clash of Civilisations and the Remaking of World Order*, this view may be nothing like as fanciful or wrong-headed as Ware so clearly implies. For example, Huntington (1996: 216) argues that after the Iranian Revolution in 1979, 'an intercivilisational war developed between Islam and the West', and is still continuing (this was written well before 9/11), and he concluded that:

> The underlying problem for the West is not Islamic funda-mentalism. It is Islam, a different civilisation whose people are convinced of the superiority of their culture and are obsessed with the inferiority of their power. The problem for Islam is not the CIA or the U.S. Department of Defence. It is the West, a different civilisation whose people are convinced of the uni-versality of their culture and believe their superior, if declining, power imposes on them the obligation to extend that culture throughout the world.

(1996: 217–18)

As in the Tamimi case, Ware's insistence on pursuing a line of questioning whose terms the interviewee clearly refuses – as indeed they are perfectly entitled to do – results merely in a pointless confrontation that tells the viewer almost nothing, as opposed to provoking an illuminating discussion about exactly why so many Muslims view the 'War on Terror' as a war on Islam. Thus:

Sir Iqbal Sacranie: The war on terror has been a failure and this …

John Ware: That's not my question, but is it a war on Islam … is it a war on Islam?

Sir Iqbal Sacranie: The war on terror has been a total failure, the way it's been perceived, the way it's been fought. When you try to occupy Afghanistan, when you see what is happening in Iraq, the people on other ground view this war on terror, this is their perception.

John Ware: Indeed. Is it not your responsibility, as the leader of the Muslim community in effect in Britain, whatever your views about the Iraq war, to disabuse the Muslim population of Britain that whatever is going on in Iraq is not a war against Islam?

Sir Iqbal Sacranie: Now, in terms of the motives behind … nobody knows about, we don't know about it …

John Ware: You are playing politics again aren't you?

Sir Iqbal Sacranie: It is.

John Ware: You are playing politics with religion.

Sir Iqbal Sacranie: We are playing.

John Ware: You are playing politics with religion.

Sir Iqbal Sacranie: We are being factual, you don't want to accept the reality of what Islam is in its daily life.

Ware's thesis, which rigidly determines both the questions that he poses to Sacranie and his responses to Sacranie's answers, is that British Muslims hold the views that they do on the 'War on Terror' because they've been influenced by radical 'Islamist' ideology emanating from certain mosques and Muslim organisations. There is, however, an entirely different, and entirely legitimate, explanation, namely that this is the conclusion that they've reached after witnessing what is happening in Iraq, Palestine and Lebanon night after night on their television screens. This explanation, however, is one that the programme quite simply refuses to countenance.

The fourth charge against the MCB is that its sincerity in condemning suicide bombings in Israel and elsewhere in the Middle East is suspect because, first, Dr Azzam Tamimi of the MCB-affiliated Muslim Association of Britain, as we have seen, regards such bombings as martyrdoms. However, as noted above, the MCB is not, and indeed could not possibly be, responsible for every utterance of every member of every one of its affiliates. The second reason given by Ware is that Sacranie attended a memorial service at the Central Mosque in London for Sheikh Yassin of Hamas after he had been assassinated by the Israelis. Here Sacranie hailed him as 'the renowned Islamic scholar', but Ware is concerned only with 'the theological justification which [he] gave to the murder of civilians' and the fact that 'he was the spiritual leader and the ideological leader of a terrorist movement'. Sacranie counters:

> In your terms, if it means fighting occupation is a terrorist movement, that is not a view that is being shared by many people. Those who fight oppression, those who fight occupation, cannot be termed as terrorist, they are freedom fighters, in the same way as Nelson Mandela fought against apartheid,

in the me way as Gandhi and many others fought the British rule in India. There are people in different parts of the world who today, in terms of historical side of it, those who fought oppression are now the real leaders of the world.

Ware, however, simply refuses to acknowledge the thrust of Sacranie's first sentence, namely that he, like vast numbers of people across the globe, Muslim and non-Muslim alike, does not accept that Hamas is simply a terrorist movement. (He could also have pointed out that it is the democratically elected majority party of the Palestinian Legislative Council.) In other words, this is another example of the problem encountered above with the 'War on Terror', and so, doggedly persisting with a line of questioning whose terms the interviewee refuses, Ware insists on leading the interview into the entirely predictable cul-de-sac, and we learn absolutely nothing about British Muslims' attitude to Hamas. The question is: who, exactly, is in denial here? The MCB about the views of some of its affiliates, or John Ware about just how widespread and sincerely held are views which he himself clearly finds anathema?

Visual style

So far, we have concentrated on what the participants in the programme actually said, although we have also touched on Ware's body language. However, two other aspects of the programme's visual style are also noteworthy.

First, in the scenes in which Ware is shown tapping away at his PC in order to unearth 'killer quotes' on the websites of various MCB friends and affiliates, a mosque dominates the view from his office window. This *mise-en-scène* is obviously not accidental (unless there really is a mosque right outside the *Panorama* office window), and, given both the content of the individual scenes in which it occurs and the context of the programme as a whole, strongly suggests Islam as a looming, and indeed threatening, presence in our society.

Second, on at least eighteen occasions, the screen is given over to dark evocations of what is presumably meant to be the inside of a mosque. This device usually occurs when a new figure is introduced, their photograph dominating the frame. The image is accompanied by a fragment of suitably 'exotic'-sounding music. On numerous occasions, quotations are superimposed on this image (and also spoken rather portentously on the soundtrack). These quotations are usually of the 'killer quote' kind, but it is the manner of their presentation that is significant in the present context. They begin as a kind of shimmering haze in the top left-hand corner of the screen, and then, in a curious snaking movement, emerge into legibility, usually accompanied by a strange rushing sound, like an electronically enhanced breath of wind. Presumably all this was intended to give the proceedings a little more visual razzmatazz (a particularly irritating TV news and current affairs tic), but visual and aural devices are never neutral and inevitably carry with them all sorts of connotations. And what we have here is a veritable battery of visual and aural clichés about the 'exotic East', a classic expression of the Orientalism defined by Edward Said as 'a political vision of reality whose structure promoted the difference between the familiar (Europe, the West, "us") and the strange (the Orient, the East, "them")' (1995 [1978]: 43).

'A closed demonstration of one point of view'

'A Question of Leadership' can be described as a classic example of thesis-driven journalism. There is nothing necessarily wrong with this kind of reportage, but the problems arise when it tips over into tendentiousness, when one has the distinct impression that the journalist is grinding an axe, that they've gone out to find the facts to fit – as opposed to test – their thesis, and that nothing they discover will sway them from the view with which they set out in the first place. This is the distinct impression left by this particular edition of *Panorama*, for all the reasons outlined above. Indeed, the judgement made by Cary Bazalgette and Philip Simpson of the British Film

Institute of an earlier John Ware *Panorama* (on the London Borough of Brent) also seems entirely apposite in the case of 'A Question of Leadership':'Any attempt at a reasoned, detached, analytic or investigative programme [was] abandoned in favour of a closed demonstration of one point of view reinforced by emotional and rhetorical flourishes' (quoted in Curran et al., 2005: 154; this book contains a lengthy and detailed analysis of the *Panorama* episode in question). Indeed, one wonders how the programme's approach to its subject can be squared with the BBC's own editorial guidelines on impartiality which, *inter alia,* state that the Corporation is required 'to produce comprehensive, authoritative and impartial coverage of news and current affairs in the UK and throughout the world to support fair and informed debate' and 'to treat controversial subjects with due accuracy and impartiality in our news services and other programmes dealing with matters of public policy or of political or industrial controversy'. The guidelines also add: 'Presenters, reporters and correspondents are the public face and voice of the BBC, they can have a significant impact on the perceptions of our impartiality ... Our audiences should not be able to tell from BBC programmes or other BBC output the personal views of our journalists and presenters' on matters of public policy or political or industrial controversy. However, in this respect even the relatively sympathetic Ehsan Masood (2005) argued that Ware may have 'allowed some of his assumptions to frame the film', and that, in the battle currently being fought out within Britain's Muslim population, 'the reporter seems to be firing some of the ammunition collected and supplied by one side for use against the other'. And the following year, Faisal Bodi, in the *Guardian,* 6 June 2006, quoted a senior ex-*Panorama* journalist as describing the programme as 'the most disgusting *Panorama* that I have ever seen. The presenter was acting like a prosecuting attorney, not a journalist.' And when Bodi tried to question Ware about a *Panorama* which he was making about alleged links between Hamas and British Muslim activists, Ware replied: 'I don't want to talk to you, you've got an agenda. Bye,' a response which some might regard as thoroughly hypocritical.

As we have seen, the MCB has never been short of critics both within and outside the Muslim community, and it would not be exactly a feat of investigative journalism to tap into this seam. Of course the MCB is not without its faults and problems – what organisation, the BBC most certainly included, isn't? – but it is, as we have seen, operating in a highly complex and delicate situation, and any programme about the Council should adequately reflect that situation, as opposed to structuring itself around the crude and misleading binary oppositions that lie at the heart of 'A Question of Leadership'. As Madeleine Bunting put it in the *Guardian*, 22 August, the impact of this film, and of the press coverage that preceded it:

> will be a powerful boost for the increasingly widespread view that there is no such thing as a moderate Muslim: underneath, 'they' are all extremists who are racist, contemptuous of the west, and intent on a political agenda. A legitimate and much-needed debate among British Muslims about a distinctive expression of Islam in a non-Muslim country has been hijacked and poisonously distorted. Journalists need to be very careful: we are entering a new era of McCarthyism and, if we are not to be complicit, we need to be scrupulously responsible and conscientious in unravelling the complexity of Islam in its many spiritual and political interpretations in recent decades.

In this respect, it's highly significant that the e-mails which the BBC received about this programme clearly show that the majority of Muslim respondents were extremely upset and angered by it, whereas for a worrying number of non-Muslims it provoked views such as 'I think for far too long Britain has been far too lenient and I welcome any tightening of immigration/deportation if it is going to make my country safer', and 'more power to the BBC for ignoring the massive pressures that must have been placed on you, from the fanatics and their supporters in World Service Television, for instance, and coming out with the truth'.[8]

In other words, it appears to have divided its audience along ethnic lines. In an increasingly divided society in ever-more fraught times, this is not exactly an achievement of which to be proud.

Part III: The Fall-Out

The sidelining of the MCB

As noted in the first part of this chapter, the thesis peddled by 'A Question of Leadership' was by no means unique to this programme and already had vociferous adherents in both liberal and illiberal national newspapers. Prominent among the former, as we have seen, was Martin Bright, the political editor of the *Observer*, and in 2006 (by which time he was political editor of the *New Statesman*), and he enlarged on this matter for a substantial publication for the right-leaning think-tank Policy Exchange entitled *When Progressives Treat with Reactionaries: the British State's Flirtation with Radical Islamism*.

Here, Bright repeated his contention that the MCB 'had its origins in the sectarian politics of Pakistan' and that its leadership 'takes its inspiration from political Islamism associated with reactionary opposition movements in the Middle East and South Asia' (2006: 11). However, rather than rehearse these over-familiar charges yet again, let us turn to Bright's conclusions. In his view:

> A starting-point would be a refusal to deal with any organisa-
> tion that is not truly representative of all British Muslims. Any
> over-arching structure is susceptible to infiltration and subver-
> sion – and the MCB is no exception. Further dialogue should
> be accompanied with serious conditions. For instance, it should
> no longer be acceptable for the British Government to deal
> with the leadership of the MCB while it refuses to accept cer-
> tain branches of Islam as true Muslims.

(2006: 29)

Bright also argued that the MCB should dissociate itself from any affiliates influenced by the Muslim Brotherhood and called for:

> An end to the Government's policy of 'engagement for engagement's sake' with the MCB. Any body that represents itself as speaking for the Muslim community must demonstrate that it is entirely non-sectarian and non-factional. The MCB has consistently failed in this area and the Government should consider cutting all ties until it has thoroughly reformed itself. For too long, the Government has chosen as its favoured partner an organisation which is undemocratic, divisive and unrepresentative of the full diversity of Muslim Britain.

> (2006: 30).

Thus by 2006, the thesis had spread from the pages of the press and into wider circulation. It is there, for example in Melanie Phillips' *Londonistan* (2008 [2006]: 153–4) and also in Michael Gove's *Celsius 7/7* (2006: 97–101), both of which quote 'A Question of Leadership' uncritically and with approval. And by 2007 Martin Bright was able to assert that 'the MCB no longer receives government funding, it no longer has the monopoly on advice to ministers and its senior officers no longer travel the world as de facto ambassadors for the UK. This is also to be welcomed. If my lobbying has in any way helped, then I am delighted.'[9] (As noted earlier, this cooling of relations also had a great deal to do with the MCB's opposition to the 'War on Terror' and Britain's involvement in the wars in Afghanistan and Iraq.) Or as the rather more sympathetic Yahya Birt (2008) put it a year later:

> Once the darling of the political establishment, the MCB has become just another voice at the table. The government has appointed a plethora of internal and external Muslim advisers, has rapidly developed its own network of local contacts, particularly with respect to 'preventing violent extremism' (PVE) funding, and set up its own panels to deal with imams and mosques, women and young people.

To talk to a wide range of Muslim organisations representative of the huge diversity of Muslim opinion in the UK is of course an admirable idea, but to make them pass some form of narrowly conceived acceptability test before admitting them to the charmed circles of the Department of Communities and Local Government or the Home Office could seem at best patronising and at worst a distinct hangover of the imperial mindset (Norman Tebbit's 'cricket test' also springs to mind). Meanwhile, to exclude the body which, for all its undoubted faults and shortcomings, does actually represent more Muslims than any other UK body, is surely simply counter-productive and completely self-defeating. Here again, it's difficult to avoid the impression that standards are being applied to Muslim organisations that would not be applied to non-Muslim ones. As Madeleine Bunting put it in the *Guardian*, 12 July 2007:

> The Muslim Council of Britain is far from perfect. Of course it doesn't score on Bright's checklist: it is not democratic, it is not representative and it can be divisive. Wake up Bright, it's called politics. Why should ethnic minority politics be any less complex and compromised than the Labour party? Is the House of Commons representative of the British population? No, of course not, there aren't nearly enough women or ethnic minorities. So why do we expect community organisations to achieve something that the world's oldest democracy can't?

The dawn of Prevent

Cut off as it was from large swathes of Muslim opinion, and listening only to a shortlist of 'approved' groupings (several of which were essentially its own creations, and thus told it what it wanted to hear, thereby losing all credibility with many Muslims), it's not altogether surprising that the government should embark on a 'rebalancing' of its relationship with Muslim communities which emphasised counter-terrorist and 'anti-extremist' imperatives. This culminated in the disastrous *Prevent* programme, discussed elsewhere in this book, which, by defining 'extremism' far too broadly and appearing to sanction the criminalisation and demonisation of large numbers of Muslims, ended up by fuelling the very extremism that it was supposed to prevent in the first place. *Prevent* was the subject of a remarkably critical report by the House of Commons Communities and Local Government Committee, and several of its conclusions and recommendations relate so directly to the issues raised in this chapter that they serve perfectly as its conclusion:

> We recommend that the Government take steps to clarify its understanding of the terms 'violent extremism', 'extremism', and 'radicalisation'. Holding extreme views is not illegal and *Prevent* should clearly focus on violent extremism. Extending *Prevent* interventions to those holding extreme views should only take place where there is a risk that an individual's adherence to an extremist ideology may predispose them to violence. The Government should ensure that this understanding is shared widely across the range of its partners in delivering *Prevent-related* projects ...

> Government interference in theological matters must be avoided. The Government's current approach to engagement with Muslim organisations has given the impression that there are 'good' and 'bad' forms of Islam – some endorsed by the Government, others not. The construction of an 'Islamic experts industry', funded and sanctioned by Government, has caused a variety of problems, including a failure to represent the views of the whole Muslim community. The issue of representation is a particular concern for young people. Empowering young people from a variety of backgrounds to take part in open and honest discussion and debate – and facilitating their influence and access to democratic institutions – is key. Initiatives such as Project Safe Space must be pursued, and backed with appropriate funding. Support and funding should also be made available to initiatives which improve communications between young people and Government ...

The Government has made clear its position on non-engagement with groups which support, or actively promote, the al-Qaeda ideology. However, there is widespread criticism of the Government's failure to engage with more 'radical' voices which do not promote violent extremism. The Government should engage with those who demonstrate a desire to promote greater understanding, cohesion and integration. No organisation – unless proscribed – should be excluded from debate and discussions.

(House of Commons Communities and Local Government Committee, 2010: 64–5)

As this chapter has demonstrated in considerable detail, however, such views are diametrically opposed to those emanating from most of the media, influential right-wing think-tanks, and indeed from the government itself. In this age of what Peter Oborne (2007) has rightly called 'client journalism' and 'manipulative populism', it will be instructive to see which views prevail when it comes to formulating, and putting into practice, future policy in this most vexed and sensitive of areas.

In the meantime, one can only be thankful that in July 2010, after the election of the coalition government, the new Home Secretary Theresa May announced that the Home Office intended to 'look at the different strands of the *Prevent* strategy and to ensure that they are properly focused on the right aims'. She said she believed 'it is right and appropriate to separate out the part of the *Prevent* strategy that is about integration from the part about counter-terrorism'. She explained further that 'one problem with *Prevent* is that those two aspects have become intertwined in too many people's thinking, which has, sadly, led to some of the *Prevent* work being rejected by those whom it was intended to help' (Hansard, 14 July 2010, column 1011).

6

The Golden Thread
Britishness and Preventing Extremism, 2000–10
Robin Richardson

Giving the annual British Council lecture in July 2004 the then Chancellor of the Exchequer, Gordon Brown, referred to a range of recent writings about Britishness. Some of the authors whom he cited with approval were journalists, scholars or influence leaders associated with the centre-left of the political spectrum – Neal Ascherson, Linda Colley, Bernard Crick, Norman Davies, David Goodhart, Andrew Marr, Herman Ouseley, Trevor Phillips. Others quoted with similar approval were associated with the political right – Simon Heffer, Ferdinand Mount, Melanie Phillips, Roger Scruton. Also he cited someone who is scrupulously unplaceable on the political spectrum – Jonathan Sacks, the Chief Rabbi. And he mentioned two influence leaders from an earlier generation who were poles apart from each other in their political sympathies, Winston Churchill and George Orwell. A thread running though all these writings, he said, was a concern with national identity. All, in their turn, saw 'a golden thread that runs through British history'. The single most important feature in the thread, Mr Brown maintained, is the 'individual standing firm for freedom and liberty against tyranny and the arbitrary use of power'.

'Britishness has also meant,' Mr Brown continued, 'a tradition of fair play.' He explained:

> We may think today of British fair play as something applied on the sports field, but in fact most of the time it has been a very widely accepted foundation of social order: treating people fairly, rewarding hard work, encouraging self improvement through education and being inclusive. And this commitment to fair play has animated British political thought on both left and right over the centuries, right through to the passion for social improvement of the Victorian middle classes and the Christian socialists and trade unions who struggled for a new welfare settlement in the 20th century.

> (Brown, 2004)

About eighteen months later, Mr Brown returned to the metaphor of golden thread, this time for a lecture delivered to the Fabian Society. By then commentary on the bombings and attempted bombings of 7 and 21 July 2005 in London had irreversibly re-shaped the context in which all public considerations of British national identity could be conducted. By the same token, discourse about Britishness and about golden threads running through British history was now irreversibly entangled with what in due course became known as the preventing violent extremism (PVE) agenda. This chapter recalls the debates about British identity occasioned by the London bombings and continues by recalling the principal criticisms that were made, as it developed, of PVE. The recurring emphasis in these criticisms was that PVE both reflected and reinforced deeply Islamophobic assumptions and attitudes and, for this reason, was likely to do more harm than good. This perception was endorsed and vindicated in March 2010 by the House of Commons Communities and Local Government select committee. But first, it is relevant to recall briefly two earlier occasions on which there was much media coverage of national identity. These dated from autumn 2000 and autumn 2001.

Autumn 2000

'Children will be told lies about their history and encouraged to feel ashamed of their country,' said Richard Littlejohn in the *Sun*, 13 October 2000, commenting on the all too likely and deplorable impact, as he saw it, of a recently published report on multi-ethnic Britain. Several other journalists issued similar dire warnings. 'British history,' wrote Paul Johnson (who is also a historian) in the *Daily Mail*, 11 October:

> is the story of freedom and respect for the law, and Britain's relationship with the world beyond our shores is the story of benefaction not exploitation, of justice not oppression, and of the desire to enlighten, to improve, to teach and to help. It is not a story of shame. Nor is it a story which needs to be rewritten. On the contrary: it can be rewritten only by inserting bias and dogma, propaganda and downright lies.

The report in question was produced by the Commission on the Future of Multi-Ethnic Britain, chaired by Lord Parekh (Bhikhu Parekh). Its members were from a wide range of backgrounds in terms of ethnicity, religion, ideology, outlook and experience, and had had distinguished careers in academia, the law, public administration, policing, education, research and the media. Between them, they were the authors of many academic works. When their report was published they were described as 'worthy idiots' in *The Times*, 'middle-class twits' in the *Star*, 'crack-brained' in the *Daily Telegraph*, 'left-wing wafflers' in the *Evening Standard*, and 'disconnected, whining liberals' in the *Daily Mail*. Their report, 400 pages of scholarly and measured discussion and commentary, with a wealth of illustrative detail, was condemned as 'gibberish', 'balderdash', 'burblings' and 'rhubarb' in the *Daily Telegraph*, 'right-on trendy trash' in the *Star*, 'an insult to history and our intelligence' in the *Daily Mail* and 'tosh' in the *Sun*.

Intemperate language along these lines was accompanied by many sheer falsehoods and misquotations (McLaughlin and Neal, 2004; Petley, 2001). There is not space here to itemise these in detail. Suffice to observe there was an emotional, abusive and wholly dismissive response to the Commission's modest and reasoned proposal that Britain's principal meta-narratives should be revisited. This response influenced Gordon Brown's subsequent speeches about the golden thread running through British history. Also, it affected the way in which disturbances in northern cities were portrayed in the following year, and the ways in which the government reacted to them.

Autumn 2001

'Ethnic communities scarred by the summer riots', ran the front-page headline in the *Independent on Sunday*, 9 December 2001, 'should learn English and adopt "British norms of acceptability".' The news item to which the headline referred was an interview with Home Secretary David Blunkett. The purpose of the interview and of the news item was to trail four reports on the disturbances of summer 2001 which were to be published two days later (Cantle, 2001; Clark, 2001; Home Office, 2001; Ritchie, 2001). The reports, in their turn, would set off what would come to be known as the government's community cohesion agenda. The key statement by the home secretary about cohesion was triggered by the question 'Have we been too tolerant of enforced marriage?' His complete answer to this question was reported as follows:

> Enforced marriages and youngsters under the age of 16 being whistled away to the Indian sub-continent, genital mutilation and practices that may be acceptable in parts of Africa, are unacceptable in Britain. We need to be clear we don't tolerate the intolerable under the guise of cultural difference. We have

norms of acceptability and those who come into our home –
for that is what it is – should accept those norms just as we
would have to do if we went elsewhere.

In the context of the four reports about to be published, and of the
Ouseley report published a few months earlier, the home secretary
appeared to be saying that Muslim communities in northern cities
typically tolerate the intolerable, for example genital mutilation and
forced marriages of children under sixteen, and that that is why some
of their younger members had been involved in public disorder earlier in the year. The further implication was that the essential purpose
of the community cohesion agenda would be to persuade Muslim
communities to mend their ways, so that they became 'acceptable'.
For people with long experience of combating racial and religious
discrimination, the remarks about 'those who come into our home'
were eerily reminiscent of many such remarks over the years by politicians and the media. To cite a single example, they echoed the
sentiment in an infamous statement made at the time of the *Satanic
Verses* affair in 1989: 'Newcomers are only welcome if they become
genuine Britishers and don't stuff their alien cultures down our
throats' (*News of the World*, 5 March 1989).

The negative and uninformed generalisations about Muslim communities in northern Britain that introduced the community cohesion agenda were of a piece with the Islamophobia that was rampant
in autumn 2001 throughout Western societies. They helped give the
impression that the reports were principally about 'self-segregating'
and 'inward-looking communities', and prevented more measured
statements in the home secretary's interview being attended to.
Further, they provoked widespread suspicion among Muslims of the
reports themselves (see Faisal Bodi in the *Guardian*, 1 July 2002). The
suspicions were in due course strengthened when it emerged that
Muslim members of the Cantle committee felt that they had been
marginalised during the committee's deliberations, and had been
unable to secure adequate attention to Islamophobia and recognition of Muslim identity (Khan, 2002). Alternative views of the

disturbances were published by, among others, the Islamic Human Rights Commission and the Institute of Race Relations. 'The fires that burned across Lancashire and Yorkshire through the summer of 2001,' said the latter, 'signalled the rage of young Pakistanis and Bangladeshis of the second and third generations, deprived of futures, hemmed in on all sides by racism, failed by their own leaders and representatives and unwilling to stand by as first fascists and then police officers invaded their streets.' The article continued:

> Their violence was ad hoc, improvised and haphazard ... The fires ... were lit by the youths of communities falling apart from within, as well as from without; youths whose violence was, therefore, all the more desperate. It was the violence of communities fragmented by colour lines, class lines and police lines. It was the violence of hopelessness. It was the violence of the violated.

> (Kundnani, 2001)

Summer and autumn 2005

At 11.12 a.m. on Thursday 7 July 2005 a teacher wrote as follows to a discussion forum at the *Times Educational Supplement*: 'This is shocking! I've just heard this news from a kid (I'm currently in ICT) and it turns out the teaching assistant's husband is working in London. She has tried to call but the network is jammed. She is worried sick!' In the following hours and days there were hundreds of further messages, the vast majority of them thoughtfully reflective about the professional responsibilities of teachers in the light of the bombings: 'Kids quite scared, but weirdly mature about it'; 'We reap what we sow. Live with it, and keep it in proportion. This is not a risk-free environment and never will be'; 'I am proud of the schools I chair in Tower Hamlets'; 'The real heroes are those who get on with it, do their jobs and do not let others derail their futures'; 'I'm sure that there were students who held him in high regard, who looked up to him [i.e. Mohammad Sidique Khan, one of the bombers] for all the "good" that he did in the school and for them as individuals. There are children whose lives he touched. They are going to have a rough time coming to terms with his actions, and I hope that they are getting the counselling and support that they need'; 'Anger's done enough already'; 'Our job now is compassion, for the families and victims of the bombs and for the children taught that suicide is glorious.'

Such quotations from teachers showed that they were able to keep their heads at a time of great crisis. Not a few commentators in the media, however, including some on the liberal left, lashed out with unfocused anger against something they called multiculturalism, and they said or implied that teachers committed to multicultural education were to blame for not preventing the attacks in London. For example, in an otherwise useful discussion of the ways in which al-Qaida has been constructed in part by the West's paranoid imagination, it was claimed in an article entitled 'A monster of our own making' in the *Observer*, 21 August, that the young bombers in London had been created by 'a half-century of a well-intentioned but catastrophically mistaken policy of multiculturalism, indifferent or even hostile to social and cultural integration'. The policy had 'produced in Britain and much of Europe a technologically educated but culturally and morally unassimilated immigrant demi-intelligentsia'.

In the web-based journal *Open Democracy* Gilles Kepel (2005) claimed that 'in Britain, multiculturalism was the product of an implicit social consensus between leftwing working-class movements and the public-school-educated political elite. Their alliance allowed one side to monitor immigrant workers ... and the other to secure their votes, through their religious leaders, at election time.' The author then added:

> The July bombings have smashed this consensus to smithereens. In one sense at least, and in spite of the massive difference in the number of deaths, British society was more deeply traumatised by the two London attacks bombings [sic] than Americans were in the aftermath of 9/11. The United States

assailants were foreigners; the eight people involved in London were the children of Britain's own multicultural society.

Similar attacks on multiculturalism were made from across the whole political spectrum. The commentators, for their part, derived succour and support from selectively quoting Trevor Phillips, chair of the Commission for Racial Equality, in order to claim that he agreed with them, having seen the error of his ways. It is true that Phillips subsequently criticised what he called 'anything-goes multicultural-ism', but in the wake of the bombings he paid handsome tribute to people working in the field of race relations among whom – inci-dentally – would have been some of the teachers quoted above:

People talk a lot about the race relations industry, usually dispar-agingly. I am proud to say that this summer, our industry did its part in holding communities together at a time of great stress. We experienced no major conflicts, and despite the fact that there definitely was an upsurge in anti-Asian activity post 7/7, we understand that this has now subsided; the GLA tells us that in London for example, the level of such activity is lower now than it was before 7/7. This is in no small part due to the work of the people often casually abused as race relations busybodies, working on the ground, calming, cajoling and conciliating. Many are paid, but tens of thousands are unpaid, and do it because they want our country to be a better place.

(Phillips, 2005)

There was a substantial gulf between the actual text of Phillips's speech about 7/7 and the way the speech was first trailed and then reported throughout the media. Whether the gulf was down to off-the-record briefings, or to a misleading press release, or to journalistic carelessness, bias or ignorance, or to sheer malice and disinformation, is not publicly known. However, the fact remains that the interesting and valuable things Phillips had to say were drowned by the headlines that his speech generated, and there was widespread disappointment and dismay, even indeed anger, among the very people whose support he most needed – for example, the people saluted in the passage quoted above. The dismay was powerfully articulated by Lee Jasper in an article headed 'Trevor Phillips is in danger of giving succour to racists' in the *Guardian*, 12 October 2005:

> Effective antiracism starts from the view that we refuse to … go along with distortions and generalisations about Islam. In these circumstances, the provocative, headline-grabbing speeches by Trevor Phillips, the chair of the Commission for Racial Equality, are counterproductive and generate many of the most unapologetic headlines in the rightwing press, giving succour to those who want to push back antiracism. Asked [by Tom Baldwin for *The Times*, 3 April 2004] whether the word multiculturalism should be killed off, he replied: 'Yes, let's do that. Multiculturalism suggests separateness.' … But the truth is that vile anti-Muslim prejudice, using the religion of a community to attempt to sideline and blame it for many of society's ills, is the cutting edge of racism in British society. Those who consider themselves antiracists need to wake up to this fact.

The new development in 2005 involved distinguishing between 'good Muslims' and 'bad Muslims', on a direct analogy with the good nigger/bad nigger distinction that was once an explicit hallmark of racism in the United States. The hallmark of good Muslims, in this demonology, is not so much that they are 'decent' or 'law-abiding' or 'peace-loving' or 'mainstream' or 'gentle' (all favourite words among non-Muslim commentators), but that they do not seek to apply their faith to social and political affairs, do not criticise British foreign policy on Iraq and Israel/Palestine, do not wear Islamic dress in public spaces, are not inclined to 'self-segregate' or seek 'separateness', are not critical of Western secularism, and do not read or offer for sale the works of, among others, Maulana Mawdudi. The convenient consequence of this demonology is that 'good Muslims' are remarkably hard to find.

In particular, the argument ran, they cannot be found in the leadership of major organisations such as the Muslim Council of Britain (MCB), the Muslim Association of Britain or the Islamic Foundation. A particularly outrageous and simplistic expression of the good Muslim/bad Muslim paradigm was presented in a *Panorama* TV programme, 'A Question of Leadership', on 21 August 2005, with substantial supporting and supportive coverage in the *Independent on Sunday* and the *Observer* (see chapter 6 of this book for a substantial discussion of this important episode).

This, then, was the atmosphere in which the government began to plan its preventing violent extremism programmes. An article by Gary Younge in the *Guardian*, 30 March 2009, headed 'Where will we find the perfect Muslim for monocultural Britain?', commented:

> For political and emotional reasons it has been necessary for some to dehumanise the bombers – to eviscerate them of all discernible purpose. Stripped to their immoral minimum, they are simply 'evil monsters' ... [But] those looking for tails and tridents on the CCTV footage of the bombers will be disappointed. They look like everybody else. If the security services are going to have any chance of infiltrating the bombers, they must first humanise those involved. They need to find out what would motivate young men who apparently have so much to live for to die – and kill. Only then can they discover how to spot the determined and stop them, and how to catch those vulnerable to their message before they fall into the clutches of the terrorists. The only extra power the police need in this effort is the power of persuasion – the ability to gain the confidence of the Muslim community by convincing them that the aim is to catch terrorists, not to criminalise their community.

The article was based in the first instance on the killing of a young Brazilian by the Metropolitan Police. It recalled also that earlier in the year, after a young British Muslim from Gloucester admitted planning to blow up a flight between Amsterdam and the US, the head of the Met's anti-terrorist branch said: 'We must ask how a young British man was transformed from an intelligent, articulate person who was well respected into a person who has pleaded guilty to one of the most serious crimes that you can think of.' The article wryly commented: 'A policy that lets the police shoot first and ask that question later will have a drastic effect on the kind of answer they are likely to get.'

A good example of appropriate reflection on key questions was provided by a symposium in late July 2005 (*Open Democracy*, 2005). 'The first generation of Muslims that came to this country,' said one of the panellists, 'did not come with dysfunctional families and polit-icised views. I can remember, being someone who is from a migrant family in the early 60s, a passive community, keeping themselves to themselves. The question to ask is how this peaceful community can have children who are full of anger, hatred and susceptible to radical ideas.' Another contributor said: 'If British society views the kids that are involved in this project [terrorism] as separate to the rest of society, a lot of problems that they are trying to solve and the young people that they are trying to address will effectively be excluded from the rest of society.'

The symposium ended with Fuad Nahdi, the founder and managing editor of *Q-News*, recalling a story about Mullah Nasruddin. Once Nasruddin wanted to learn how to play the guitar so he went to a teacher who told him 'It's very easy, but you have to pay £10 for the first lesson and then £5 for each of the other lessons.' Nasruddin thought about this and then said OK, can I start with the second lesson. All too much of the debate about 7/7, Nahdi emphasised, particularly the debate initiated by the government and developed by journalists, had been about the second and subsequent lessons, not the first. What, though, is the content of the first lesson? Introducing the symposium, Isabel Hilton, *Open Democracy*'s editor, enumerated some of the points which the lesson plan needs to contain. She mentioned the Sykes–Picot agreement of 1916 for the dismemberment of the Ottoman Empire; the 'War on Terror'; the jihad in Afghanistan; the Zia regime in Pakistan; Kashmir; oil; patterns of migration and ensuing social alienation; theological and doctrinal debates within Islam, both in Britain and globally; intergenerational strains in migrant communities; and integration and multiculturalism. Her underlying point was that there are 'overlapping and competing narratives' and that 'each of us tends to attach ourselves to the story that we most recognise as the prime explanation'. She concluded: 'If we confine ourselves to the narrative that we are most comfortable with, and we are not open to new facts, then we will be tethered to explanations that don't necessarily work' (in *Open Democracy*, 2005).

It was a timely warning to the government, but – alas – was ignored. During the rest of the autumn of 2005, and then throughout 2006, the attack on multiculturalism continued. At the end of 2006 a review of the year by Brian Appleyard in *The Sunday Times*, 17 December, announced multiculturalism's final demise:

> Multiculturalism is dead. It had it coming. An ideology that defined a nation as a series of discrete cultural and political entities that were each free to opt out of any or all common orthodoxies was never a serious contender in the Miss Best Political System pageant. But, with Jack Straw's startling statements about the veil, with Trevor Phillips, the then head of the Commission for Racial Equality, trashing the ideology and with the spectacle of a Labour peer trying to persuade me she had never believed any of it and that it was time Muslims joined the mainstream, it is safe to say that Miss Multi–Culti was finally booted off the catwalk in 2006. In her place are a various attempts to emphasise a British way of doing things and a deep governmental impatience with the shoddy intellectual and political credentials of Muslim so-called 'community leaders'. Will it work? Let's hope so.

Preventing violent extremism

A cartoon shows the prime minister and the home secretary walking along the backstreets of an urban area somewhere in northern

England (Sims, 2009). Each is pushing a wheelbarrow loaded with bags of money. It is early summer 2009 and apparently these two very senior politicians are about to distribute the contents of their barrows with the minimum of deliberation. In preparation for their arrival, and presumably with a view to being in receipt of their largesse, a local resident is hastily changing the sign outside his house. Until a few minutes ago it said 'Community Youth Centre'. It is now about to say 'Post-Jihadi, Counter-martyrdom, Therapeutic, De-radicalisation Workshop'. Meanwhile another local resident, standing outside another building, one that is still called Community Youth Centre, looks on in dismay. Is this other resident dismayed by the irresponsibility, short-termism and ignorance of the politicians? Or is it the cynical opportunism of his rival co-religionist that disturbs him? Or is he ruefully reflecting on his own slowness to take advantage of a new funding stream? It is not clear.

As of summer 2009, the most substantial government publication on PVE was *Pursue, Prevent, Protect, Prepare*, subtitled *The United Kingdom's strategy for countering international terrorism* (HM Government, 2009), published a few months earlier on 24 March. Summarising and revising the counter-terrorism strategy launched originally in 2003, it was known in shorthand as CONTEST 2. It ran to over 170 A4 pages, had more than 200 detailed and informative footnotes, was attractively and expensively designed and formatted, and contained a lengthy and well-written executive summary. It cost £34.55. As indicated by the document's title, the overall strategy had four arms or, in different metaphors, four streams, prongs, pillars or strands – 'pursue', 'prevent', 'protect' and 'prepare'. It was the second of these, 'prevent' that drew extensive criticisms. In response to the criticism from many quarters, the House of Commons Communities and Local Government Committee set up an inquiry.

The aim of the *Prevent* strategy was 'to stop radicalisation, reduce support for terrorism and violent extremism, and discourage people from becoming terrorists', and was aimed at 'the group of people who are vulnerable to persuasion to provide tacit or silent support to terrorists in certain circumstances and possibly reject and undermine our shared values and jeopardise community cohesion' (HM Government, 2009: 14, 15). In 2008–9 the budget was over £140 million. The objectives were itemised as follows:

> to challenge the ideology behind violent extremism and support mainstream voices;
> to disrupt those who promote violent extremism and support people living in the communities where they operate;
> to support individuals who are vulnerable to recruitment, or have already been recruited by violent extremists;
> to increase the resilience of communities to violent extremism
> to address grievances which ideologues are exploiting;
> to develop supporting intelligence, analysis and information
> to improve strategic communications;

> (HM Government, 2009: 82)

The House of Commons committee received over 70 memoranda, held five oral evidence sessions and paid a visit to Birmingham to meet local frontline *Prevent* workers, academics and religious leaders.

Criticisms of *Prevent* were based principally on lived experience. Also, however, critics were aware of leaked drafts of the document published in March and of a range of documents from think-tanks which appeared to have the government's ear (Kundnani, 2008). They were articulated in many or indeed most of the 70 submissions received by the House of Commons committee and were strongly expressed by, among others, widely distributed papers from the An-Nisa Society (2009) and the Institute of Race Relations (Kundnani, 2009). It was alleged that the *Prevent* agenda:

> reflected and legitimised a mindset which sees all Muslims as much the same, regardless of their ethnicity, nationality, social class, life experience, geographical location and political

outlook, and regardless of how observant and religiously oriented they are, or are not, and which in addition sees all Muslims as a threat, namely as potential terrorists, or as potential supporters of terrorism – all constitute 'a suspect community';

might therefore encourage, or anyway not discourage, hate crimes against people perceived to be Muslims and against their property; desecration of mosques and Muslim cemeteries; discrimination in employment and workplace practices; inertia and insensitivity towards Muslims in public services; casual rudeness in public places; negative and ignorant stereotypes of Muslims in the media; and electoral support for political parties which both explicitly and with dog-whistles play on fears about the creeping 'Islamification' of Britain;

distracted attention, resources and energy from the provision of services, support and opportunities which *all* young people need, regardless of their faith background or ethnicity, if they are to develop as active citizens, locally, nationally and internationally;

fostered or exacerbated tensions and rivalries between different Muslim groups and organisations; encouraged simplistic distinctions between deserving ('moderate', 'Sufi') Muslims and undeserving ('extremist', 'Salafi'); used patronage, favouritism and grants to divide and rule; and operated through a colonial-type system dependent on so-called community leaders;

de-professionalised teachers and youth workers, as also staff in other public services, by co-opting them into surveillance and intelligence-gathering on behalf of the police and security services and undermining relationships of trust;

made little or no use of insights, wisdom and moral teachings and exemplars in Islamic traditions of education and learning, and in the writings and reflections of scholars and researchers of Muslim heritage concerned with issues of citizenship, identity, pluralism, youth culture and globalisation;

popularised words which remained undefined, and therefore
meant different things to different people and contained
different nuances in different contexts – words such as
'extremism', 'radicalisation', 'resilience', 'Islamism' and
'fundamentalism';

devolved responsibility for implementing the programme to local
authorities and other public bodies without checking whether
they have relevant expertise, experience, capacity and contacts,
and with inadequate accountability and transparency;

obstructed implementation of the letter and spirit of equalities
legislation, including in particular race equality legislation,
and of expectations and statutory requirements relating to
community cohesion;

did not even mention Islamophobia and anti-Muslim racism,
let alone discuss anti-Muslim hostility in public institutions
and the media as likely to affect disaffection, alienation and
anger among young Muslims;

was most unlikely to achieve its own aims of preventing violent extremism by winning the hearts and minds of Muslim
individuals, communities and organisations.

(Akram and Richardson, 2009)

The following quotations give a flavour of how the arguments
were summarised in the critics' own words:

The most glaring concerns of the *Prevent* strategy are the targeting of the whole Muslim community as potential terrorists,
the fusion of counter terrorism with community cohesion and
community development initiatives, and the mainstreaming of
Prevent in the core services of local councils. The strategy has a
heavy surveillance focus, which has considerable risks involved
and is morally dubious … The strategy is confusing and unclear.
It aims, for example, to strengthen the 'capacity' of Muslims
to resist violent extremism and to build 'resilience'. Whatever

that means is open to differing understandings. At one level, the euphemistic and vague terminology serves the purpose of getting the strategy past the Muslim community with little protest. The loose definitions also leave the strategy open to interpretation at the risk of being counter-productive. It gives officers substantial leeway in implementation with no account-ability to Muslims, who are the subject of it.

(Khan, 2009)

Where does the image of the dysfunctional, marginalised and resentful Muslim minority come from? In two words – moral panic ... Problems occur when a perpetually morally indig-nant press is associated with a weak government which only appears to stand for whichever populist measure will guaran-tee its re-election. This appears to be the case in today's Britain and Contest 2 is evidence of this. The government seems to have ceased to seek out real solutions to the problems it faces and opted to legislate their way through a moral panic ... Contest 2 has the potential of becoming a socially divisive document that seeks to marginalise normal Muslims with its fatally flawed dual approach to tackling terrorism by attacking Islam. The worry is that if Muslims were not isolated, cynical and abandoned at the launch of Contest 2 they may well become so by the time Contest 3 is rolled off its moorings.

(Hamdan, 2009)

People have started to feel that Contest and PVE were from the beginning taking Muslims step by step towards denouncing their faith. At first it was about only targeting extremists, but the defini-tion of that has broadened so much that any activity you do could be taken as extremism. Of course you need to spend money on security, but taking a blanket approach towards every member of the Muslim community is wrong, a fallacy and a waste of resources.

Because you are delivering something to people who really don't know anything about extremism or terrorism.

(Chair of Lancashire Council of Mosques,
quoted in Sims, 2009)

Instead of trying to deny or sweep under the carpet the real impact of Government policy on the Muslim community, we need to consciously engage with it. We must create the space within the community where our young people feel free to speak openly about how they feel as young Muslims growing up in a country where their identity is constantly contested. The best antidote to the appeal of extremism is to create a model of critically engaged citizenship. That will only happen when more young Muslims engage in the political process and are confident and assertive about expressing their concerns, irrespective of whether it offends the Government or not. To that end we need more Muslim role models prepared to speak out, not stooges prepared only to do their masters' bidding. It is a waste of PVE funding if it is used simply to finance tokenistic, window dressing initiatives that simply reinforce Government spin and increase cynicism in the democratic process.

(Yaqoob, 2008)

The term *Prevent* lends itself to the idea that there lies a dormant terrorist within Muslims; that somewhere, entwined in their instincts and licensed by their religious beliefs, there is the possibility that some, albeit very rarely, will turn to terrorism against the state. And so we must do something to 'prevent' that from happening. Such can only stigmatise Muslims, it can redirect attention to Islamic teachings being the identifying factor, and this has created vicious cycles of mistrust and demonising, in a language of otherness.

(Islamic Society of Britain, 2009)

The atmosphere promoted by *Prevent* is one in which to make radical criticism of the government is to risk losing funding and facing isolation as an extremist, while those organisations which support the government are rewarded. This in turn undermines the kind of radical discussions of political issues that would need to occur if young people are to be won over and support for illegitimate political violence diminished. The current emphasis of *Prevent* on depoliticising young people and restricting radical dissent is actually counter-productive, because it strengthens the hands of those who say democracy is pointless.

(Kundnani, 2009: 6)

The House of Commons Communities and Local Government select committee indicated in its report (March 2010) that it agreed with the vast majority of the critical submissions that it received. It expressed its agreement in the following terms:

Our inquiry has shown that the current overall approach to Prevent is contentious and unlikely ever to be fully accepted in its existing form by those it is most important to engage.

We agree with the majority of our witnesses that Prevent risks undermining positive cross-cultural work on cohesion and capacity-building to combat exclusion and alienation in many communities.

The single focus on Muslims in Prevent has been unhelpful. We conclude that any programme which focuses solely on one section of a community is stigmatising, potentially alienating, and fails to address the fact that no section of a population exists in isolation from others.

Regarding the Government's analysis of the factors which lead people to become involved in violent extremism, we conclude that there has been a pre-occupation with the theological basis of radicalisation, when the evidence seems to indicate that politics, policy and socio-economics may be more important factors in the process. Consequently, we suggest that attempts to find solutions and engagement with preventative work should primarily address the political challenges. We therefore recommend that opportunities be provided for greater empowerment and civic engagement with democratic institutions, to strengthen the interaction with society not only of Muslims, but of other excluded groups.

(House of Commons Communities and
Local Government Committee, 2010: 3–4)

In summer 2010, following the general election in May and the formation of the coalition government, it was reported in the *Guardian*, 14 July, that the Prevent programme would be dismantled as part of an urgent review of counter-terrorism work. Later the same day the Home Secretary Theresa May stated in the House of Commons that, as set out in the Home Office structural reform plan, the government's intention was not to dismantle the programme but to 'look at the different strands of the Prevent strategy and to ensure that they are properly focused on the right aims'. She said she believed 'it is right and appropriate to separate out the part of the Prevent strategy that is about integration from the part about counter-terrorism'. She explained further that 'one problem with Prevent is that those two aspects have become intertwined in too many people's thinking, which has, sadly, led to some of the Prevent work being rejected by those whom it was intended to help' (Hansard, 14 July 2010, column 1011).

Concluding note

There is a golden thread running through British history, Gordon Brown maintained, to do with fair play and the rights of the individual vis-à-vis state power. He contended further that the thread is recognised in all parts of the political spectrum. His speeches on

these points were delivered within the context of profound uncertainties and disagreements about the legacy of British history. The
media could have played a constructive part in encouraging and
resourcing deliberative democracy. By and large, however, they
signally failed in this responsibility. Among those who suffered
most from this failure were British Muslims. They were consistently
misrepresented in the media, as – more generally – were issues of
pluralism, multiculturalism and democracy. There are signs of hope,
however. Large numbers of British Muslims thought it worthwhile
to put their concerns in thoughtful and temperate ways to the
Communities and Local Government select committee. The committee, for its part, showed that it had listened and heard. In so far as
the committee thus amplified the voices of individuals against the
state and the state-supporting media, it showed that, indeed, there is
a golden thread in British culture which celebrates fair play.

7

Muslim Women and Veiled Threats

From 'Civilising Mission' to 'Clash of Civilisations'

Gholam Khiabany and Milly Williamson

oday, the language used across Europe to debate the issue of Muslim women and the veil is conducted by politicians and the media in the most vitriolic of terms – ones that would roundly be considered to be unacceptable were they to be applied to the religious practices of Christian or Jewish women (El Hamel, 2002: 299). It has been noted that discussions about Islam in the West have become 'fixated' on practices of veiling (Macdonald, 2003: 169–73) that carry with them a legacy of colonial discourses on veiling, including an obsession with unveiling. It has become impossible to talk about Islam without reference to women, and impossible to talk of Muslim women without reference to the veil. Indeed one commentator suggests that the 'image of a veiled Muslim woman seems to be one of the most popular Western ways of representing the "problems of Islam"' (Watson, 1994: 153). It is of importance to understand how the highly emotive and charged language about the veil has come to be so acceptable among media commentators, left of centre and liberal intellectuals, mainstream feminists and neoconservative politicians alike. It is the contention of this chapter that the debate about the veil cannot be understood outside the broader context of colonialism and imperialism. However, the controversy over the veil in Europe also cannot be understood outside contemporary domestic politics. This chapter examines the link between definitions of the Muslim veil that have emerged since 9/11 in the broader context of the 'War on Terror', and the mobilisation of a particular image of the veil forged in that moment, in support of exclusionary domestic politics and attacks on civil liberties. We suggest that the tone of righteous indignation (not dissimilar to missionary language) that dominated the discussion of enforced veiling under the Taliban in 2001 has left a framework of interpretation of the Muslim veil that operates now in the quite different context of European Muslim women and the veil. We will argue that, even at the time, the indignation expressed allowed commentators to avoid important contextual discussions to produce a notion of the veil that always stands for 'un-freedom' for Muslim women and, by association, in Europe today, has come to stand as a threat to non-Muslim women and to the 'Western values' that are purported to protect gender freedom.

The narrative of 'salvation'

Running in tandem with the long-standing colonial context for interpreting the Muslim veil, there have been key moments in recent history which have shaped the contours of perception of the veil in the West. Both Leila Ahmed (1992) and Lila Abu-Lughod (2006) demonstrate the way that Western colonial powers have long used the idea of the liberation of Muslim women from Muslim men as a justification for imperialist adventures in the Middle East, such as the British occupation of Egypt in the 1880s. These discourses have been developed in recent times in order to distinguish the values of the West in binary opposition to those of Islam, on the basis of the issue of gender equality. However, in this century, a key instance in defining the veil was the US and British invasion of Afghanistan. It was the Bush administration's identification of the liberation of women in Afghanistan from the Taliban as a key objective in its invasion and occupation of Afghanistan that 'brought gender to the forefront of global politics' (Thobani, 2007: 170). The administrations of Bush and Blair used the veil as a symbol of un-freedom in their cynical attempt to use the Taliban's (previously ignored) disastrous treatment of women as an excuse to invade the country (Sreberny, 2004; Stabile and Kumar, 2005). It was at this moment that the veil became *the* most prominent symbol in discussions about gender equality. Annabelle Sreberny argues that during and after the invasion of Afghanistan, the *burka*[1] became 'the key symbol of women's oppression' (2004: 172). She points out that the West took no interest in Afghanistan and the plight of its women from when the Soviet-backed government fell in 1992 and through the rise of the Taliban in 1996: 'Western countries did little while an entire generation of girls and young women were removed from the education system and rendered illiterate and unskilled' (2004: 175).

Certainly, the British press ran very few articles about the plight of women under the Taliban prior to 9/11. The eight daily newspapers (and their Sunday editions) ran a total of thirty-three articles on women in Afghanistan in 1997. By 2000 it had grown to 217. However, the number of articles leapt to 2782 in 2001 leading up to and following the US and UK invasion of Afghanistan. This picture was repeated in the US. In 1999 only twenty-nine articles on women in Afghanistan were to be found in the US press, and in 2000 only fifteen articles were written (compared to the 113 articles about the destruction of statues of Buddha by the Taliban in the same period) (Stabile and Kumar, 2005: 772). Stabile and Kumar argue that these figures demonstrate that 'when it comes to "breaking news", craven news media take their leads from political elites', and the figures support their analysis that 'suffering women are subjects for political and public concern only insofar as their suffering can be used to advance the interests of US elites' (2005: 772).

Sreberny points out that both the US and British governments 'sought quite cynically to use their first ladies to make rare political interventions to focus on women in Afghanistan' (2004: 176). Both Cherie Blair and Laura Bush made statements in the media denouncing the *burka* as a symbol of the oppression of women in Afghanistan. On 17 November 2001 Laura Bush presented her Radio Address to the Nation:[2]

> Good morning. I'm Laura Bush, and I'm delivering this week's radio address to kick off a world-wide effort to focus on the brutality against women and children by the al-Qaida terrorist network and the regime it supports in Afghanistan, the Taliban. That regime is now in retreat across much of the country, and the people of Afghanistan – especially women – are rejoicing. Afghan women know, through hard experience, what the rest of the world is discovering: The brutal oppression of women is a central goal of the terrorists ... Fighting brutality against women and children is not the expression of a specific culture; it is the acceptance of our common humanity – a commitment shared by people of good will on every continent. Because of our recent military gains in much of Afghanistan, women are no longer imprisoned in their homes. They can listen to music and teach their daughters without fear of punishment. Yet the terrorists who helped rule that country now plot and plan in many countries. And they must be stopped. The fight against terrorism is also a fight for the rights and dignity of women.

In addition to trying to enlist women as a way of justifying the bombing of the very same women that the US Marines were supposed to be saving, Bush's overt linkage between 'terrorism' and the oppression of women was accompanied by a concealed assertion of racial superiority which relies on a notion of white Western identity as the norm (as in defining 'our common humanity') (see Dyer, 1997), the liberator ('our recent military gains' freeing women) and the defender of the 'dignity of women'. This is an articulation of the old colonial intentions, what Edward Said calls the 'civilising mission', 'the idea that some races and cultures have a higher aim in life', which justifies military action 'not in the name of brute force or raw plunder, both of which are standard components of the exercise, but in the name of a noble idea' (2001:574). Soon after Bush's speech, Cherie Blair and prominent female members of the British Labour government (including two cabinet members, International Development Secretary Claire Short and Education Secretary Estelle Morris) echoed these sentiments when they launched a campaign to improve the rights of Afghan women, with Blair commenting that 'nothing symbolises the oppression of women' as much as the *burka*. As Sreberny points out:

> Thus the burqa was used as part of a Western propaganda campaign, here addressing audiences sympathetic to women's rights. The burqa became the synecdoche for fundamentalism, antimodernism, and suddenly a ruthless pursuit of the terror network behind the September 11 events was transformed into a war of liberation with women as the main victors.
>
> (2004: 176)

Said's 'noble idea' thesis is borne out tragically in this instance, for women's rights have not been a priority of the US-backed interim or new Afghan governments; no money was allocated from the US government's 2003 budget towards rebuilding Afghanistan and much of the pledged money from other countries has not been forthcoming. In the meantime, five US companies have swallowed up half of the aid budget to Afghanistan, paying extortionate salaries to executives and making up to fifty per cent profits on contracts. Over half of the £1.1 billion given by the Italian government to rebuild a maternity hospital in Kabul went to the profits of subcontractors (Jerome Starkey and Ross Lydall, *Scotsman*, 25 March 2008). If aid to Afghanistan has not been a priority, installing former Unocal oil corporation consultants in positions of power has been – including the president of Afghanistan, Hamid Karzai, in order to restart the negotiations for the construction of an oil pipe line.

The imperialist intervention and its callow justification provided the conditions under which the explosion of articles about women in Afghanistan occurred. Indeed, the rhetorical framework produced by political elites and government was taken up and elaborated by well-known feminist commentators and columnists in broadsheet newspapers in the UK in subsequent weeks, who rallied in solidarity with the women of Afghanistan and, in the process, lent the language of feminism to military invasion and to their male counterparts in both the broadsheet and tabloid press. The issue of 'women's liberation' generated an alliance of right-wing and liberal-left commentators, with many on both sides taking up virtually identical positions. One of the most voluble voices has been that of Polly Toynbee, who is a columnist for the liberal *Guardian* newspaper. Thus, in an article on 28 September 2001, Toynbee presented herself as the voice of Western feminism, pointing out (unlike the authors of other articles) that the Northern Alliance had a record on women's rights as awful as the Taliban, and promoting the Afghani women's organisation RAWA. Despite this, however, her language and tone are filled with bile and binary oppositions which do the job of 'othering' Islam per se, all under the banner of Western, secular, feminist ideals:

> The top-to-toe burka, with its sinister, airless little grille, is more than an instrument of persecution, it is a public tarring and feathering of female sexuality. It transforms any woman into an object of defilement too untouchably disgusting to be seen. It is a garment of lurid sexual suggestiveness: what rampant desire and desirability lurks and leers beneath its dark mysteries? In its objectifying of women, it turns them into cowering creatures demanding and expecting violence and victimisation. Forget cultural sensibilities.

> More moderate versions of the garb – the dull, uniform coat to the ground and the plain headscarf – have much the same effect, inspiring the lascivious thoughts they are designed to stifle. What is it about a woman that is so repellently sexual that

she must diminish herself into drab uniformity while strolling down Oxford Street one step behind a husband who is kitted out in razor-sharp Armani and gold, pomaded hair and tight bum exposed to lustful eyes? ... Islamophobia! No such thing. Primitive Middle Eastern religions (and most others) are much the same – Islam, Christianity and Judaism all define themselves through disgust for women's bodies ... Religions that thrive are pliable, morphing to suit changing needs: most Christianity has had to moderate to modernise. Islamic fundamentalism flourishes because it too suits modern needs very well in a developing world seeking an identity to defy the all-engulfing west. And the burka and chador are its battle flags.

Alongside her nasty description of a Middle Eastern man, which is filled with racist stereotypes, her language of disgust at the *burka* is quickly transformed into disgust at the Muslim veil of any variety and at Islam in general. Her suggestion that she is equally opposed to all religions' treatment of women is disingenuous – Christianity 'has had to moderate to modernise', while Islam is becoming fundamentalist in order to oppose the West, with the veil as its 'battle flag'. Toynbee thus moves in this article from sympathy with the oppressed women of Afghanistan to a view of the veil as part of the terrorist threat against the West and its values. Despite superficially sounding 'modern' and 'progressive', the article is in fact an early contribution to the construction of a thoroughly reactionary binary opposition between Islam and the West, one which hijacks the cause of women's liberation in order to produce an account of Islam and the veil as barbaric and uncivilised, and which is produced almost entirely within the logic of Samuel Huntington's 'clash of civilisations' thesis. A year later (on 13 November 2002), having actually visited Afghanistan, her tone is exactly the same when she attempts to explain why the women of that country have not lifted their veils:

The women are indoctrinated so deep ... that their own inferiority is branded on their brains. Every time sophisticated

Muslims in the west use sophistry to explain that the prophet was actually a great liberator of women, every time they fail to condemn outright some of the Koranic laws themselves and demand reformation, they help condemn women across the Islamic world to this self-immolating damage.

Here she is linking the threat of Islam 'out there' with Islam (and the threat it poses) here 'at home' when she refers to the 'sophistry' of Muslims in the West, who are being held to blame for the plight of women in Afghanistan and across the 'Islamic world'. In this apparent slip of the pen, all Islam is associated with fundamentalism and is thus deemed blameworthy, signalling Toynbee's early contribution to the rise of the twenty-first century's fastest growing form of racism – Islamophobia.

Similar sentiments were expressed by Alice Thomson in the *Daily Telegraph*, 23 November 2001:

First I went to Iran to talk to a few of the 2.5 million Afghans living in mud houses and tents. Zarah showed me around. She had been so hungry in Herat that she'd started sucking her hair and had been stopped by the Taliban. They accused her of chewing a sweet, beat her and raped her. 'I am lucky; there is food and water in Iran', she told me. The situation of the refugees in Tajikistan was far worse. On an island stuck in the middle of no-man's-land in the Pyandzh river, two women in white burqas floated across the reeds like swans. They had so little food that they had come to beg for eye ointment to cook with.

This description of the dire circumstances that face Afghan refugees, while offering a graphic (if belated) glimpse of the catastrophic lives of Afghan women, is, like most articles on this subject in the British press, empty of any contextual content, including the role of the US in the rise of fundamentalism in the region and in the developing humanitarian crisis there. Instead, the article uses the very real horrors that face Afghan refugees in order to produce hatred for the

Taliban and from thence for Islam. These 'feminist voices' were joined by male counterparts not normally celebrated for their defence of women's rights. Thus in the *Sunday Express*, 23 September 2001, Robert Kilroy-Silk wrote:

Consider this: what do you think would happen if we discovered that there was a country that oppressed and humiliated its black population and decreed they were second-class citizens? What if it transpired that all the black people were forced to wear clothes that identified them as black and were required to hide all of their black skin on pain of being beaten, that they were not allowed to be educated or to work and were compelled to carry out all menial tasks. And if they were found to have committed adultery they would be publicly stoned to death. The whole world would be outraged, wouldn't it? The UN would pass resolutions, the Afro-Arab countries would be demanding that the US mount a liberating invasion. The world would not rest until the blacks had been freed.

Yet this is what the mad Taliban in Afghanistan have been doing to women for years. And this is the country we must attack? This is the wicked regime some young British Pakistanis publicly applaud, boast that they are prepared to fight and die for? They call this a noble cause? It says a great deal about them and their attitude to women, doesn't it? It also says something about the priorities of the West that we will allow women to be oppressed in a way that we would never tolerate if they were black or Jewish.

This pretty selective defence of human rights once again brings the threat home. One suspects that one will wait in vein for similar attitudes to be expressed in the British press towards the women of Palestine (most of whom are Muslims) and for condemnations of Israel's treatment of the Palestinian population as a whole.

The plight of women of Afghanistan was also a key concern of an article by Laura Barton in the *Guardian*, 4 December 2001:

After five years of repression under the Taliban, the women of Afghanistan are attempting to claim their right to participate. Since 1996, they have endured an existence virtually unimaginable to those of us living in Britain. They have been banned from appearing on television. They were not permitted to work or go to school, and were forced to obey a strict curfew ... Women were expected to wear a burka – an all-enveloping garment, with a small, veiled opening for the eyes. Inside and outside Afghanistan, some people argue that the burka frees a woman from the lecherous glances and unwanted attentions of men. But its use was formalised under the Taliban as part of the control of women's lives by men ... Religious fanatics would throw acid in the faces of unveiled women. They were subjected to random beatings for laughing in public or for revealing too much ankle. It was forbidden for women to visit a male doctor unaccompanied, and as most female doctors had fled or been sent home it became extremely difficult for women to get medical attention. Women were not allowed to venture out of doors without a male companion. Those without male relatives had to remain at home and paint their windows black.

Again, while this provides an overdue account of the harsh treatment of women in Afghanistan, each of the articles quoted above revels in its supercilious indignation at the treatment meted out to women by the Taliban, and the collective tone is of moral superiority. Yet where was this indignation in 1995 when Amnesty International released a report describing the situation of Afghan refugees as 'the worst in the world' (Stabile and Kumar, 2005: 771)? Why was there a deafening silence (only two articles) in the British press in 1996 when both RAWA and the Feminist Majority published on the internet evidence of the abuses of the Taliban? And where were the articles in the British press on the rise of fundamentalism in the region prior to the rise of the Taliban, which was a direct consequence of earlier US intervention? This silence about inconvenient facts, coupled with a general lack of historical and geo-political context, allows the press to present Islamic fundamentalism and Western governments as if they belong to two completely separate and unconnected worlds, whereas in point of fact, as Stabile and Kumar (2005) among others have pointed out, Western governments, and in particular that of the US, have played a key role in the development of fundamentalism in Afghanistan (and indeed elsewhere).

What cannot be missed, however, is the hyper-rhetorical and emotive language routinely used in press discussions of the veil, based on a false binary between the 'modern' West, protector of women's rights and civilisation, and 'sinister', 'primitive' Middle Eastern Islam. This language was formed in a moment of history which was defined by neo-imperial adventures undertaken above all by the governments of the USA and the UK, who stand accused of cynically exploiting the issue of women's oppression in Afghanistan, which they had long ignored, to obscure their real aims, not only in that country but elsewhere in the Middle East. In this first phase of the 'War on Terror', its intellectual justification comes from Huntington's 'clash of civilisations' thesis, which sets out a binary opposition between Islam (as a whole) and the West (also as a whole) and which positions Islam as violent, fanatical, atavistic and despotic, in contrast to the West. In this context, the veil is a symbol of Islam's barbarism and Muslim women its victims: objects of pity. But this is an image of Muslim women outside the West.

The narrative of 'threat'

However, the context has shifted and the meanings of the veil in phase two of the 'War on Terror' have moved from an external image of victimhood and a justification for military intervention to an internal sign of fundamentalism and a visible threat at home. The end of the Bush/Blair era brought to a close the confident first phase of the 'War on Terror' and was marked by the increasing unpopularity of their military adventures. The neocon rhetoric of 'exporting democracy' has been shown to be a failure and its intellectual premises, never exactly convincing, have increasingly been challenged. In the UK, the controversy over the 'Dodgy Dossier' about the alleged existence of weapons of mass destruction in Iraq was re-ignited in 2009 by the Chilcot Inquiry, further undermining the case for going to war. In this context, Bush and Blair's militaristic language has gradually been replaced by calls for a new kind of 'War on Terror' based on the 'soft power' of cultural influence. However, as Arun Kundnani points out, at the same time as this *kulturkampf* has been launched by governments in the US and Europe, it has been matched by an aggressive new form of 'liberalism' which seeks to redefine the clash of civilisations thesis at a time when its initial manifestation looks increasingly bankrupt. And after the terrorist attacks on 7 July 2007 the 'War on Terror' shifted from an external question to an internal one. While members of the anti-war movement and some other sections of the population accepted that the 7/7 terrorist attacks were at least partly a consequence of Britain's involvement in the invasion and occupation of Iraq, the government and much of the press identified an 'evil ideology' as being the cause (Kundnani, 2007: 97). Conveniently this denied the role played by the injustices perpetrated throughout the war and occupation in fuelling the rising anger among Muslims in the West and instead sought explanations that were in accord with a new right-wing attack on multiculturalism, an attack which attracted a number of erstwhile liberals as well.

Significantly Huntington and his enthusiastic followers are prime examples of this ideological shift. Indeed, it is worth remembering that when Huntington pointed at Muslims and Islam as the principal threat to what he calls 'Western Civilisation' he was in fact concerned not only with Muslims and Islam in the Middle East and North Africa but also large Muslim communities (of all nationalities and ethnicities) who were living in the West. That his next major project, *Who Are We? America's great debate* (2004), turned to immigrants in the United States, and specifically to members of its Hispanic communities, should thus be no surprise. And one of his admirers, Francis Fukuyama (2006), was similarly disturbed by demographic changes within North America and Europe. Indeed, even when he began to distance himself belatedly from the disastrous invasion of Iraq he argued:'Meeting the jihadist challenge needs not a military campaign but a political contest for the hearts and minds of ordinary Muslims around the world. As recent events in France and Denmark suggest, Europe will be a central battleground.' The clash of civilisations was no longer going to take place 'out there' but at home.

The context of this new 'liberalism' is twofold: one is that the West has a permanent population from the postcolonial world, many of whom are now second- and third-generation citizens of their country of residence. As many have reminded us (Al-Azmeh, 2007; Zubaida, 2003), Islam, which for long was perceived in Europe as 'external', is a highly visible internal social actor in European countries. Said (1995 [1978]) suggested that many centuries ago 'the Cross faced down the Crescent' with devastating consequences, but one consequence of the colonisation and imperialism which followed was that, in the West, the 'Crescent', or a rather small slice of it, took up residence. However, colonialism is neither an isolated entity nor a trans-historical moment and, as such, cannot be understood without reference to modern capitalism. It is this system that explains the competition for colonies and the ensuing conflicts, as well as the social relations that have shaped and reshaped both the colonised and the colonisers. As Dirlik suggests:

> The present world is a world that is radically different from the world of decolonisation in the immediate aftermath of World War II. Capitalism has reinvented itself and opened up to the formerly colonised, who are now participants in its global operations. Former colonials are in the process of colonising the 'mother' countries, bringing the earlier 'contact zones' of the colonies into the heart of formerly colonialist societies. These motions of people force a rendition both of nations and national cultures.

> (2002: 439)

And it is through this process that those unable to 'integrate' are marginalised.

Twinned with this are the neocon economic projects which are trying to dismantle welfare systems as part of their determination to impose 'free market' economic policies on Western societies. Migrants, refugees and 'asylum seekers' (as well as the poor in general) have been fingered as the main beneficiaries of these systems and, as part of the justification for destroying all forms of state welfare, have been comprehensively stigmatised and 'othered', a process in which the press, particularly in Britain, has played a key role.

The veil has come to play a significant role in the process of identifying an internal 'other', and although its meanings have shifted in this new context, the central meaning of the veil in the first phase of the 'War on Terror' – Islamic female oppression – continues in play and has been grafted onto this context with new meanings. But the practice of the veil is neither 'Islamic' nor exclusive to Islamic communities. It may have escaped the attention of many people, but many women in southern Europe cover their heads, and the issue of 'modesty' is by no means exclusive to Muslims. Discussions of the veil usually reveal assumptions that religion is the determining factor in, and the all-encompassing aspect of, 'Muslim' identity; similarly, it is frequently assumed that the meaning of 'Islamic' and what counts as 'Islamic' in terms of sartorial practices and piety are fixed, given and uncontested among 'Muslims'.[3] What underlines such readings of 'Islamic culture' is the perception of a timeless and homogeneous Islam and Islamic community, regardless of class, nationality, politics and location. As Reina Lewis (2007: 428) argues:

> There are several misconceptions about the veil that need to be addressed: first, although the veil is today predominantly associated with Islam, it is a garment that is pre-Islamic in origin and one that has been adopted by diverse religious and ethnic communities, especially in the Middle East. Secondly, in the Middle East, the veil often signified status rather than piety or ethnic allegiance. Thirdly, there is no single garment that

equates to the veil: different versions of clothing that are held suitably to preserve modesty in gender-mixed environments have been adopted by different communities (often with different names for the same garment). Furthermore, the form of these garments or combinations of garments changes over time, quite often within the lifespan of a single woman. Thus, attempts to legislate which type of body covering is properly Islamic can only be seen as partial and located.

The objection and opposition to the veil (which has been badly misunderstood) has historically been expressed in humanitarian terms. If internationally the opposition is expressed in terms of the humanitarian concern to liberate women (a duty which in Afghanistan has been given to US marines), and therefore the form of expression has been strikingly 'internationalist', inside 'Fortress Europe', as the debate about the veil in the UK all too clearly demonstrates, the concern and the language are clearly nationalist. Labelling Islam as 'unique' and 'exceptional' and in diametrical opposition to what 'the West' stands for, the debate about the veil is effectively no longer about 'liberation' but about the anxiety over the perceived threat to 'national culture', 'our way of life' and the very future of the nation.

Images that are circulated in the media of Muslim women often brush aside the variety of their experiences, lives, histories and contexts in the interests of erecting the false binary of 'us' and 'them' and promoting the idea of the incompatibility of 'Islam' with 'modernity'; a form of 'exceptionalism' that sets Muslims aside as the truly alien other. That such images have been used relentlessly to manipulate public opinion into supporting neo-imperial adventures in the Middle East is beyond doubt, and we have already touched on this. But, increasingly, such images are also used to drum up support for the most right-wing purposes in domestic policies in various European countries. The controversy over the veil in European countries cannot be understood outside colonial history, but more significantly, outside domestic politics. Historically the veil (or lack of it) has been regarded as a shorthand for nation and national loyalty (as in the cases of Iran and Turkey in 1920s, and again since 1979). 'The women's question' has in fact been a central concern of the historical debate about the boundaries of the public sphere and the fault line between 'public' and 'private'. The issue of the extent and limits of the 'visibility' of women in public life has been one of the main battlegrounds in modern societies and a contentious issue among varied social interests and political projects. For centuries women's emancipation has been central to the 'modernisation' project, and is usually associated and equated with 'national progress' and the brushing aside of outdated traditions which are seen as impeding that progress (Gole, 1997). Such arguments are now being rehearsed once again in Europe as European states demand the loyalty of their Muslim citizens to their national culture and way of life, and the veil plays a key role in such arguments. However, the dominant narrative of the veil, playing as it does to notions of 'us' and 'them', 'the West' and 'Islam', modernity and tradition, ignores the complexity of the veil in various national and political contexts. But, more significantly, this mainstream narrative ignores the very specific context of the veil within Europe.

Even though press commentators were trying to link the idea of 'War on Terror' with the 'woman question', and in particular the *burka* and *hijab*, as early as September 2001, it was the terrorist attacks in July 2005, and in particular Jack Straw's intervention and comments about the veil in October 2006, which turned it into a really significant national debate.

On 5 October 2006, Jack Straw, then Labour Leader of the Commons and ex-home secretary, called on Muslim women in Britain to remove their veils in order to help community relations, in his weekly column in the *Lancashire Telegraph*. His comments were moved to the front page and were immediately taken up by the rest of the British media. Straw's suggestion that the veil is 'a visible statement of separation and difference' contributed enormously to the rising tide of Islamaphobia in Britain (and across Europe), and exemplified a growing tendency in government and the media to demonise Muslims in Britain and to mark them out as a particularly problematic section of the population. Straw's intervention came at a time when multiculturalism (now associated particularly closely with Muslims) was under attack in Britain and across Europe (as it still is), in a push towards what is called 'integrationism', but which really means 'assimilation' (Fekete, 2006; Werbner, 2007; Wilson, 2007). Parliamentary and press debates on this issue frequently stress the 'alien culture' of Muslims, insist that Islamic and European values are incompatible, and suggest that Muslims in Europe refuse to 'integrate'. Since 9/11, Muslim-directed citizenship reforms have been introduced in every European country, immigration laws have been tightened and the rights of both citizens and long-term residents have been curtailed (Fekete, 2006). The image of the veiled Muslim woman has been an important symbol in this climate of Islamophobia and racism, for it is presented as visual evidence of 'difference', and Muslim women's continued use of the veil is constructed as an overt refusal of 'our way of life'. Indeed, a number of important rulings under the European Convention on Human Rights have actually denied Muslim women the right to wear the headscarf in certain public places on the grounds that, by using the veil, Muslim women interfered with the 'rights and freedoms of others' (Vakulenko, 2007: 187). In 2004 the wearing of the headscarf in schools in France was banned (ostensibly on the grounds that French state schools are secular institutions).

Understanding the shifts in perceptions of the veil

The public controversy generated by Straw's comments took on a life of its own that continues to this day. The issue was not just a dispute over a garment, it was far more acute than that.

Today, the coverage of veil use among Muslim women is organised through four interlocking themes that combine in a particular trajectory. The predominant theme is that the veil is constructed as a deliberate refusal of 'our way of life', which is presented as part of a more general erosion of the 'British way of life'. This construction has recourse to a prevalent monoculturalism which presents a falsely singular image of British culture, of Islam and of the veil (Fekete, 2006). Linked to this is a second theme related to the notion that British attitudes towards multiculturalism are excessively tolerant. The variety of veiling garments have been reduced to a single sign in which the *veil in general* is a symbol of that which can no longer be tolerated: an example of the way in which 'too much' tolerance has produced threats to the 'British way of life'. The veil has been reconfigured through two tropes: the veil as act of refusal, and the veil as act of resistance. The 'veil as act of refusal' relates to the first two themes above: excessive tolerance and the refusal of 'our way of life'. The 'veil as act of resistance' takes us into the two final themes – the notion that Britain is suffering from the tyranny of a culture imposed by a minority, and the linking of the use of the veil to the threat of terrorism. Here we can see that the veil acts as a link between ideas of Muslim 'backwardness' and ideas of 'extremism' (Khiabany and Williamson, 2008).

In the mainstream account of the *burka* and *hijab* in recent years, and especially since Straw's intervention, the issue is framed repeatedly, indeed obsessively, as a matter of life and death, in which a minority is not only putting British culture at risk but also the security and indeed the very existence of the country itself, and in which British citizens (white, Christian, law-abiding, silenced due to 'political correctness' and misguided multiculturalism) are considered to be the main victims.

After Straw's comments many papers used a number of stories to link the veil overtly to issues of security. On 26 December 2006, the *Star* (just like the *Sun*) printed ten faces in the *niqab* on one page and asked readers: 'Can you go one better than Britain's security staff and spot the villain in the veil?' The story was about the escape of the killer of policewoman Sharon Beshenivsky, who was reported to have passed through airport security wearing full veil. The paper claimed that the escape of the killer (Mustaf Jama) 'has highlighted the poor state of Britain's airport security and raised fears that political correctness is preventing full checks from being carried out on veiled passengers. But despite the public outrage, the Government is refusing to order checks on ALL veiled passengers.'

The *Daily Mail* cover story on 16 January 2007 also concerned the veil and security. The story, under the headline of 'Bombing suspect fled in a burka', stated that:

One of the alleged July 21 bombers fled London after the attempted attacks disguised as a woman wearing a burkha, their trial heard. Yassin Omar was captured on CCTV at Golders Green coach station in north London and at Birmingham coach station disguised in the traditional Muslim women's dress ... Prosecuting counsel Nigel Sweeney said: 'CCTV shows him and his fiancee at Golders Green coach station and him at Birmingham coach station that evening disguised in the burkha.'

A further story in the *Daily Mail*, 8 February 2007, under the head-line 'School veils allow new Dunblane, similarly collapsed the issue of security into that of 'threats to our way of life'. This reported the comments of a judge to the effect that allowing veil-wearing in schools could allow a recurrence of the primary school massacre which took place in Scotland in March 1996. According to the arti-cle: 'Allowing Muslim girls to wear full-face veils to school could make Dunblane-style massacres more common, a judge suggested. Judge Stephen Silber was hearing a case brought by a 12-year-old Muslim girl against her headmistress's ban on her veil. The judge suggested veils would make it hard to identify intruders in schools, making murderous attacks more likely.'

Paul Ross focused on the same issue on 25 February 2007 in the *Star*. After it was reported that the judge had ruled against a pupil demanding to wear a *niqab* in school, Ross hailed the action of the judge as a victory for 'common sense' and noted that:

On the same day the niqab decision was announced Britain's most prominent Islamic organisation, the Muslim Council of Britain, said that Muslim kids should have separate changing rooms for swimming and sport with individual cubicles – even for primary school kids – prayer rooms and single sex classes for biology lessons, which should stress 'Islamic morals'. Oh, and they also want different uniform rules, a plea which has already been booted out. Of course these demands are not just unreasonable – they are downright impossible. And the Muslim Council of Britain must know that if they read even the occasional infidel's newspaper or have an ounce of sense in their bearded bonces … But it's not really about getting what they want – it's about making a lot of noise and nuisance and promoting a sense of grievance among Muslims – to keep the anger and resentment simmering.

Ross's article was part of a vociferous press campaign against the so-called 'dictatorship of minorities' and the 'PC brigade', which are represented as attempting to curtail the freedom of the law abiding British, the 'us' who cannot open their mouths for fear of being called racists. (This topic is discussed at length in Chapter 4.) As Robin Richardson has pointed out, 210 comments appeared on the *Daily Express* website between 21 and 23 February 2007, most of the comments' authors believing they 'were responding to a new publication from the Muslim Council of Britain (MCB). In fact, they were responding to a monstrously distorted and inaccurate depiction of the MCB publication in the *Daily Express*' (Richardson, 2007). None of the issues that Ross and many of the contributors to the *Daily Express* website attributed to the MCB publication (2007) actually appears in that document.

Frances Childs also applauded the victory of 'common sense' when it came to banning the veil in schools. Writing in the *Daily Mail*, 22 March 2007, under the headline 'Why banning religious dress in schools is a lesson in common sense', she appeared to have something of a personal axe to grind, based on her experience teaching at a sixth-form college in which her class contained three girls who wore the full face veil:

In the year that I taught the class, the girls never sat next to anyone else. They never entered into class discussion and

I admit that I never asked them their opinions about the books that we read. Simply, they embarrassed me. Unable to see their faces, they had no individuality. I couldn't call them by name unless I assumed they would always sit in the same order. Not being able to see their faces, I couldn't read their emotions. I had no idea if they smiled when a joke was cracked. I didn't know if an account of slavery moved them to tears as it did some of the other students, let alone if they understood what I was teaching ... They sat in the classroom with us, but they weren't part of the group. They were effectively invisible ... So it was with delight that I read this week that schools will be able to ban pupils from wearing the full-face veils.

Given that both Ross and Childs use the term 'common sense' as an automatic argument-clincher, it is worth pausing for a moment to recall Gramsci's analysis of the operations of 'common sense' in the creation of consensus. For Gramsci, common sense is 'the folklore of philosophy' and as such is made up of the 'diffuse, unco-ordinated features of a general form of thought particular to a particular period and a particular popular environment' (1971: 330). As such, according to Gramsci, it is 'an ambiguous, contradictory and multiform concept', although one of its hallmarks is that it is always 'crudely neophobe and conservative'. For all these reasons, Gramsci argues, 'to refer to common sense as a confirmation of truth is a nonsense' (1971: 422–3). However, common sense 'works' in popular discourse precisely because it seems to contain a kernel of undeniable and obvious truth. Thus, drawing on her own personal experience of teaching veiled students, Frances Childs constructs a more general argument which suggests that Islam stands in opposition to British values. Of course, it needs to be noted that, primarily due to the anti-war movement and the increased political engagement of British Muslims, there are views and arguments that run counter to this 'common sense' view. However, it's also important to understand that consensus is built not through a monolithic ideology but through a *dominant* one, and, as Elizabeth Poole has noted (2002: 81), and as other chapters in this book make clear, the majority of articles in the British tabloid and broadsheet press depict Muslims as having difficulties in assimilating and relating to mainstream society.

However, the sense of triumph for 'common sense' did not last long, as a subsequent ruling upset the tabloids. The *Daily Express* reacted angrily on 25 April 2007 after senior judges ruled that wearing the veil in courts should be allowed. According to the *Daily Express*, the ruling 'could lead to a suspect criminal being allowed to give evidence without the public or press hearing it'. Tory MP David Davies said: 'This is another nail in the coffin for this country. We have reached the point where we are bending over backwards to pander and forget the culture and laws that made this country what it is.' The paper's editorial, headed 'Disgraceful veil rule will only fuel further anger', called the ruling a crazy act of 'cultural surrender', and argued that 'the decision to give the green light for full-face veils to be worn in court by lawyers, witnesses and even defendants drives a coach and horses – or should that be a camel train? – through British legal tradition'.

In this and in many other articles, the veil is thus used as a signifier in the 'common sense' argument that Britain is excessively tolerant. This is a key plank in attacks on multiculturalism. Thus, in an article headed 'Fear of giving offence is killing our culture', Minette Marrin in the *Sunday Times*, 7 October 2007, cited the veil judgement as 'some strange abandonment of common sense' and blamed this and various other events on 'a decadent loss of belief in ourselves, in our own culture and in its superiority – warts and all – to others that may threaten it'. One of the events she cited was taken from a story in the previous week's paper, which alleged that a number of Muslim workers in Sainsbury's had refused to check out purchases of alcohol, and on the same day that Marrin's article appeared, the *Sunday Times* published another story on the same theme, headed 'Muslim medics get picky' which alleged that:

Some Muslim medical students are refusing to attend lectures or answer exam questions on alcohol-related or sexually transmitted diseases because they claim it offends their religious beliefs ... Some trainee doctors say learning to treat the diseases conflicts with their faith, which states that Muslims should not drink alcohol and rejects sexual promiscuity. A small number of Muslim medical students have even refused to treat patients of the opposite sex. One male student was prepared to fail his final exams rather than carry out a basic examination of a female patient.

The article adds that 'the religious objections by students have been confirmed by the British Medical Association (BMA) and General Medical Council (GMC)', but signally fails to reveal where and when these alleged events took place. Adding to the increasing hall of mirrors effect, it also repeats the previous week's story 'that Sainsbury's is permitting Muslim checkout operators to refuse to handle customers' alcohol purchases on religious grounds'. However, even the initial report in the *Sunday Times* (30 September 2007) could identify only one member of staff who had asked not to handle alcohol, and this was during Ramadan. This tends to throw the veracity of the whole carefully constructed edifice into some doubt.

In the *Daily Mail*, 25 October 2007, Stephen Glover linked the notion of an 'oppressed majority' to the issue of security, the veil and immigration in an article entitled 'Britain will be scarcely recognizable in 50 years if immigration deluge continues'. Glover cannot actually be blamed for the headline, nor for the fact that a photograph accompanying the article was of a street in which a woman in a veil could be seen, but what is significant in the present context is his remark that:

British culture, whatever it represents, is evidently not worth preserving in the view of some on the Left. It is a curious paradox that some of its adherents believe that foreign cultures are worth safeguarding, but not our own. One of the Left's best arguments against colonialism is that it involved placing a foreign culture above indigenous ones. But when our own indigenous culture is threatened, we are told that it is parochial and small-minded to think about trying to defend it.

This then leads him to argue that 'unless we acquire American habits of assimilation, I very much doubt that Britain can painlessly absorb the numbers of immigrants that are projected over the next 20 years'.

Meanwhile, the *Daily Express* dedicated its front page on 19 July 2007 to a protest by a number of Muslims outside the Old Bailey, where four members of the Al Muhaj group were on trial. Under the banner heading 'Outrageous' the paper claimed: 'This was the extraordinary scene on the streets of Britain yesterday as burka-clad protestors demanded the release of four extremists. Swarming outside the Old Bailey, the Muslim hate mob poured scorn on the nation that guarantees their freedoms.' But whatever the rights or wrongs of the case, the accompanying picture showed that the 'mob' 'swarming' outside the court consisted of only six women in the veil. Shifting the image of Muslim women from victims to aggressors, the lead article on the same day was headed 'Wearing of burkas is a threat to our way of life' and suggested that the *burka*:

> is becoming the Islamic equivalent of the mugger's hooded top or the armed robber's balaclava. Anyone sincerely wishing to integrate into the British way of life would never wear such an alien and threatening outfit … Make no mistake, the proliferation of burka-wearing is a direct threat to the British way of life and in all too many instances is intended to be just that.

The failed terrorist attacks in London and Glasgow early in July 2007 gave the press the opportunity to link the *burka* and the *hijab* with terrorism. Thus the headline of a story in the *Sun*, 2 July 2007, about the arrest of a 'terrorist suspect' was headed 'Nicked: Doc and wife in a burka'. And a leader in the *Daily Express*, 2 July 2007, headed 'We should abandon failed policy of multiculturalism', linked the issue to the *burka,* terrorism and the question of integration. According to the *Daily Express*:

> It is becoming increasingly clear that many of the Islamist terrorists trying to bring death to our streets are born and bred in

Britain. Because of the mistaken doctrine of multiculturalism, British Muslims have been allowed to live an existence entirely separate from their non-Muslim neighbours. This has added to the confusion many young Muslims have over their identity. In some it is resulting in a hatred of the wider society in which they live but do not take a full part. In response to the latest attempted terror outrages, the Government should certainly consider new powers for the police. But, more importantly, it should examine its own policies and abandon those which are making matters worse. That may mean no state funding for Muslim faith schools and must mean an end to so-called 'chain migration' under which young British Muslims are pressured into marrying foreigners to afford their extended families a route into the UK. Ministers should be encouraging Muslims to integrate, not separate. It is surely also time for the Government to consider a legal ban on the burkha in public places. This is a nation where law-abiding citizens are not ashamed to show their faces. The era of politically correct cultural surrender must be brought to an end.

The 'debate' over the veil has continued since Straw's comment, but it took on a new momentum in 2009 with similar concerns about the veil being raised by other European governments, particularly that of France. Matthew Parris, in an article in *The Times*, 28 May 2009, suggesting that he has seen more people covering their face in Tower Hamlets than in Damascus, offered a more 'cultured' version of the 'us' and 'them' thesis:

Spitting is a cultural feature in China but we discourage it here. In Syria I took my shoes off to enter mosques, though that is not in my culture; and wouldn't have worn clothing like skimpy shorts or vests, or drunk alcohol in the streets: practices offensive not to me but to the mainstream culture where I was. Knowingly to disturb people's feelings is to be offensive. In Western European society, to go out in public with your face masked is (unless done for comic effect) disturbing. Hiding the face is felt to be threatening, and slightly scary, and subliminally this goes way back, and quite deep I think: it certainly frightens children.

He then went on to ask: 'Would it be wrong to try to convey to communities in Britain who adopt the full hijab that, though it is a woman's legal right to dress as she chooses, she should recognise that she's in a country where many people will find a masked face disturbing, and that (without meaning to) she is acting in a culturally inappropriate manner, which may offend?' While the implication is that it is part of the British national character to respect other people's culture, the underlying assumption is that all Muslims living in Britain are not British.

The veil is now an issue that is constantly in play in the British press; when it is not in the headlines, it simmers in the background waiting to be revived. Thus, for example, French President Sarkozy's call in June 2009 for the ban on the *niqab* and *burka* sparked a whole rash of articles. Typical of these was an article in the *Daily Express*, 24 June 2009, headed 'Even Muslims say: Ban the burka here in Britain'. However, the Muslim groups cited were only those hostile to the *burka* such as the Quilliam Foundation, Iraq Solidarity UK and the Iranian and Kurdish Women's Rights Organisation (this last not exactly a regular guest on the pages of the *Daily Express*). Also quoted was Douglas Murray, director of the right-wing Centre for Social Cohesion, which has a very particular agenda on matters pertaining to Islam and Muslims, and 'a poll for the *Daily Express* yesterday [in which] 98 per cent of people said they agreed that Britain should ban the garment'.

One of the hottest topics surrounding the veil, and one of the key battle-grounds for defining 'our way of life', has been the issue of education and the veil. One incident, in which three Muslims wearing the *niqab* were refused entry to a Catholic college in Jack Straw's constituency in Lancashire, was taken up by a number of national newspapers. The three women (a teacher and two pupils) from a sixth-form college were attending the Catholic college open day when they were asked to remove their veils. The students did so but the teacher refused and was barred from entering the college. On 30 June 2009, the *Daily Mail* reported the incident under the headline 'Catholic school bars Muslim teacher who refused to remove face veil so staff could identify her'. Reminding its readers of previous similar incidents, the *Daily Mail* referred to the Jack Straw controversy to Sarkozy's attempt to ban the *burka*, and quoted David Cameron to the effect that 'You can't wear the full garb and be an effective teacher'.

As it happens, the *Daily Mail*'s reporting of this event was relatively balanced and free from editorialising. However, one does need to ask why an incident such as this was deemed nationally newsworthy in the first place, and what this says about the news values of the British press. And when small, local incidents such as this, or a student taking legal action against her school's uniform policy, are routinely reported and then cumulatively recycled, frequently to the accompaniment of editorials and other comment pieces which link the veil with the global threat of terrorism and even to so-called 'rogue' states such as Iran and Lebanon, then it is clear that this is not simply a matter of mere reportage but of waging an ideological campaign.

Conclusion

The debate on the *burka* and the *hijab* cannot be understood outside history; that is, the history of colonialism and imperialism, the process of the neoliberal restructuring of Europe and the rest of the world, and the worsening of living conditions for many at the heart of Europe and indeed elsewhere. In this context, the recent emphasis by politicians on celebrating Empire, stopping 'apologising for our past' and attempting to reassert a certain idea of 'Britishness' are highly ideologically significant. The increasingly strident reassertion of what are claimed to be 'our values' is a clear sign of a deliberate strategy to safeguard the privileges of socially advantaged groups; it is not simply a cultural matter. In using the *burka* and the *hijab* to set yet another test for ethnic communities to show their loyalty to and identification with the 'host' culture, what is usually forgotten is the clear evidence of the long cultural identification between the colonised and the coloniser. What was ignored, for example, in the debate about Lord Tebbit's famous 'cricket test' to determine the loyalty and cultural affinity of British Asians, was that the very existence of the love for cricket among Asians was itself a sign of shared interests and cultural preoccupations. But the intention of the test was not really about accepting 'our culture' but reviving colonial supremacy.

8

'This Idiotic Man'

The British Press, Sharia Law and the Archbishop of Canterbury

Claire George

On 7 February 2008 the Archbishop of Canterbury, Dr Rowan Williams, publicly discussed the legal issues that surround the formal accommodation of Sharia within secular civil law. His words created a media storm that was characterised in the bulk of the press by inaccurate reporting, Islamophobic comment and personalised attacks. This chapter looks at what Williams actually said and why his words attracted so much press attention. It also shows how the Sharia law controversy highlights the existence of considerable press hostility towards both Islam and the liberal intellectualism represented by Williams.

In 2008 Rowan Williams was in his sixth year as Archbishop of Canterbury. The former Oxbridge academic was a well-known theologian, poet and active promoter of interfaith dialogue. It was in this spirit that he was invited to deliver the opening lecture of a year-long series of talks and discussions on Islam in English Law. The series was held at the Royal Courts of Justice. The lecture, 'Civil and Religious Law in England: A Religious Perspective', was a tentative exploration of the issues raised by the accommodation of aspects of religious law within secular civil law. Williams did not call for the legal system to be altered but, rather, looked at what would need to be considered if changes were made. He discussed the possibility of a system under which some parts of religious law were formalised by the state, offering believers an optional, supplementary jurisdiction in carefully overseen incidences, without barring them from their rights as secular citizens. Williams focused on Islamic law but stated clearly that the issues he spoke of were relevant to all religious communities.

Williams' lecture was written specifically for the audience of legal experts who attended the event that evening. His ideas were communicated to the general public at lunchtime on the same day in a pre-recorded interview with Christopher Landau on the BBC Radio 4 *World at One* programme. It was this interview which sparked the first wave of press coverage.

In order fully to understand the affair, it is first necessary to look at the content of the four principal sources of written information which the Lambeth Palace press office made available on its website. These were the lecture text, the radio interview transcript and the two related press releases.

The press releases

Journalists had direct access to Williams' words through the press releases, which were heavily laden with quotations from his radio interview and lecture. The limited amount of paraphrasing and summation in both press releases went against modern public relations practice, which is to condense information into a concise format that can be directly quoted in newspaper articles. It was particularly unfortunate for any reporter in a busy newsroom who needed to read the press releases quickly but was not familiar with the cultural, legal and religious issues covered by Williams. To make matters worse, neither press release followed the usual PR convention of presenting all the key points in the opening paragraphs. Instead the Archbishop's ideas were spread evenly throughout each text, which thus demanded careful reading.

Despite the evident lack of public relations finesse, it would be too simplistic merely to blame the press releases for what journalists subsequently wrote. The press releases may have been unconventional, but they were a perfectly comprehensible account of Williams' ideas. Journalists could also refer to the lecture text and the radio interview transcript which, as noted above, were both clearly displayed on the Lambeth Palace website. Journalists should have had time to read all of the material carefully before discussing it in the public domain. If they did not, it supports the 'churnalism' thesis put forward by Nick Davies in *Flat Earth News* (2008), in which he argues that many newspapers now recycle press releases in a factory-like fashion without adequate research and fact-checking.

The press release for the radio interview began with a paraphrase of the first point discussed by Williams and Landau. It stated Williams' view that 'UK law needs to continue to find accommodation with religious legal codes such as the Islamic system of Sharia if community cohesion and development are to be achieved.' It then went on to state that the formal recognition of religious law was relevant to all faith communities, including Christians, and that in some cases this was already happening. It cited the example of Orthodox Jewish courts in operation in the UK, and Williams' statement that certain provisions of Sharia were already recognised under the law: 'It's not as if we're bringing in an alien and rival system. We already have in this country a number of situations in which the internal law of religious communities is recognised by the law of the land as justified conscientious objections in certain circumstances in providing certain kinds of social relations.'

The press release for the radio interview also underlined Williams' opposition to the brutal punishments sanctioned under Sharia in some countries, and his concern that the accommodation of Sharia should not deprive anyone of their legal rights as secular citizens. In this respect, Williams was quoted as saying:

Nobody in their right mind, I think, would want to see in this country a kind of inhumanity that sometimes appears to be

203

associated with the practice of the law in some Islamic states [with] the extreme punishments, the attitudes to women as well … I think it would be quite wrong to say that we could ever license so to speak a system of law for some communities which gave people no right of appeal, no way of exercising the rights that are guaranteed to them as citizens in general.

The press release which publicised the lecture also stressed that Williams' ideas were relevant to people of all faiths, and that this was not a specifically Muslim issue. Utilising a direct quote from the lecture, this press release underlined the Archbishop's opposition to the oppression of women. Thus, in response to the fear that the recognition of religious law could reinforce 'retrograde elements' in minority communities 'with particularly serious consequences for the roles and liberties of women', Williams said that there needs to be a 'rubric' that no ' "supplementary" jurisdiction could have the power to deny access to the rights granted to other citizens … or to punish its members for claiming those rights'.

In addition, this press release highlighted the cultural focus of Williams' lecture, which was the concept of plural identity. Williams challenged the assumption that a person cannot be equally both a secular citizen and a member of a religious group. The release quoted Williams' statement that:

The danger arises not only when there is an assumption on the religious side that membership of the community (belonging to the umma or the Church or whatever) is the only significant category, so that participation in other kinds of socio-political arrangement is a kind of betrayal. It also occurs when secular government assumes a monopoly in terms of defining public and political identity.

Williams then expressed his hopes for a scheme 'in which individuals retain the liberty to choose the jurisdiction under which they will seek to resolve certain carefully specified matters … This may include aspects of marital law, the regulation of financial transactions and authorised structures of mediation and conflict resolution.' It is particularly important to note this passage because Williams was misrepresented, or at least misunderstood, as someone who wanted to introduce Sharia wholesale into the administration of criminal law among British Muslims. The press release also repeats Williams' idea for a body to oversee the administration of Sharia in order to prevent 'vexatious appeals to religious scruple'.

In summary, then, the press releases made it clear that Williams opposed brutal punishments and the oppression of women. They showed that the accommodation of religious law was relevant to *all* faith groups, and that it was not a new idea in the UK. They also made it very clear that Williams wanted religious people to retain their secular rights as citizens. Furthermore they showed that Williams was not arguing for a replacement of secular law, or for two systems running alongside each other, but rather for a carefully monitored supplementary jurisdiction for particular civil law situations.

The *World at One* interview

One element of the radio interview that was not covered in the press release was Williams' view on plural identity. In the interview the Archbishop told Christopher Landau that there was 'a bit of a danger' when people thought that there was 'one law for everybody' and that 'anything else that commands your loyalty or your allegiance is completely irrelevant in the processes of the courts'. This was later misrepresented by the press as supporting the idea that Muslims in Britain should be able to live under entirely separate laws.

Williams pointed to the existence of prejudice against Sharia caused by the misunderstanding of it as a 'single fixed entity'. He underlined the fact that Sharia is diverse and flexible, saying: 'Where it's codified in … very brutal and inhuman and unjust ways, that's one particular expression of it which is historically conditioned'. Williams emphasised that Sharia is a method rather than a code of law, that it takes a case-by-case approach, and that it is capable of change. He also explained that it is the subject of debate within the Islamic world and warned: 'I don't think we should instantly spring to the conclusion that the whole of that world of jurisprudence and practice is somehow monstrously incompatible with human rights simply because it doesn't immediately fit with how we understand it.'

In short, the radio interview should have caused journalists to question whether common accounts of Sharia, which tend to be projected by the majority of the press, were in fact accurate. In several cases, however, it most definitely did not. Indeed, one of the most striking aspects of this incident is that it was actually a specialist religious journalist, *The Times'* Ruth Gledhill, who was one of the first to seriously misrepresent what Williams had actually said. This was in her *Times* blog 'Articles of Faith', in which her response to the interview was headed 'Has the Archbishop gone bonkers?' and in which she complained: 'Now it seems he wants women, children, all of us in fact, to have to kow-tow to some of the strictest, harshest and most draconian laws dreamed up by any religious system, ever, anywhere in the world.' And yet anyone following the hyperlink from her blog to the Lambeth Palace website page carrying a transcript of the radio interview would have quickly discovered that Williams had stated precisely the opposite!

The lecture

The lecture raised many of the same points that were outlined in the press releases and covered in the radio interview, but it also contained a much deeper discussion of legal issues. Its main subject was the nature of law, legal universalism and plural identity. It is in the lecture that we see that Williams' chief interest was actually in the subject of the accommodation of religious law within secular civil law, and that he was simply using Sharia as an example to illustrate a more general argument.

Crucial to an understanding of why Williams wanted to talk about the accommodation of religious law, why he considered this matter

to be relevant to all faith groups, and why he thought it was important for social cohesion, is what he had to say about plural identities:

> Societies that are in fact ethnically, culturally and religiously
> diverse are societies in which identity is formed, as we have
> noted by different modes and contexts of belonging, 'multiple
> affiliation'. The danger is in acting as if the authority that man-
> aged the abstract level of equal citizenship represented a sover-
> eign order which then allowed other levels to exist. But if the
> reality of society is plural – as many political theorists have
> pointed out – this is a damagingly inadequate account of
> common life, in which certain kinds of affiliation are margina-
> lised or privatised to the extent that what is produced is a
> ghettoised pattern of social life.

He then went on to argue that the law should contain provision for
religious belief in order to communicate effectively with citizens:

> If the law of the land takes no account of what might be for
> certain agents a proper rationale for behaviour – for protest
> against certain unforeseen professional requirements, for
> instance, which would compromise religious discipline or
> belief – it fails in a significant way to communicate with some-
> one involved in the legal process (or indeed to receive their
> communication), and so, on at least one kind of legal theory …
> fails in one of its purposes.

And in a passage which should have signalled unequivocally that he
most certainly did not want Muslims in Britain to live under entirely
separate laws, Williams stated: 'Recognising a supplementary jurisdiction cannot mean recognising a liberty to exert a sort of local
monopoly in some areas.'

Thus the clear picture that emerges from Williams' words is that
he supported secular civil law and the protections that it offers, but
that he also wanted to question the assumption that it was the only

law to which religious believers should formally relate. He most emphatically did not propose that religious believers should ignore secular law, but merely that they should have access to a second system on certain occasions.

The press reaction

In this age of 24-hour breaking news, the Archbishop's views sparked an instant media reaction. On the day of the radio broadcast and subsequent speech, the BBC website reported on the *World at One* interview with a story entitled 'Sharia law in UK "unavoidable" '. This BBC report then fed into news and comment across the web, radio and television. British national newspapers picked it up in their print versions the following day, and it was front-page news and featured in editorials for several days after the speech. On their websites the story maintained a very high profile for a week, resurfacing in the following months whenever the issue of Sharia became topical.

Unsurprisingly, the overall tone of coverage in the liberal newspapers such as the *Guardian* and the *Independent* was noticeably different from that of illiberal newspapers such as the *Sun* and the *Daily Telegraph*. This is not to say that liberal newspapers were uncritical of Williams' ideas, nor that they were entirely free of stereotypes of Islam, but they did tend to avoid the overt hostility towards Muslims and Islam all too evident in many articles in the illiberal press.

Since very little actually happened once Williams had given his Radio 4 interview and made his speech, apart from his commenting on the controversy when he addressed the General Synod on 11 February, it is hardly surprising that newspaper coverage was dominated by comment and opinion. News reports tended to concentrate on gathering various people's views of the Archbishop and Sharia. The British press being notoriously comment-driven, journalists were not exactly shy of airing their own opinions in numerous comment pieces, and, as will be demonstrated later in this chapter, they also on occasion inserted them into what purported to be news reports. A pessimist might describe the controversy as a media circus based on the misunderstanding of the Archbishop's intentions, fuelled by prejudice against Muslims and Islam and driven by opinion-led journalism. A more optimistic view, taking into account coverage in the liberal press, would be to think of the affair as a public discussion of the place of Islam, Christianity and secularism in British society.

An idea of the sheer volume of press coverage and its largely opinion-driven character can be seen by examining the coverage in *The Times* and the *Daily Mail*.

The Times followed the affair in daily leader articles from 8 February to 11 February. Much of the non-leader coverage was written by religion correspondent Ruth Gledhill, sometimes in partnership with other reporters. *The Times'* reaction was dominated by comment and opinion. Under *The Times* website's own system of article classification, the majority of articles were comment pieces. On 8 February the newspaper published six articles: one news report, one legal background story, three comment pieces in the faith section and one leader. On 9 February there were again six articles, all classified as comment: one was the leader, another was a column by Matthew Parris, the third was the letters page and the rest were comment pieces in the faith section. On 10 February there were four comment pieces and one news report. The comment pieces were the leader, one article in the faith section, a column by Minette Marrin and a passing reference in a column by Roland White. The news report largely focused on a government minister's comments on first-cousin intermarriage in rural Pakistani Muslim families. On 11 February the Sharia story appeared in six articles categorised as comment. One was a leader, one was the letters page and the remaining four were placed under faith. From 12 February to 15 February the affair was mentioned in two articles on each day. All of these were classified as comment pieces, and it was evident that by this time the story was moving away from the controversy itself and towards wider issues concerning Islam.

The volume of coverage in the *Daily Mail* was similar to that of *The Times*. The newspaper published six articles on 8 February, six articles on 9 February, six articles on 10 February, two on 12 February, one on

13 February and one on 14 February. However, none of the *Daily Mail*'s coverage was written by religious affairs correspondents.

Under the *Daily Mail* website's system of classification, stories are classed as either news or debate. Yet news stories were often far from neutral. For example, on 8 February in an article classified as news but with the snide headline 'He regards himself as a unifier. Pity his own Church is so divided', Geoffrey Levy, in a clear case of substituting comment for fact, wrote of Williams that he had 'posted an astonishing warning notice to his own religion to move over and make space for Islam'. He then stated, equally misleadingly, that Williams had 'forecast – indeed, virtually recommended – the adoption of some aspects of Islamic law in Britain'.

On 9 February an article classified as news but published under the editorialising headline 'Equality before the law is not negotiable, Dr Williams' again mixed news with comment by referring to Williams' allegedly 'bumbling support for Sharia law being allowed to co-exist alongside the British legal code' and stating that 'the beleaguered Archbishop of Canterbury resorted yesterday to the oldest stand-by in the book – "I have been misinterpreted"' – which, of course, he had, by papers such as the *Daily Mail*.

A key feature of newspaper coverage during this controversy was the quoting of people who did not appear to have read or heard what Williams had actually written or said, and who seemed to be relying on the dominant press version of events. Thus the *Independent*, 7 February, an article entitled 'Archbishop ignites Sharia law row', quoted Alistair McBay, spokesman for the National Secular Society, as stating that: 'In a plural society, all citizens are equal under the law and the Archbishop's comments directly undermine this. We have segregated schools, segregated scout groups and even segregated toilets for Muslims, and now the Archbishop says we should have different laws, it's madness.' And similarly Liberal Democrat leader Nick Clegg was quoted by *The Times*, 8 February, in an article co-written by Ruth Gledhill and headed 'Archbishop argues for Islamic law in Britain', as mistakenly claiming that Williams was calling for entirely separate jurisdictions: 'Equality before the law is part of the glue that binds our society together. We cannot have a situation where there is one law for one person and different laws for another.'

Room for misunderstanding

One of the key problems was that newspapers reported that Williams had called for the implementation of Sharia, when in fact all he had done was tentatively explore a number of ideas. It may well be the case that, in these circumstances, certain phrases which he used were not entirely clear and left room for misunderstanding. And indeed, this point was made in a leading article in the *Independent*, 10 February, which complained that Williams had 'allowed many people to read a subtext to his words, which is that there is "one law for us and another law for them". It is a widespread sentiment, tinged with racism.' Similarly, a leader in *The Times* pointed out that 'in today's cacophony there is no guarantee that any view will be heard without distortion. Its message must be clear, available and loud enough to compete for the nation's attention.' In such a situation, the leader argued, 'much turmoil could have been avoided if Rowan Williams had thought more about the potential media impact' of his speech. It continued:

> Reports rarely print a full text: was it not inevitable that partial quotation would remove the caveats? And did not Dr Williams himself contribute to what is claimed as distortion by agreeing to a radio interview that inevitably boiled his argument down to a few soundbites? Dr Williams eschews spin. As an academic, he believes he has the vocabulary and articulation to make himself understood. As Archbishop, he speaks, however, not from the lecture podium but from the nation's pulpit. His words must be clear to all. It is failing of the speaker, not the listener, if they are not … If the Archbishop finds himself misunderstood, he has only himself to blame.

Meanwhile in the *Daily Mail*, 8 February, Stephen Glover also sought to shift part of the blame for the media furore onto Williams himself, arguing that 'Rowan-speak' was like 'wading though cold porridge with a lead weight attached to one's feet'.

Indeed Williams himself admitted that even he saw problems with his language, as he made clear in his address to the opening of the General Synod: 'I must of course take responsibility for any unclarity in either that text or in the radio interview, and for any misleading choice of words that has helped to cause distress or misunderstanding among the public at large and especially among my fellow Christians.' Indeed, as the quotations from Williams already presented in this chapter show, his manner of speaking was academic and not always immediately accessible. Furthermore, it is possible to see how Williams' opening words in his interview with Christopher Landau could be seen as calling for the introduction of Sharia into Britain. Landau questioned Williams, saying: 'Your words are that the application of Sharia in certain circumstances, if we want to achieve this cohesion and take seriously peoples' religion, seems unavoidable?' Williams replies: 'It seems unavoidable.' The opening statement in the press release for the radio interview could also be read in a similar fashion: 'The Archbishop of Canterbury, Dr Rowan Williams, has said that UK law needs to continue to find accommodation with religious legal codes such as the Islamic system of Sharia if community cohesion and development are to be achieved.'

Now, it is conceivable that a journalist working in an understaffed newsroom and under considerable time pressure might take these statements literally, and be genuinely mistaken in believing that Williams had issued a call for Sharia. However, in the second paragraph of his lecture Williams stated clearly that he was exploring a legal issue and using Sharia as an example with which to illustrate a broader argument. What he actually said was: 'There are large questions in the background ... I shall therefore be concentrating on certain issues around Islamic law to begin with, in order to open up some of these wider matters.' These words were there for journalists to read, but either they failed to do so, or they chose simply to ignore them. And the same applied to the statement published on 8 February by Lambeth Palace on its website, which provided hyperlinks to the lecture and the radio interview transcript and stated that:

The Archbishop made no proposals for Sharia in either lecture or the interview, and certainly did not call for its introduction as some kind of parallel jurisdiction to the civil law ... the Archbishop was not suggesting the introduction of parallel legal jurisdictions, but exploring ways in which reasonable accommodation might be made within existing arrangements for religious conscience.

But whatever the case, time constraints and lack of resources are no excuse for journalists to fail to inform themselves fully about their subject before writing about it – particularly if the subject is as fraught and sensitive as this one most certainly is. One of the main jobs of the journalist, surely, is to explain complex subjects and issues to non-specialist audiences and readerships. And, in particular, this is the job of the specialist correspondent such as, in this case, Ruth Gledhill. However, as already noted, she was actually one of the very first journalists to misrepresent what the Archbishop had actually said, and, when it became apparent that he had been misunderstood (to put it charitably), to argue that he was the agent of his own misfortune. Thus in *The Times*, 9 February, she argued that, shortly after his appointment, 'it quickly became apparent that his words were as woolly as his eyebrows', adding that:

> The vast majority [of his speeches] are difficult for the layman to understand. This does not matter when a cleric is a tutor or professor of theology. It is even expected. But when he is Archbishop of Canterbury, discussing aspects of a religion which have given rise to some of the greatest threats to world peace, the world needs to be able to understand him.

Increasing public understanding of the Archbishop's words would be, one would have thought, an important element of the job of a religion correspondent, particularly on a serious paper such as *The Times*, but apparently not in this case.

It may well be that journalists wrote that Williams was calling for the introduction of Sharia, because that is what it looked like at first glance. However, this is simply sloppy, lazy journalism. And then to carry on repeatedly making the same mistakes, even when these have been clearly pointed out as wrong, is a classic example of the rat-pack mentality at work, or of what Nick Davies calls Ninja Turtle Syndrome (1998: 145–7). One also strongly suspects that pre-existing prejudice against and ignorance of Sharia played a role in journalistic misrepresentations of what Williams actually said. This topic will be explored further below.

'Crude stereotypes of Islam'

By 8 February it was already being presented as an established fact that Williams had called for the implementation of Sharia. Thus *Daily Telegraph* religion correspondent Jonathan Petre and political editor Andrew Porter confidently wrote: 'Dr Rowan Williams, the Archbishop of Canterbury, has sparked a political storm by calling for aspects of Sharia law to be adopted in Britain.' Meanwhile Steve Doughty of the *Daily Mail* reported: 'Political leaders poured scorn on the Archbishop of Canterbury yesterday over his call for Sharia law in Britain.' And Bob Roberts, political editor of the *Daily Mirror*, wrote: 'The Archbishop of Canterbury faced a barrage of criticism yesterday after he called for Britain to accept some parts of Islamic Sharia law.' In similar vein, the *Sun* website on 8 February carried a comment piece by its columnist Anila Baig in which she criticised Sharia criminal penalties. This was accompanied by a background article headed 'Brutality that sickened the West', which contains photographs of victims of extreme Sharia punishments and focuses on harsh applications of Islamic law in Saudi Arabia and Iran. However, as Williams had never proposed the introduction of Sharia criminal laws, neither piece bears any real relation to what he actually said.

But it was not simply Sharia law that the illiberal press had in their sights.

Coverage in such newspapers was frequently characterised by comment which was hostile to Islam in general. Islam was depicted as a threat to Christian and/or British values, and there was a widespread assumption that Islam was alien and other. (Note, for example, the headline on the *Sun* website on 8 February: 'Williams: victory for terrorism'.) The faith was painted as monolithic, backward and barbaric. Thus on 10 February the *Observer's* leading article felt compelled to note that the 'haste with which some opponents of the archbishop have reached for crude stereotypes of Islam is dispiriting'.

The publication by the press at this time of such a large amount of comment hostile to Islam strongly suggests that hostility to Muslims was the reason why the Archbishop's words attracted so much attention in the first place. Such a conclusion is strongly suggested by *The Times* leader of 11 February, which criticised Williams for raising 'this most sensitive of issues' with insufficient clarity, and denied that the furore was the result of the media distorting what he had actually said. In the leader's view: 'Newspapers, radio and television journalists have well-honed instincts for what issues matter. In reporting the rising tensions between faith groups and the new political importance of faith itself, the media have given extensive coverage to the moral and political debate.' However, what *The Times*, along with every other illiberal British newspaper, habitually omits to note in items such as this is their own role in helping to render these issues 'sensitive' and their own contribution to 'rising tensions', thus rendering their own agency conveniently invisible.

The overt nature of anti-Muslim coverage in the illiberal press is exemplified by Melanie Phillips' column in the *Daily Mail* on 10 February. Headed 'The church should have the guts to sack the Archbishop … and pick a man who truly treasures British values', the article argued that 'Islamism' was attempting a takeover of Britain and that Williams 'has gone down on his knees to welcome it'. Quite ignoring the fact that Williams had specifically suggested safeguards to oversee the administration of Sharia, and failing to recognise that the Qur'an gives equal value to male and female life and that violence against women is a cultural issue rather than a religious one, Phillips proceeded to rage on about 'Muslim women whose second-class status under Islamic law subjects them to systematic injustice, violence and "honour killings"'.

In a *Daily Express* blog post on 12 February headed 'Sharia law!? Why should we trust Britain's Muslims?', Patrick O'Flynn described Muslims as a 'troublesome minority with a record of disrupting our national life and ostentatiously refusing to fit in with the overall culture'. He continued: 'We do not think they can be trusted to run even a diluted version of Sharia to settle inter-family disputes. We fear this will be another step in the Islamification of Britain.' O'Flynn thus not only depicted Islam as an alien threat, but also infantilised Muslims in a way reminiscent of the old imperial prejudice that the peoples of the British Empire were too immature to govern themselves.

In the *Daily Telegraph* on 9 February Simon Heffer criticised Williams as leader of the Church of England, stating: 'If the Church of England has any point, it is to stand up for the prevalence of English and Christian values. We like our country as it is.' In one brief sentence Heffer thus manages to misrepresent two religious communities. He excludes Muslims from Englishness, wrongly assuming that they cannot be both Muslims and secular citizens. But he also wrongly implies that the Church of England exists to uphold national values, when in fact Christianity is internationalist.

The view that Islam is alien to Britishness and that Christianity is synonymous with the latter was also expressed in an article by Amanda Platell published in the *Daily Mail* on 10 February. Here she accused the Archbishop of being 'barmy', although she added: 'Perhaps Dr Williams should be applauded for highlighting this creeping Islamisation of parts of Britain.' She continued: 'If one good thing is to come out of the Archbishop's absurdly naïve comments, it should be to provoke a debate over the need to fight for our Christian nation before it's too late.' In describing Williams as 'barmy' and his comments as 'naïve' Platell simply descended into personalised name-calling and displayed her ignorance of the highly complex nature of his arguments.

Meanwhile in the *Daily Telegraph*, 9 February, Charles Moore stated that it is:

blindingly obvious that the current state of Islam is quite different from that of Christianity. Western societies are hosts to large numbers of Muslims, who quarrel fiercely among themselves and include extreme, sometimes violent minorities. Goodness knows, the history of Christianity is scarred with such things, but at the moment, in the West, Christian violence is not a big problem. Muslim violence is.

Moore's words contain a number of worrying assumptions about the position of Muslims in Britain. In his view Muslims appear not to be part of Western society, rather they are *hosted* by it. It is also debatable whether 'large numbers of Muslims' in Western societies quarrel fiercely among themselves – any more than the Protestant/Catholic conflict in Northern Ireland can be used to generalise about conflicts among Christians. It might also be added that, by Moore's logic, if violence carried out by Muslims is 'Muslim violence', then violence committed by Christian countries such as the UK ought to be called 'Christian violence', a label which one suspects Moore would strongly reject.

'Intellectual arrogance' vs. illiberal populism

It is undeniable that Lambeth Palace could have done a better job with its media management, but as the first part of this chapter shows, the material was there for journalists had they cared to read it. The fact that they chose to ignore it in one way or another suggests very strongly that this was one of those all too familiar occasions on which the bulk of the press was determined not to let the facts get in the way of a good story, and that the reasons why they perceived this as a 'good story' have deep cultural and ideological roots.

The evidence cited elsewhere in this book shows that by February 2008 negative perceptions of Muslims and Islam abounded in large sections of Britain's press, and indeed were largely taken for granted there and regarded as 'natural'. But, crucially, these negative perceptions also extended to liberal intellectuals such as Williams, who were represented as at best naïve and, at worst, treacherous – an all too familiar charge in Britain's populist and illiberal newspapers. A typical example of this approach was provided by Simon Heffer in the *Daily Telegraph*, 9 February, in an article headed 'Sharia courts? Off your knees, Archbishop', in which he asked: 'Why, then, has this idiotic man suggested that some elements of Islam's Sharia law should be recognised in Britain? ... He is doing it for the traditional, British liberal reason: he seeks to capitulate to anyone who offers to challenge the status quo.' And writing in the *Daily Telegraph* on 9 February, Matthew d'Ancona echoed exactly the same illiberal prejudice expressed by Heffer:

> Forty years after Enoch Powell's 'rivers of blood' speech, the Archbishop of Canterbury has delivered its liberal mirror image: let us call it 'rivers of blather' ... In the name of liberal co-existence, the Archbishop took arms against the very principles that give our ever-more diverse, cacophonous and mobile society what cohesion it has ... I see instead liberalism kowtowing to fundamentalism, liberalism eating itself.

Anti-liberalism also raised its head in an article of 11 February by Ruth Gledhill in *The Times* in which, not for the first time, as we have seen, she in effect attacked the Archbishop for being an intellectual, and a liberal one at that. The article was headed 'The intellectual arrogance that pervades the heart of Lambeth Palace wisdom', and it begins:

> The Archbishop of Canterbury rarely lets anyone amend his speeches. Unlike his predecessor, George Carey, Rowan Williams is confident enough of his intellectual gifts to consider that he does not need the wisdom of others in guiding the public expression of his thoughts.

> This illustrates the divergent backgrounds of the two men – one is working-class, self-taught, rooted in the simplicity of an evangelical faith, the other is Oxbridge to the depths of his

complicated soul, espousing a Christianity at once liberal, catholic and ascetic. Lord Carey reads the *News of the World*, and
likes to write for the paper. Dr Williams prefers Dostoevsky,
and is writing a book about him.

Given the headline, the rest of the article, and Gledhill's other pro-
nouncements during the course of this saga, it is not exactly difficult
to see where the author's sympathies lie in this particular ecclesiastical
beauty contest. They are also readily apparent in her remarks that:

> Although he is a holy and spiritual man, danger lies in the
> appearance of the kind of intellectual arrogance common to
> many of Britain's liberal elite. It is an arrogance that affords no
> credibility or respect to the popular voice. And although this
> arrogance, with the assumed superiority of the Oxbridge
> rationalist, is not shared by his staff at Lambeth Palace, it is by
> some of those outside Lambeth from whom he regularly seeks
> counsel. Neither the Archbishop nor his staff regard his speech
> as mistaken. They are merely concerned that it has been mis-
> understood. This characterises the otherworldliness that still
> pervades the inner sanctums of the Church of England.

Anti-intellectual populism of this kind, accompanied by its inevitable companion, a thoroughly patronising endorsement of the 'popular
voice' and the 'common man', has of course long been a staple of the
Murdoch press, for which 'giving the people what they want' per-
forms both a money-spinning economic function and a conservative
ideological one, but it is perhaps rather more surprising to find it in the
'Holy Smoke' blog of the editor of the *Catholic Herald*, Damian
Thompson, which is hosted on the *Daily Telegraph* website. However,
on 12 February he wrote that 'even in a moment of public humiliation,
Rowan Williams can't pass up the opportunity to display his intellectual superiority over other members of the General Synod', while
on the following day he called the Archbishop and the Prince of
Wales, another promoter of interfaith harmony, 'intellectually vain

men who, encouraged by flattery from non-Christian religious leaders, believe they can transcend their constitutional obligations to the Christian faith'. So much for ecumenicalism then.

As we have seen in this chapter, the line taken by the illiberal press, either implicitly or explicitly, during the Sharia law furore was that Christian values and Islamic values were diametrically opposed to each other, and that Williams had effectively acted as a traitor by speaking up for Sharia. Christianity was thus typecast as something British, whereas Islam was seen as alien. Yet, many people of faith would point to Islam's shared roots with Christianity, Islamic reverence of Jesus and the Virgin Mary, and the emphasis that both religions place on caring for the poor and the marginalised. In speaking up for the rights of a minority population who daily face Islamophobic prejudice, Williams was in fact acting within his obligations to the Christian faith. If you like, he was a modern version of the Good Samaritan. It is thus perhaps appropriate to end this chapter with a thought from *Times* columnist David Aaronovitch, who suggested in the paper's 12 February edition that 'perhaps it's the fact that the Archbishop genuinely is holier than us that has contributed to the exuberant pleasure it has given so many people to misrepresent so violently what the poor man was saying'.

9

Keeping Your Integrity – and Your Job

Voices from the Newsroom

Hugh Muir and Laura Smith

Text, talk and imagery in the media arrive each day in people's hands, and on their TV and computer screens, after lengthy and elaborate processes of selection. 'Every day people die or are born,' noted the commentator Atif Imtiaz on his blog 'Bradford Muslim' in 2005, 'goods are bought and stolen, people make speeches and write books'. But, he continues, 'all of these events are filtered by those who decide on the extent of newsworthiness, such that some of these events are more important than others – that is, they become more available within the public conscience'.

The first filter as events move towards the public conscience, Imtiaz notes, is:

the minute-by-minute news wire of Reuters or Associated Press, which is itself dependent upon a variety of factors: the close proximity of their correspondent or associate to the event, its relevance to the current narrative canon, and the competition of other events that may be viewed as more important. All of these factors at the stage of the first filter decide what ultimately becomes news.

Next, 'the journey from this point to the *News at Ten* or the tabloid front page is similarly dependent on … decisions and processes at different levels of editorial hierarchy, and their relationships with proprietors and government officials'. Even after publication, whether in the press or on television, processes of selection continue, as viewers and readers attend to specific aspects of a story, often seeking confirmation of the understandings they already have rather than things that would challenge them to re-think.

What role, in these multifaceted processes of selection, is played by relatively junior staff in the editorial hierarchy? Does it make a difference if, at all levels of the hierarchy, there are journalists who happen to be Muslims? If so, in what ways? Do Muslim journalists experience distinctive stresses, difficulties and dilemmas? These are the questions explored in this chapter.

The chapter is based on in-depth interviews with six journalists. The interviews were conducted by people who are journalists themselves and whose backgrounds and experience enabled them to establish a ready rapport with those whom they were questioning. Almost certainly they elicited more frank and detailed responses than would have been forthcoming in conventional academic research. All six journalists were of Muslim heritage and work or have worked on mainstream papers. Quotations from the interviews provide a vivid and essential complement to the other chapters in this book. Among other things they show the importance and value of employing people of Muslim heritage as journalists. At the same time they demonstrate the ethical, professional and personal dilemmas and stresses that Muslim journalists experience, and in which they need support.

Though they were happy to share their thoughts and experiences, and in some cases were clearly relieved to do so, most of the six felt too fearful of the possible repercussions to allow themselves to be identified. None of their names, therefore, are given. Nor are there any other personal details here that might enable them to be identified. They were all asked the same series of questions (shown in Box 5).

All six had worked at mainstream national newspapers and all but one still worked within the mainstream media at the time of their interview. Between them they had also worked on mainstream local and regional newspapers, on wire services and in television. They ranged in age from their early twenties to their mid-forties and were both male and female. Their stories described the complications, concerns and occasional advantages that accrue from being a Muslim journalist trying to progress in one's career and, at the same time, trying to retain personal integrity in the newsrooms of national newspapers.

Box 5 The experiences of Muslim journalists: the interview questions

Did you believe the news media's portrayal of Muslims and Islam was fair before you entered journalism?

Was part of your motivation in becoming a journalist to address that?

Do you believe you are treated differently from other reporters who are not Muslim and/or from an ethnic minority?

Have you ever been asked to do something you felt uncomfortable with because of your background or faith?

Have you ever refused to do something on that basis? What was the reaction?

Have you ever felt a conflict between your profession and your faith? Do you feel you have ever compromised your beliefs to get a story?

Have you ever been unable to sell a story to the newsdesk or your commissioning editors on Muslim issues or Islam that you felt was important?

Do you feel adequately supported and understood by your newsdesk/commissioning editors and your colleagues? If you

---

ever feel isolated within your organisation, are there colleagues you can talk to about this?

Have your views and beliefs been influenced by the process of being a journalist?

Have your views about whether the news media are fair to Muslims or Islam changed as a result of working within the mainstream press?

Did things change for you at work after 11 September and/or 7 July? If so, how?

Do you believe there is an expectation that you will somehow represent 'the Muslim community' and its views?

Do you feel you can make or have made as much of a difference to the coverage of Muslim and other issues as you might have hoped?

What are your plans for your future career? Do you intend to stay within the mainstream media?

Do you ever feel angry or offended by stories you read within your own newspaper or others about Muslims or Islam?

Do you believe mainstream British newspapers are institutionally Islamophobic?

The first two questions in the interviews, as shown in Box 5, were about expectations and motivations before people became journalists in the first place. Much of what respondents said about motivation would have been said also by young non-Muslim journalists. They wanted to write, to tell stories, to meet people, to have a varied and interesting career. This is a selection of what our interviewees said:

I became a newspaper journalist because I'm really nosey, I like talking to people and I like telling stories. I have a thing about the underdog and people who don't have much of a voice in the media but I don't think that is much to do with being Muslim.

(Reporter B)

I went into journalism because I like words, I like writing. The idea that you go in to change things or to address things is putting the cart before the horse. That's not the reason you go into it. I write from the heart. I am as interested in music as much as I am in religion. I went into it because I thought it was an interesting career.

(Reporter F)

My motivation was a slightly naïve wish to try and save the world. These were instincts I could see in people who weren't Muslim, so they weren't intrinsically Muslim, although they clearly were shaped by my parents' background. There are things that you are aware of as somebody with multiple cultural heritage which enable you to be quite empathetic to lots of different situations in an argument.

(Reporter D)

Although their motivations to become journalists were not, for the most part, connected to their sense of themselves as Muslims, they were already aware, when they embarked on their careers, that there was a mismatch between their own personal experience on the one hand and what they encountered in the media on the other. Several had been brought up with a suspicion of newspapers and a belief that they were biased against Muslims and Islam. There was reference to coverage of international issues such as the Bosnian War and the Israeli–Palestinian conflict, and, closer to home, to *The Satanic Verses* affair at the end of the 1980s.

I was brought up to be suspicious of the British media. Perhaps this is culturally what Asians and Muslim children of immigrants are brought up with. I remember my dad saying the press was biased and that it was all against us. There was a real sense of injustice in how things like Palestine and Bosnia were reported and how many of the victims were not shown. Even when they were, they would be mentioned in passing at the end in a way that dehumanised them. I gradually switched off the news because I found the portrayal so depressing. So culturally there was suspicion. I expected the news to be biased against Muslims.

(Reporter A)

I was first aware of the perception of Muslims after the Salman Rushdie affair. It was during my first years at secondary school and some of the things that were reported were really bad. It made Muslims out to be total barbarians who because they didn't have an understanding of literature were one step away from being wild animals. The media didn't realise that religion is not something that Muslims do once a week. It's a way of life and they take it really seriously, more seriously than anything. And if you insult their religion you've had it. The rot set in from that because it was the first time that British Muslims had been in the public eye and it was for entirely the wrong reasons.

(Reporter B)

When I was growing up I was very aware that the picture painted of Muslims … was nothing that I really recognised in my own upbringing. At school and at college I did notice that my peers were very aware of a media image of what Muslims were and what they did. But my experience didn't really accord with that picture. I don't know why that is. It may be because being Muslim was one element of my cultural make-up but there were lots of other things too. Seeing the Rushdie thing happen, I remember not necessarily feeling comfortable with what people who looked like you were arguing but nonetheless also being annoyed at how it seemed that it was acceptable to generalise about the group of two million people that you belonged to.

(Reporter D)

Unease and mixed loyalties

All the journalists interviewed had experienced a sense of unease about how to balance their personal integrity, and at times their religious or cultural beliefs, with the demands of being a journalist. On the one hand, they experienced as positive the possibility of bringing in stories that would be otherwise absent from the news pages – a useful strategy for a young reporter trying to make their mark. On the other, they often felt a sense of being used and pushed into the cul-de-sac of writing about minority issues. Coping strategies, ranging from acceptance to refusal, were fraught with difficulties, as outlined in the stories and recollections described below. The journalists knew that they were expected, like anyone in their profession, to use any wiles they could in order to get the story, including their ethnic or religious identity. They did not on the whole object to this, but all had been asked to do things they felt uncomfortable with. At least two had been asked, as a professional assignment, to infiltrate al-Qaida. Quite apart from the difficulties and dangers of attempting this, there was a sense of responsibility not to reinforce stereotypes when it came to reporting on the community with which they were identified. They had learnt to draw their own lines – some through painful lessons, others by setting their own limits when they were starting out. (See, for example, the story in Box 6.)

For some, formative experiences in their careers came in the aftermath of 11 September 2001. For others, equivalent experiences came after the London bombs of July 2005. In all cases a significant crunch came when they forcefully realised that they could not escape the expectations and perceptions of their colleagues. 'When I started my journalism course,' one recalled,

> I lived in a state of denial about my race and my religion. I felt I was growing up having to apologise for being an Asian because Asians were greedy and smelly people who came over here and took people's jobs. Religion was something I rarely spoke about. I didn't drink but I didn't have the confidence to speak up about it. The way I learnt to cope was to make every

effort to make people forget my difference. I thought that because no one referred to my colour at all before I became a journalist that it wasn't an issue. As a result I went into journalism thinking I am going to be treated just like everyone else.

The reality was different:

> At my first local paper, I started making friends among Asians and suddenly realised there was a whole thing here I had turned away from. My first job was in a city which has a large Pakistani community and is very racially divided. I was suddenly being asking to write about forced marriages (which were then called arranged marriages) or great curry restaurants or festivals, when they'd print a photo of an exotic woman in an ornate sari – real stereotypes of Asian women. They'd send me out to talk to the community. I would turn up and wouldn't know how to speak Urdu or how to relate to people. The newsdesk didn't discuss this with me. They just looked at me and made the assumption that I was Asian so I could access this very private community.

> (Reporter A)

Reporter A also recalled that the paper served an area where there was much outright racism among white people and reflected: 'It was the first time I had encountered real, real racism. There I was confirming quite a lot of the stereotypes for this racist audience. I quickly realised I didn't like doing these stories. I was in shock that they were asking me to do such clichéd stuff.' Reporter B similarly reflected on September 2001 and July 2005:

> After September 11 loads more people started asking me about being Muslim. I was saying 'I'm not a spokesperson for the faith, I can't tell you why these people did this.' But they would ask 'Would you do it?' and 'Do you know any terrorists?' ...

After 7 July it was so much worse because they were British. It was all right before because they were foreigners. But now it was one of ours. One of us had decided to shit on their own doorstep. And you had all these programmes being made about why these men had turned to extremism. It was like the Salman Rushdie row all over again.

Conflicting loyalties at a personal level were mixed with growing awareness of external commercial pressures on newspapers and of the internal organisational culture in newsrooms. Reporter D, for example, recalled twice being asked to do 'undercover stuff, like infiltrating a radical mosque'. One could argue, the recollection continued, 'that it was a classic channelling of a minority reporter into the cul-de-sac of reporting about ethnicity – but I don't think it was. I can see why it is reasonable for me rather than Bob Jones to go undercover at Finsbury Park. So yeah, I didn't mind so much.' The fact was, Reporter D continued, that there was in the office a very one-dimensional view of Muslims in Britain and around the world:

> The idea was that they were all part of the same tree and it could all be explained through a set of common behavioural characteristics in a way that would be absolutely shocking if it was said about any other ethnic group. Even though Muslims are the most racially diverse group around – both politically diverse and theologically diverse – it seemed to be okay to make these astonishing sweeping generalisations that were pretty insulting.

'I felt it was more a case of ignorance than of spite', said Reporter D, who then commented on the sources of ignorance and the pressure from readers and society more generally to create and promote bogey figures:

> The crucial fact is that the leader writers, decision-makers, columnists didn't have any Muslim friends. So you lacked

fundamentally the empathy to be able to say, well we can't just group an entire two million people as all the same. The idea that there was this Islamic monolith that was about to take over, and all thought the same and had this rabid anti-intellectual inability to reason, seemed quite prevalent, even in the very highest decision-making parts of the media … The biggest problem for me came in realising that being scared shitless by this big group of people that are out to get you is actually quite a good story. People have an interest, and always have had, in having bogeymen. That's more or less what is happening.

Similar points about the public's interest in bogey figures were made by Reporter B: 'I was rung up by friends on other newspapers and I was asked if I knew anyone that would comment on the bombings. And I said, how do you mean "comment"? I knew exactly what they were after — they wanted someone that would praise them, and they thought that I'd have a good idea of where you could go to get that kind of quote.'

Reporter B continued:

There is a certain pressure on a paper to shock and to frighten and to scare. And there's a tiny constituency of Muslims in Britain that are quite happy to acquiesce with that. So you have the bizarre situation where you have journalists desperate for a terrifying story talking to nutcases who represent nobody but themselves and everyone else kind of left in between thinking what on earth's going on … I can see that it makes good copy and I can see that if you have no connection with the community concerned that you wouldn't really care as to the effect of that … The media is not an impartial observer. It's playing a role and it's creating a market for frightening news. And there are certain comic, scary and villainous British Muslims who want it as well.

Other anecdotes about and recollections of this theme are described below. In Box 6 there is a description of a heated argument with a

230

news editor, in Box 7 an account of an assignment in Leeds shortly after the 7 July bombs, and in Box 8 a reporter recalls visiting a Muslim home and his subsequent shock when the resulting article was changed and distorted.

Box 6 'One day I just snapped'

It was at a national newspaper. After September 11, I think I became quite a valuable commodity to them. My identity provided me with a role. There was a part of them thinking I would look really good for them. We don't have an Asian, we don't have a Muslim. For years I just went ahead and did those stories. I wrote them with insight but I was writing for a white, non-Muslim community.

It was more than a year before things started to change. I realised that my voice was a very small but powerful tool. I could go to Regents Park mosque and they were saying stuff that was really thoughtful and I could actually write a big piece on it and people would read it. That was really positive. I realised it was a powerful thing and saw I should write about them honestly.

But the negative thing is our paper became fixated on the Asian community. They wanted to give them more inclusion in the paper but the way they found to do that was by looking at arranged marriages vs. forced marriages, rapes, suicides, domestic abuse. They were absolutely obsessed. For a while I thought, this is interesting. But then I noticed it was happening every week. I would get phone calls and be sent on every Muslim story. Some of it was really challenging and interesting, but at the same time I was still being given regular stories about forced marriage. Then one day I just snapped and blew up. The news editor went really red and embarrassed and didn't want to discuss it. Because it was about race I think he was very worried about being seen as racist. So overnight I stopped getting any of those stories and suddenly I was stripped of that access.

> I had no opportunity to discuss it. I tried to broach the sub-
> ject with the news editor but he was so embarrassed it seemed
> impossible to talk about it openly. By that stage I wasn't being
> given anything because what they had made me do for the past
> year was just Asian and Muslim stuff.
>
> I ended up regretting ever saying anything because it had a
> snowball effect. He obviously thought it was wrong and racist
> for me to be given any Asian stories. It felt like a punishment
> for speaking up.
>
> (Reporter A)

Pros and cons of being a Muslim journalist

In all the interviews there was discussion of whether journalists who
are of Muslim heritage have distinctive professional advantages, or
whether on the contrary their background is a kind of burden or pen-
alty. This has already been touched on in several of the quotations
above. Reporter B argued that 'I want to be seen as a reporter first and
foremost. I don't want to be seen as an ethnic minority reporter … I
don't want them to think of me as Asian or Muslim. I just want them
to think of me as a reporter.' Meanwhile Reporter E revealed that:

> I find there are differences in how I've been treated compared
> to reporters who are not Muslim or from an ethnic minority.
> One positive is that people are interested to know what I think
> because they want to tap into that knowledge. Not just on
> Muslim issues, but also because I'm South Asian … But it can
> be negative in the way people think you are only hired for one
> reason. I never thought that at all when I worked at a local
> paper. But when I went to the nationals it was different …
> There was a raid in the local area and the paper weren't going
> to send anyone. Then they sent me and it went really well. I
> got some reasonably decent stuff. Then they called me to go

and do other stories like that and I got a slight sense that I was being used for a single purpose.

(Reporter E)

On balance, Reporter E felt the dangers of being used and exploited were outweighed by the opportunity to challenge and remove negative stereotypes: 'I have been thrown into writing about Muslim issues rather than having a massive interest in them. But I'd rather do it than let anyone else do it because I am more aware of the issues. Otherwise you get stuck with stereotypes.' Reporter B, meanwhile, stated that:

There needs to be an understanding that there is no homogeneous Muslim community in Britain. First you need to look at Shi'as and Sunnis, then you need to look at where they came from. Then within Pakistan there are people from different areas. You can't just lump them all together. You need someone to understand that there is segregation within the Muslim community. You will get Pakistani Muslims living in one part and Bengali Muslims in another and they will never meet.

Several others similarly felt that they had been successful in challenging the worst kinds of stereotype, both in their writing and in their interactions with colleagues. 'I don't think I've changed the news agenda', said Reporter A, 'but I think I've added to things by not doing stories in a stereotypical way and in that way I might have slightly changed people's perspective on Asians and the Muslim community. At the same time I'm not sure if I left that the influence would continue.' There was a danger, though, of being pigeon-holed and typecast. 'I am a professional journalist,' said Reporter C, 'not a professional Paki.' The ambivalence of this reporter was expressed more fully as follows:

I have broadly steered clear of so-called Muslim stories. In some ways I am interested because some of the subjects are such lunatics. I was given a watching brief on some of these extremist groups, which was quite interesting for a while.

233

But then it started veering towards the hocus-pocus and it became annoying. The thing is I don't want to be pigeon-holed ... I am a professional journalist, not a professional Paki. I suppose it's primarily because I've been brought up in quite a Western and secular way and I felt uncomfortable because I had to seem enthusiastic about projects I was being asked to do simply because of my name. Newsdesks wanted me to have some insight into the ethnic communities but in the end that petered out because I wasn't interested.

Other comments on this theme included:

People ask my opinion on anything that happens to do with Muslims. If it's a Muslim academic or a certain newsy personality, they'll say, do you know this guy? Is this a story? They'll see something on the wires or in a newspaper and ask me whether it's crucial to cover or total bollocks ... I think I have made some difference, especially with certain features I've written. Some people are scared of going into a mosque or approaching people with beards. I used to have no interest in ethnic affairs but as you get older you notice things a lot more. Now it would be hard not to get involved in reporting these things.

(Reporter E)

One of the things that happens is if you are a Muslim you are offered more opportunities to write about things where the prime reason you are being asked is because you are a Muslim. It's not that I've been asked to do something I'm uncomfortable with ... Some people who have that experience want to do it because they feel passionate about it. With me I feel I have to keep a sense of perspective. For every one article I write about Islam or Muslim issues I have to write at least one or two more that are not about that. I don't want it to look like here you are banging on about being Muslim again.

(Reporter F)

Reporter F added the crucially important point that Muslim-ness was not by any means the totality of their personality and identity:

> I don't think that being a Muslim is the most important thing and the only thing about me. It can be a gilded cage to get into that kind of writing. I am not only interested in that. It genuinely is not the only thing that defines me. I only think about it professionally. I don't think about it socially. I sit around thinking about Philip Roth or Superman films or any number of other things rather than that.

Box 7 'Ludicrous projects'

After the London bombings, there was more pressure for stories about terrorism which you were expected to get using your supposed ethnic identity. I did really well out of July 7. I went up to Leeds. I wouldn't say I enjoyed it exactly but it was one of the most exciting times of my journalistic career. I came back and my colleagues said I did well and I felt a great sense of professional pride.

Leeds was absolutely insane. People there had the look of people who'd been invaded by a medieval army. We were interrogating people, saying 'Who is Mr Big?', and they were like 'I don't know mate, I'm just on my way to the mosque.' It was pretty mad.

Because I had done a reasonable job … I got sent off on all these wild goose chases without any proper sense of thinking things through. I got a bit pissed off. I'd had quite a good run doing mainstream stories, then July 7 happened and I didn't get any of the other stuff any more. I just got sent on these ludicrous projects.

(Reporter C)

Box 8 'The next day I was appalled'

After one of the terrorist attacks I was sent to door-knock a suspected extremist. The office knew it was a long shot but I was quite determined and I knew my Muslim background could get me in. I knocked on the door and said Assalamu Aleikum and told them I was a Muslim. After a few minutes they let me in.

I was a journalist just beginning. I would have done the story very differently now but I didn't know what the paper was looking for then. I just took what he was saying at face value. What I wrote was exactly what he had told me without any slant on it. It was neutral. It was probably not written in the most sophisticated way but I was really pleased with what I'd done. The next day I looked at the paper and I was appalled. It had been rewritten in a way that made him seem really slippery. It was really cynically done. I was really disappointed and scared about what he might think. But I didn't have the confidence to say I was really upset about it. It was a real wake-up call for me. I felt I had gone in there and used my Muslim background for my own glory. I felt very guilty because I was complicit in stitching him up.

That incident has left me questioning everything. It left me questioning my position as a Muslim and as a journalist. Sometimes I am comfortable with using my faith as a means of getting in. Sometimes I say I am a Muslim so therefore I understand. But I won't push it to get a story any more. There are now many more Muslim journalists and I think the Muslim community is far more canny about it. Muslim journalists still work for papers that are very hard on Muslim communities. People are learning not to open up just because a journalist is a Muslim.

I did use my ethnic identity after the July bombings. I got a lot of stuff from Muslim people who spoke to me in Urdu in a very unguarded way. I do use my Asian-ness, the way I look, my name.

But I have changed the way I do things. Sometimes now on the way to a story I'll draw my own lines. I have had to really fight with the newsdesk about the reality on the street so now I will challenge them. I have compromised myself in the past and now I think I never would because it had such a big impact on me. I am forever finding myself anxious about being responsible to the people I've spoken to and not resorting to stereotypes. There are times when I censor a tiny amount because someone in their anger will say something like 'I'm really glad the bombings happened.' To some extent I feel I need to protect them.

(Reporter A)

Relationships and organisational culture

In all the interviews there was consideration of everyday professional relationships, including relationships with senior staff, and of the general climate of opinion and outlook in newspaper offices. Comments included:

I don't make a big song and dance about being Muslim. I talk about it quite freely with some of my colleagues and my friends but it's not something I bring up in the workplace. I leave it at the door. There are times when I feel angry but I feel I don't want to make it an issue at work. You should never become the story. I like to think I've never put myself up as a Muslim reporter. It's not my job to explain or defend my religion.

(Reporter B)

I was given some good advice once by a colleague which was 'Go through the hoops and you'll be all right.' Most people have been pretty good and pretty decent to me. However, some people didn't have a clue, particularly those on the back bench [a team of senior journalists overseeing the production of the newspaper, responsible for assigning particular stories to particular slots on particular pages] and now in very senior positions in journalism. I never felt isolated in a big way.

(Reporter C)

One news editor wanted me to go undercover in the firm of someone in the public eye and find out if they were employing illegal immigrants. They didn't have anything on the guy, they just wanted to catch him out. I didn't like it. If there was a tip-off it might be different but it really was like finding a needle in a haystack. You don't need a journalist, you need an actor. You can always find something bad about someone if you really want to. But there was no indication that he had done anything wrong and you really are out to get someone. It's very tabloid to campaign against an individual. It's very personal but morally I didn't think it was right.

(Reporter E)

I was very lucky in that I got ahead quite quickly. If I didn't like a story I'd tell them, I'd say it's rubbish and I was listened to. I think some people would be surprised how much they would be listened to if they went and had the conversation at the right time. If they chose their moment. I've never done any story that I am ethically unhappy about. I wouldn't do it. There are stories even now that other journalists do where I work and I've said very clearly that I think they're rubbish stories and I wouldn't do them.

(Reporter D)

In most cases the interviewees had been the only journalists from Muslim backgrounds working at their newspaper. In many cases, they were also one of only a handful of non-white journalists at their place of work. Asked whether they had ever felt isolated, their responses appeared to vary according to their level of seniority and professional confidence. Those who believed they had the support of their news editors and could talk to their colleagues felt they could balance their background with their job. Those who did not felt frustratingly powerless to resist an organisational culture that expected them to somehow represent 'their' community. Responses included the following:

I know the editors I deal with and I feel I am adequately understood. As for isolation, you can be isolated in a room full of brown faces. I have been with Asians and felt I have nothing in common with them. To be perfectly honest, I can be around a whole load of Muslims and feel I have nothing in common with them. The feeling of being the only ethnic minority person is very difficult but it's been a while since I felt that because I think it's a lot about a certain level of confidence based on my profile and my work. If I don't feel happy with something I don't do it.

(Reporter F)

I now have a great news editor who I feel I can talk to if I need to. With the previous newsdesk I felt very isolated. I felt people didn't know what to make of me because I was Muslim and Asian and not posh. I felt like a fish out of water. I felt I had to fit in as much as possible for them to accept me. I felt very isolated. There were no other Asians. If I object to doing anything I could say so now. Before, I didn't have the support of the newsdesk, I couldn't talk to them at all. They were suspicious and afraid of that difference. It's amazing to think I work for the same people because it's changed so much. I feel more supported and feel I can bring up stuff I want to bring up about race. I have written comment pieces that have given me a voice. I have had a really abusive reaction but also some really positive letters. It's in my hands. If I want to do stuff about that, I can.

(Reporter A)

Views of media coverage

Since entering newspapers, all six journalists had developed a pragmatic understanding that commercial considerations often come before social responsibility in the newspaper industry. But all except one believed newspapers should acknowledge their role in shaping the views of their readers. Although they hesitated to use the word 'Islamophobic', they felt that the tendency of newspapers to portray Muslims as either a problem or a danger was unhelpful. Their solutions? A move away from lazy journalism and its reliance on stereotypes and scaremongering; better informed reporting on the issues facing areas outside London; more balanced foreign coverage; and, especially, greater diversity in employment. It would also be helpful, several of those interviewed pointed out, if opinion leaders within Muslim communities had a better understanding of how the media operate, and if they were to see more clearly that there is a wider range of views within and between newspapers than they tend to realise, and more goodwill among individual journalists.

Reporter E acknowledged that 'there is some pretty shady reporting', adding: 'I don't know what the point of a lot of it is. Some papers only seem to do knocking stories. Some of them border on being libellous. They are stirring up the issue for no reason and it makes it difficult for other reporters because now certain people won't talk to the press at all because they think they are going to be stitched up.' There was comment on the pressures that newspapers experience from readers and the general climate of opinion and it was pointed out that there had been much responsible journalism at the time of the bombs in London in summer 2005:

If a story's there and it's the biggest story in town they have to cover it. If it's what your readership asks for, you will respond. If you are a news editor getting letters saying you need to be stronger on this stuff, you will ... Some of the reporting after the London bombs was very good. It was reported very well and very sensitively. Generally, in the immediate aftermath, newspapers were responsible. They realised they couldn't inflame the situation too much because it was a powderkeg. People were scared that something could happen because nobody knew how people were going to react.

(Reporter E)

Other comments on how stories are selected and treated, and on pressures in this regard to conform to readers' expectations, included the following:

I remember wanting to do a story about a Muslim organisation and the way it was being demonised. I tried to do a hard sell on my newsdesk but they said 'Do 400 words and we'll see where we can put it.' In the end it made a 300-word story. I felt very disappointed. I felt it was important to put it in. But it wasn't sexy enough because it was not about extremism. The focus at that time was all on allocating blame and getting to the bottom of where extremism was happening. Everyone was being tarred with the same brush.

(Reporter A)

I can see the frustration of normal people who think 'Why am I tarred by association?' We didn't badger on about David Koresh and the Waco cult being Christians or about Timothy McVeigh being Christian. But equally I don't like endless stories about Muslims being victims. It's a really difficult area. No one demands that Christians all have to answer for all other

Christians. But what you get in the Muslim community is that people feel a sense of collective guilt about what happens. If any Muslim commits a crime or acts badly or the odd one becomes a terrorist everyone feels guilty. They are only identified as Muslims when it's a bad news story, it seems. It's pretty rare in other circumstances.

(Reporter D)

What I do feel frustrated about is there is still a tendency to only report about Muslims as a problem. It seems to be always a question of 'What are we going to do about Muslims? What are we going to do about terror? About fundamentalism? This new wave of young people who are rediscovering their religion?' What I would like would be to have Muslims represented in a way where their Muslim-ness wasn't the reason that they were being reported on.

(Reporter F)

Now I work at a newspaper I can see how unfair some media organisations are. But I also see there are some papers that are endeavouring to do something different and be more questioning. That response of 'all you media are bad' has gone. Now when I hear Muslims say that I think 'You are really not helping yourself.' The Muslim community sometimes hasn't distinguished between liberal papers and the media as a whole. It just means it won't get its voice in the paper. I don't want to get so chippy that I shoot myself and the Muslim community in the foot.

(Reporter A)

If coverage is to improve there is also a role for opinion-leaders in Muslim communities. As Reporter C put it: 'I think the press has been pretty fair to Muslims. They don't really need to stitch people up, they do a good enough job of that themselves. My view is Muslims have got to address issues themselves, things like anti-semitism and homophobia that seem to be unchallengeable within Muslim communities. As far as I'm concerned newspapers just report them as they are.'

At the same time, though, newspapers could and should be far more responsible in their portrayal of opinion-leaders and give a louder voice to majority moderate opinion. In this respect, Reporter D argued:

The London bombings said it all really. Carried out by four Yorkshire British Muslims that killed six or seven Muslims in the process. What kind of questions does that raise? For a start, just how relevant is the label 'Muslim'? The point is that the extremists and those who carry out criminal actions are a subset of the Muslim world yet there seems to be an applicability of what they do across the entire religion that fits the agenda of fundamentalists on all sides. 1.995 million British Muslims are utterly irrelevant to this whole terror story. But you wouldn't get that impression from the papers. It's clumsy journalism.

I take issue with many things done by British Muslims. If the media was doing its job it would help Britain's two million Muslims to be able to develop a kind of reasoned, questioning attitude within itself. And you are beginning to see that a bit. But instead it's far easier and a more potent story to paint a picture of this kind of green peril on your doorsteps. The real danger of that is that one fears it might become a self-fulfilling prophecy.

Recurring scare stories about 'the green peril on your doorstep', it was agreed, were among the biggest problems to be addressed. As Reporter D said: 'There does seem to be a kind of narrative which many newspapers are playing off: that a rampant Muslim lobby are controlling the leaders of a politically correct establishment to force Christian Britain to hand over everything that's sacred to Britain, which is just rubbish.'

Employment issues

Despite a range of personal difficulties, as illustrated above, all the interviewees were certain that improved coverage of Muslim issues in the media would be immensely helped if there were more good journalists of Muslim background employed in the media:

> Papers don't live in a bubble. They represent government policies, popular prejudices, popular opinions. Editors and journalists are just part of society. Ideally they should be representative socially but because it's such a white, middle-class industry those views will predominate. And that view is that Muslims are scary and a problem so that's what gets projected in the media. I still feel so amazed at how white it is. I would love it if there was another Asian reporter in the newsroom. There are times when I just want to leave and do something where I am not this minority and not this token Asian.

> But there is a problem with representation in terms of employment. I think it's an absolute obscenity how few Asians and Muslims there are working full-time within the British press. How papers can claim to report on modern Britain and have so few is mind-boggling. It's just basic good journalism to have a more representative workforce.
>
> (Reporter A)

> I was surprised by the reaction of papers to the bombings, surprised people didn't realise what was going to happen in places where second-generation people were growing up. You could see it a mile off – the social fracture. It's up to the journalists to be more aware about the country we live in. There are very middle-class people in the media – public school educated, red-brick universities. They are completely unaware of normal life. They talk about 'Muslims' but they're not willing to engage with them.
>
> (Reporter F)

I still think you need more people who actually are from that background who are able to report on it. There is a generational problem. Quite a lot of reporters are people in their forties and fifties. The world in Britain has changed since their formative experiences. There are also class issues. There are too many people who are Cambridge educated and from private schools, who may be Muslim in name but wouldn't recognise a working-class Muslim if they had them in their face. There is too much nepotism and old ways of doing things. Middle class–ness seems to overpower Muslim-ness. There has been a death of working-class voices. If journalism is about finding out the view from the ground then class is as important as race or religion.

(Reporter E)

In addition to issues of social class in the organisational culture of an office, there are also issues of religious faith, as Reporter F noted:

Newspapers want to sell copies of newspapers and what they are interested in is interesting stories. Commercial considerations are more important to them than idealism. They want to hear why Britain is the way it is. There are journalistic imperatives going on. What newspapers have a problem with is people who have an absolute faith. Papers are run by people who are secular so they find people who have an absolute faith fascinating and horrifying in equal measure.

More young people of Muslim backgrounds should be advised and encouraged, it was said, to think seriously about taking up journalism as a career. Such thinking should start at school, not college, as Reporter B argued:

You've got to get journalists to go into schools because the super-bright kids can't find their way into newspapers. We need to be saying: 'Have you thought about this as a career?' It's got such a bad reputation in Pakistani communities. Parents think it's a waste of time and energy, it's got bad prospects and

245

it's badly paid, and it's not putting anything back into your community. I wanted to be a journalist when I was fourteen and my mum said no. It was white, middle-class kids at school and university who did the student newspapers. I never felt posh enough or connected enough. My parents didn't buy newspapers. If you get kids when they are young and say, 'This is a career option and you can make a difference' … It's something that can be done by regional newsrooms.

Having been appointed, journalists of all backgrounds throughout Britain – particularly those outside London – need to extend their knowledge of Muslim communities. In this respect, Reporter B stressed that:

> Journalists need to understand communities outside London and how different they are. Every city will be different, with different practices and ways of life. It's about people being good journalists and not being lazy. There is an element of truth in every stereotype but that doesn't mean you have to accept it. Getting out there and talking to people and mosques and schools and making friends with your local councillor would be a good start.

The essential thing, to emphasise the point made above, is that journalists should be good at their jobs. 'I think', one of the interviewees said, 'papers need to employ people who are good journalists and if they happen to be a Muslim then great.'

Conclusions

This chapter has shown through vivid personal testimony some of the challenges faced by journalists from Muslim backgrounds working within mainstream newspapers. The challenges are recalled in Box 8, which consists of short highlights from the interviews.

Box 9 'I'm a professional journalist, not a professional Paki'

Papers need to employ people who are good journalists and if they happen to be a Muslim then great.

I haven't got a magic hotline to Osama or Bakri Mohammed. People think I must know people and I'm hiding it. Of the Muslims I know, 99 per cent of them are my relatives.

I felt people didn't know what to make of me because I was Muslim and Asian and not posh. I felt like a fish out of water.

You can be isolated in a room full of brown faces ... To be perfectly honest, I can be around a whole load of Muslims and feel I have nothing in common with them.

The only conflict I have is feeling a sense of responsibility to not merely confirm the worst stereotypes people have over Muslims.

I wouldn't now pitch a story about Ramadan and lots of lovely Muslims. Because there's no story there. It's not Islamophobic to say that.

The thing is I don't want to be pigeon-holed ... I'm a professional journalist not a professional Paki.

I feel I have to keep a sense of perspective ... I don't want it to look like here you are banging on about being Muslim again.

I feel slightly conscious when I am sitting in a mosque because of work ... Suddenly I am in there being really pious with everyone else and I feel like a bit of a charlatan.

The media is not an impartial observer. It's playing a role and it's creating a market for frightening news. And there are certain comic, scary and villainous British Muslims who want this as well.

This was just shit-stirring in the hope of finding something and I didn't want that on my conscience ... All that would happen in return is I would get a byline. Big deal.

I knocked on the door and said Assalamu Aleikum and told them I was a Muslim. After a few minutes they let me in ...

The next day I looked at the paper and I was appalled ... It
was really cynically done.

After September 11, I think I became quite a valuable commodity to them. My identity provided me with a role.

I don't make a big song and dance about being Muslim. I talk
about it quite freely with some of my colleagues and my
friends but it's not something I bring up in the workplace. I
leave it at the door.

I've become much more politicised. I thought my race and
identity were something I could put in a box away from my
role as a journalist. I have become much prouder of my
religion and race.

Although most of those interviewed had entered the profession
with consideration of their Muslim-ness only dimly in the background, their job has yanked their ethnic and religious identity firmly
into the foreground and forced them to consider how it affects the
work they do. Some have coped by accepting responsibility for
changing the way their paper reports on Muslim issues. Others have
responded more obliquely, by trying to change opinions within
their workplace but deliberately avoiding covering such stories
themselves.

The willingness of the six journalists quoted in this chapter to
speak so personally about their feelings and experiences shows how
hard they have had to think about what their background means for
their job, and about what it means to be a 'Muslim journalist' in an
era when coverage of Muslim issues is often skewed by ignorance
and prejudice. Their hopes for the future are clear: that newspapers
accept their responsibility for forming public opinion in this area and
attempt to address some of their failings; and, more personally, that
journalists from similar backgrounds entering newspapers in years to
come might be freed from the tokenism and pigeon-holing they

have struggled against. As one of them put it: 'There's no reason why a Muslim journalist shouldn't be writing about music, or sport, or anything else.'

In the light of the discussions and quotations in this chapter it is clear that if media coverage of Islam and Muslims is to be improved, there are practical advantages in employing journalists who are themselves of Muslim backgrounds for the reasons below.

When writing about issues concerning Islam or Muslims they are more likely to do so with sensitivity, fairness, and an awareness of complexity.

When interacting with members of the public who are Muslims they are more likely to establish a rapport and to win people's trust and confidence.

They are able to advise and challenge colleagues, including senior editors, about ways certain stories should and should not be covered.

They can have an impact on the organisational culture of the paper, making it more open-minded and self-critical.

It is also important, however, that senior managers in news organisations should:

understand that there is a wide range of opinion, outlook and practice among journalists of Muslim backgrounds, as among people of Muslim backgrounds more generally. Not all practise the religion, for example, and no single individual should be treated as a representative or ambassador;

recognise that journalists of Muslim backgrounds are keen to be treated essentially as journalists who happen to be Muslims rather than Muslims who happen to be journalists;

resist pressures to limit people's career prospects by pigeon-holing and typecasting them into a narrow range of work.

10

Responsible Journalism

Julian Petley and Robin Richardson

The previous chapters of this book have suggested that in most though not all of the UK print media, and for most though not all of the time:

the dominant view is that there is no common ground between the West and Islam, and that conflict between them is accordingly inevitable;

Muslims in Britain are seen as a threat to traditional British customs, values and ways of life;

alternative worldviews, understandings and opinions are not mentioned, or are not given a fair hearing;

facts are frequently distorted, exaggerated or oversimplified;

the tone of language is frequently emotive, immoderate, alarmist and abusive;

the coverage is likely to provoke and increase feelings of insecurity, suspicion and anxiety among non-Muslims;

the coverage is at the same time likely to provoke feelings of insecurity, vulnerability and alienation among Muslims, and in this way may actually weaken the government's measures to reduce and prevent extremism;

the coverage is unlikely to help diminish levels of hate crime and acts of
   unlawful discrimination by non-Muslims against Muslims;

the coverage is likely to be a major barrier preventing the success of
   the government's integration and community cohesion policies
   and programmes;

the coverage is unlikely to contribute to informed discussion and
   debate among Muslims and non-Muslims about ways of working
   together to maintain and develop Britain as a multicultural,
   multifaith democracy.

This final chapter considers ways of improving the situation. The
discussion is organised under six headings:

- Freedom of expression
- Dealing with anxiety
- Religious literacy
- Critical literacy
- Complaints and complaining
- Professional codes of practice.

Freedom of expression

It is relevant to recall the Danish cartoons controversy – more accurately and tellingly the Danish *caricatures* controversy – in 2006. No
national paper in the UK chose to reprint the caricatures. The reasons they gave for this decision reflected principles of responsible
journalism which all UK media claim to be guided by and according
to which they invite assessment, criticism and judgement. Admittedly, in the light of the reporting of Muslims and Islam detailed in
this book, such protestations on the part of papers other than the
Guardian, the *Observer* and the *Independent* could be regarded as pretty
inconsistent with their past record, not to say downright hypocritical.
On the other hand, for the purposes of this chapter, let us take their
stated reasons for non-publication at face value.

All agreed that freedom of expression is not absolute. In the words of a leader in the *Independent* (3 February 2006): 'There is no doubt that newspapers should have the right to print cartoons that some people find offensive ... But there is an important distinction to be made between having a right and choosing to exercise it.' The same point was made by Gary Younge in the *Guardian* (4 February 2006): 'The right to freedom of speech equates to neither an obligation to offend nor a duty to be insensitive. There is no contradiction between supporting someone's right to do something and condemning them for doing it.' A leader in the *Daily Mail* (3 February 2006) stated that: 'While the *Mail* would fight to the death to defend those papers [abroad] that printed the offending cartoons, it disagrees with the fact that they have done so.'

So under what circumstances, the question arises, is it appropriate for the media to exercise restraint rather than to exercise their right of free expression? In relation to the Danish caricatures, UK newspapers in effect proposed three broad principles. First, there was a desire not to cause distress, insecurity and fear. The caricatures were hurtful to many people, particularly, but not only, to Muslims, and papers chose not to distress substantial numbers of their actual or potential readers. Doubtless there was a strong element of self-preservation and commercial self-interest here, but, whatever the papers' motives, the actual words used had to do with principles of respect, civility, courtesy and human concern. 'The cartoons are intended to insult Muslims,' said the *Sun* (3 February) , 'and ... [we] can see no justification for causing deliberate offence to our much-valued Muslim readers.' 'There is no merit in causing gratuitous offence,' said *The Independent* (4 February), 'as these cartoons undoubtedly do.' 'To present them in front of the public for debate is not a value-neutral exercise,' said *The Times* (3 February). 'The offence destined to be caused to moderate Muslims should not be discounted.' 'We prefer', said the *Daily Telegraph* (3 February), 'not to cause gratuitous offence to some of our readers.' Freedom of speech, said the same day's *Daily Mail*, is 'a treasured characteristic of a civilised society. But great freedoms involve great responsibilities. And an obligation of free speech is that you do not gratuitously insult those with whom you disagree.'

Second, the principle of avoiding gratuitous offence was seen as particularly important with regard to people who are vulnerable to hate crimes on the streets and to discrimination and exclusion in employment and public life. People should have the right, said the *Independent* (3 February), 'to exist in a secular pluralist society without feeling as alienated, threatened and routinely derided as many Muslims now do'. 'It would be senselessly provocative', said the same day's *Guardian*, 'to reproduce a set of images, of no intrinsic value, which pander to the worst prejudices about Muslims.' In other European countries, incidentally, there was markedly less concern to avoid further distress to those who are already vulnerable and excluded. A group of French writers, for example, defended publication of the cartoons on the grounds that 'picking on the parish priest has long been a national sport'. However, it should be noted that anti-clericalism and anti-Muslim racism are extremely different from one another, not least with regard to the relative power and standing of those who are attacked.

In an article in the *Guardian* (13 February), the philosopher Onora O'Neill recalled that the concept of freedom of speech in newspapers derives in part from the work of J.S. Mill in the nineteenth century. But in Mill's day, she continued, a free press was seen as the champion of the weak in the face of overweening governments, and as augmenting and giving voice to the powerless. It is less easy to justify the same freedom of expression being permitted to the immensely more powerful media organisations that dominate the modern world. She concluded:

> Once we take account of the power of the media, we are not likely to think that they should enjoy unconditional freedom of expression. We do not think that corporations should have unrestricted rights to invent their balance sheets, or governments to damage or destroy the reputations of individuals or institutions, or to deceive their electorates. Yet contemporary

liberal readings of the right to free speech often assume that we can safely accord the same freedom of expression to the powerless and the powerful.

Third, explicitly or implicitly, papers presented themselves as responsible for upholding standards of courtesy and respect, with a view to promoting thoughtful discussion in a diverse but inclusive society. 'Our restraint is in keeping with British values of toler-ance and respect for the feelings of others,' said the *Daily Telegraph* (3 February). 'The right to publish,' said the same day's *Guardian*, 'does not imply any obligation to do so,' especially if putting that right to the test inevitably causes offence to many Muslims at a time when there is 'such a powerful need to craft a more inclusive public culture which can embrace them and their faith'. The limits to free expres-sion, said Ziauddin Sardar in the *Independent on Sunday* (5 February), 'are to be found in the social consequences, the potential harm to others of an exercise of free speech'. He continued:

> Tolerance is easy if there is nothing to offend. We become toler-ant only when we defer to the sensitivities of those with whom we profoundly disagree on matters we do not believe can or should be accepted. Forbearance is the currency of peaceful coexistence in heterodox society ... Freedom of expression is not about doing whatever we want to do because we can do it. It is about creating an open marketplace for ideas and debate where all, including the marginalised, can take part as equals.

The cartoons themselves, wrote Tariq Modood in *Open Democracy* (2006), developing this theme, were 'a trigger rather than the main issue'. What was really at stake, he argued, was how to build and maintain an inclusive but diverse society. For Muslims, the underly-ing causes of anger surrounding the cartoons included:

> A deep sense that they are not respected, that they and their most cherished feelings are 'fair game'. Inferior protective legislation,

socio-economic marginality, cultural disdain, draconian security surveillance, the occupation of Palestine, the international
'war on terror' all converge on this point. The cartoons cannot
be compared to some of these situations, but they do distil the
experience of inferiority and of being bossed around. A handful of humiliating images become a focal point for something
much bigger than themselves.

He then compared the responses of the UK press with those of
papers elsewhere in Europe, noting that:

> Europe is having to choose which is more important, the right
> to ridicule Muslims or the integration of Muslims ... While
> we [in the UK] could not be said to have made a decisive
> choice there is greater understanding in Britain about anti-
> Muslim racism and about the vilification–integration contra-
> diction than in some other European countries. This is not to
> say that Muslim sensibilities must be treated as fixed. They too
> will rightly change and adapt to new contexts. The point is
> that this cannot be a one-way process. Civic integration and
> international interdependence – let alone anything as ambi-
> tious as a dialogue of civilisations – means that there has to be
> mutual learning and movement on both/all sides, not just the
> hurling of absolutes at each other. This is not just a matter of
> compromise but of multicultural inclusion.

There are parallels between the way in which the press dealt with
the cartoons and its behaviour in the aftermath of 9/11 and 7/7.
Certainly there was a clear possibility, on Tuesday 11 September 2001
and the ensuing days, that violent hatred of all Muslims in Britain
would be whipped up. Phrases in email messages sent to the Muslim
Council of Britain that week included: 'You don't belong here and
you never will. Go back to fornicating with your camels in the desert,
and leave us alone'; 'Your religion is a joke'; 'The US will soon kill
many Muslim women and children. You are all subhuman freaks';

'I no longer have any respect for you. None at all. I am so sorry, but I just despise you and your cruel God. You are not people. Just get out of the UK'; 'I have never considered myself to be a racist – but I am now ... Your kind knows nothing but force ... well you've sown the seed, now reap the whirlwind, you have woken us up to what you all stand for'; 'What a vile evil race you load of Muslims are ... Get out of my country now! England is for white civilised English people'; 'Your satanic religion. We will kill you all ... may Islam burn under US bombs'; 'The rest of the world will now join to smash the filthy disease infested Islam. You must be removed from Britain in body bags', and so on and on.

There were literally hundreds of such messages. But the tone in the press was much more calm. This, we know now, was at least partly down to a mixture of government pressure and pleading. The most striking example, arguably, was in the *Sun*. On Thursday 13 September there was a two-page editorial with the banner headline 'Islam is not evil religion.' This declared:

> If the terrorists were Islamic fanatics [at that time it was suspected, but not yet known, that those responsible for the bombs had associations with Islam] then the world must not make the mistake of condemning all Muslims ... The men who hijacked packed passenger planes and flew them into the World Trade Centre and the Pentagon were evil. But the religion they practise is one of peace and discipline ... The Muslims in Britain ARE British. They may have a different culture to most of us but they love this country and they respect democracy.

In relation to 7 July 2005, a report from the European Monitoring Centre (EUMC) commented:

> The strong and united stand taken by the UK Government, police and community leaders, including leaders of the Muslim community, in condemning both the bombings and any retaliation, has played a major part in preventing an anti-Muslim

backlash. This joint action was decisive in countering a short-term and disturbing upsurge in anti-Muslim incidents in the immediate aftermath of the bombings. Such incidents have now dropped back to levels before the bomb attacks.

The EUMC report noted further that the UK press 'went to great lengths to report in a balanced and objective way, for instance by putting in focus Muslims as having been among the victims of the bombings'. In the immediate aftermath the press warned against a possible backlash and the hate crimes that followed in the wake of the attacks were given broad coverage. However, it noted too that once the initial coming together of different communities had faded, hostile coverage in parts of the media was resumed. Thus it's important to note that the distorted and mischievous stories about banning Christ and Christmas in order not to offend Muslims, analysed in Chapter 4, occurred within four months, while the tendentious coverage of the MCB and other such umbrella organisations, described in Chapter 5, occurred even sooner.

Dealing with anxiety

'In many influential circles in Europe', notes the political philosopher Bhikhu Parekh, 'it is widely held that its over 15 million Muslims pose a serious and political threat', and most of the chapters in this book show how the threat is portrayed in the UK media. Parekh continues:

Sometimes this view is explicitly stated; more often it is implied or simply assumed. On other occasions it takes the form of an attack on multiculturalism for which Muslims are held responsible and which is a coded word for them. It cuts across political and ideological divides, and is shared alike, albeit in different degrees, by conservatives, fascists, liberals, socialists and communists.

(Parekh, 2008: 99)

Parekh's use of the concept of anxiety, rather than – for example – phobia, means that there can be measured reflection and deliberation around questions such as:

- Is an anxiety rational and well founded, or is it based on insufficient or inaccurate information or on misperception?
- If the latter, what are the real reasons for the anxiety?
- Where misperceptions exist, what factors have influenced their formation?

In the light of the answers to such questions there can be debate about sensible measures, as distinct from panicky, harmful or self-defeating measures, to remove or reduce anxiety.

One of the ethical responsibilities of journalists lies in seeking to acknowledge and understand anxiety but not to pander to it and inflame it into the kinds of moral panic discussed in chapter 2. This, of course, can conflict with newspapers' commercial imperatives, since it is one of the clichés of the journalistic world that bad news sells papers. There are in consequence real ethical dilemmas in the reporting, selecting, editing and publishing of stories about relationships between Muslims and non-Muslims at the present time, whether in the UK or in the world more generally, when, for the reasons explained in this book, this is a particularly fraught subject. In so far as the media get this wrong, they exacerbate the very conditions about which they are reporting, although precious few media outlets are prepared to admit to their own agency in this matter (or indeed any other). As John Lloyd has observed, the media 'have an unwritten rule not to divulge their power … They make and re-make the versions of the world with which we live – and yet when the news media represent the world, they largely excuse themselves from it' (2004: 15–16). Contemporary life is inexplicable without an account of the part the media play in it, and yet in most media accounts of the world, media institutions and their activities are largely invisible, and where their presence is actually acknowledged, they are habitually represented as mere neutral observers, a 'window on the world' as opposed to a refracting lens or distorting mirror. This is an area in which a great deal more critical self-awareness, not to mention honesty, is urgently required. As Will Hutton put it in the *Observer*, 17 August 2003: 'Britain's least accountable and self-critical institutions have become the media.'

The Parekh report, *The Future of Multi-ethnic Britain* (2000), did not use the concept of moral panic. It did, however, maintain that all considerations of race, ethnicity and religious diversity nowadays should be constructed with an acute awareness of the wider context of rapid social and cultural change which our society, and indeed the wider world, is undergoing, a process which many find distinctly disturbing, unsettling and threatening. In this context, the report identified seven interacting trends: globalisation; Britain's decline as a world power; the increasing importance of the European Union; devolution within the UK; the end of empire; the rapid advance of social and moral pluralism, linked to the shift from an industrial to a post-industrial and service economy; and post-war migration (2000: 23–6). These are the major *underlying* causes of malaise and unease, the report argued, not the specific events, groups or communities that are all too often pressed into service by the media as scapegoats. The anxiety-inducing effects of globalisation have already been discussed in chapter 2, but it is worth summarising these again, along with the other six causes of anxiety, as these are extremely important to any consideration of the way in which responsible journalism should report the modern world.

Globalisation

The growing interdependence of the world's major regions results from the rapid movement of global capital and investment, neoliberalism and the deregulation of financial and other markets, the rise of multinational corporations, the spread of new information and communications technologies, the new cultural industries, and changing global consumption patterns. One effect has been to weaken aspects of national sovereignty, the nation-state as an exclusive political focus, national economies, and the idea of nation as the guarantor of citizenship.

The long-term decline in Britain's position as a world power

Militarily, Britain is dependent on alliances for effective influence. The country is no longer the centre of a worldwide empire and no longer leads in the technologies of the new global age. Overall, Britain has slipped to the position of a middle-ranking power. This has under-mined the long-standing sense of the inevitability of British 'greatness'. There is widespread concern that Britain has lost its historical vocation, and the country is tempted to look back, nostalgically, to past glories.

Britain in Europe

This is part of an inevitable trend towards larger regional associations. However, the idea of an island people with an island destiny has been central to British, and especially English, national identity. Indeed, Britishness has been most effectively described negatively, in terms of what it is not – especially 'not European'. In this respect, Euroscepticism (of which British newspapers are a particularly significant carrier) can most usefully be considered not as a specific policy but as a form of gut nationalism, a last-ditch refusal to make any further concessions to 'foreignness'.

Devolution

Many factors have conspired to stimulate pressure to devolve power from England to Scotland, Wales and Northern Ireland. The process is said by its supporters to represent a loosening of ties, not a breaking of ancient bonds. However, as the new parliaments and assemblies flex their muscles, significant divergences between Westminster and the devolved institutions are developing. These inevitably weaken the centralised idea of a united kingdom, and in some cases have fuelled a resentful form of English nationalism. What symbolic glue can hold these increasingly autonomous entities together?

The end of empire

This relates closely to the long-term decline of Britain as a world power, and is seen by some as the shedding of a burden whose time has passed. However, expunging the traces of an imperial mentality from the national culture, particularly those aspects of it which see the white British as a superior race, is a much more difficult task. This mentality has penetrated everyday life, popular culture and consciousness, and remains active (if largely unacknowledged) in projected fantasies and fears about difference, and in racialised stereotypes of otherness.

The rapid advance of social pluralism

The shift from an industrial to a post-industrial and service economy has been accompanied by the breakdown of older class hierarchies, diminished respect for traditional sources of authority, shifting gender and sexual norms, erosion of the established cultural canon, more emphasis on individualism, hedonism and personalised ethics, a greater sense of diverse religious and non-religious world views, and a growing sense of moral relativism. Some or all of these are sources of anxiety for the traditionally minded.

Post-war migration

Migration is a worldwide phenomenon; indeed, it is one of the most obvious and visible forms taken by globalisation. It affects every metropolitan Western country, for all have needed influxes of labour from outside. It is also driven by poverty, exploitation, underdevelopment, natural disasters, famine and civil war. Migration to Britain from the Caribbean, the South Asian subcontinent and Africa, and more recently Eastern Europe, has raised many questions about British identity and British institutions.

Religious literacy

There is an increasing need for people in public bodies, particularly those with leadership and senior management responsibilities, to possess 'religious literacy'. It is not unreasonable to expect responsible and socially aware media to help to develop this skill. A crude measure of the need is the number of stories in the media that mention the words 'Christian' and 'Muslim'. According to Ian Mayes, the then readers' editor of the *Guardian*, writing in that paper on 5 December 2005, the word 'Christian' appeared in the *Guardian* 770 times in 1985; 1221 times in 1995, and 2341 times in 2005. The word 'Muslim' appeared 408 times in 1985, 1106 times in 1995, and 2114 times in 2005.

A working definition of religious literacy might include the following:

> Skills in understanding and assessing religious statements and behaviour; discerning the difference between valuable and harmful aspects of religion and religions; appreciating religious architecture, art, literature and music without necessarily accepting all the beliefs that they express or assume; and making reasonable accommodation between people holding different religious and non-religious worldviews.

As the above makes clear, the concept of religious literacy does not imply holding a set of distinctively religious beliefs, but understanding the range of ways in which religion may affect a person's values and perspectives. It implies also that a religious tradition should be understood in its own terms, so far as is possible, and not through templates and assumptions derived from another, presumably 'superior', tradition. For example, it is religiously illiterate to suppose that imams in Islam have the same range of roles and responsibilities as clerics in Christianity. Equally, it is illiterate to equate an attack on a bishop of the established church with an attack on a cleric in a marginalised community subject to racist violence. Thus, for example, it was religiously illiterate for the French writers mentioned above, *à propos* the controversy about the Danish caricatures in early 2006, to defend them on the grounds that 'picking on the parish priest has long been a national sport'. It could also be concluded that some of the religious commentators cited in chapter 8 were guilty of such illiteracy.

Religious literacy also involves recognising that within every tradition there is a tension and conversation between pressures to maintain the heritage and pressures to re-interpret it. For example, it is religiously illiterate to suppose that all people with a strong commitment to a certain tradition have much the same orientation towards it. Further, religious literacy involves understanding the pressures in every tradition that lead to the emergence of 'fundamentalism' and 'extremism', and that may cause people to use religious discourse to justify, or to try to justify, immoral acts.

When people 'religionise' a conflict by claiming a divine seal of approval for their own actions, which is frequently what those labelled 'fundamentalist' do, their discourse has one or more of the following five functions: (a) to justify actions and policies that would otherwise be difficult or impossible to justify; (b) to motivate combatants to perform acts that they would otherwise be reluctant to perform; (c) to provide solace and comfort for defeats, uncertainties, risks, dashed hopes and privations that would otherwise be intolerable; (d) to mobilise tacit or active support among onlookers that would not otherwise be forthcoming; and (e) to provide legitimacy for authority figures who would otherwise be distrusted or opposed. Claiming divine support for one's own side frequently involves demonising – more accurately, perhaps, satanising or devilising – one's opponents, and doing so with the aid of religious imagery and frames of reference.

In all religious traditions a distinction is made between 'true religion' and 'false religion'. Sometimes it seems easy to make the distinction, or minimally to recognise false religion when one sees it – planes being flown into the Twin Towers, for example, or the cavalier equation of 'true religion' with 'us' and 'false religion' with 'them'. But traditional teachings throughout the centuries have also stressed that telling the difference between 'true' and 'false' religion is seldom straightforward, for human capacities for self-deception, false security and unhealthy defences against anxiety seem limitless. 'We'd better acknowledge the sheer danger of religiousness,' wrote the Archbishop of Canterbury shortly after 11 September 2001.

> It can be a tool to reinforce diseased perceptions of reality, a way of teaching ourselves not to see the particular human agony in front of us; or worse, of teaching ourselves not to see ourselves, our violence, our actual guilt as opposed to our abstract 'religious' sinfulness. Our religious talking, seeing, knowing, needs a kind of cleansing.

> (Williams, 2002: 4)

We may seem to have strayed from the subject of responsible journalism here, but it is surely obvious that religious literacy is required when journalists deal with issues relating to the subject matter of this report, particularly in tense times such as our own. But it should also be noted that it is similarly required from certain individuals and groups in Muslim communities too. A report by the Department for Communities and Local Government (Choudhury, 2007) identified a range of factors that affect whether or not young British Muslims become attracted to extremism and fundamentalism. One of these was:

> a lack of religious literacy and education [which] appears to be a common feature among those that are drawn to extremist groups. The most vulnerable are those who are religious novices exploring their faith for the first time as they are not in a

position to objectively evaluate whether … [a] radical group represents an accurate understanding of Islam.

(2007: 6)

The development of religious literacy in young Muslims is a task for Muslim organisations, including mosques, and has to do with leadership and scholarship. The government can also facilitate the task and the media arguably have a role in supporting it. The principal responsibility of the media, however, is to avoid putting obstacles in its way. The Department of Communities and Local Government report indicated that other factors affecting whether someone becomes attracted to extremism include experiences of discrimination and blocked social mobility, and 'the public devaluation and disparagement of Muslims and Islam' (Choudhury, 2007: 9), which leads to feelings that they do not belong and are not wanted. In this connection, the media most certainly have a part, for it is they who play a very considerable role in the process of public devaluation and disparagement. Journalists are unlikely to change their ways in this respect unless they too develop religious literacy.

Critical literacy

'Pupils need to be able to interpret reports,' argues a consultation paper issued by the Department for Education and Skills, 'and develop skills to interrogate and make judgements about how their meaning is constructed and conveyed. While different localities may have different contexts, the media, especially the press and the broadcasters, are universally available and afford all pupils opportunities to explore diversity and its representations. Critical literacy is crucial' (Ajegbo, 2007: 69). It continues:

If you are white … living in a white area, how do you relate what you see on the television to your idea of being British and the nature of British society? If you are black, how do you interpret programmes on AIDs and famine in Africa, or inner city issues in America? If you are Muslim, how do you cope with the barrage of media images about terrorism or the veil? Schools must play their part in recapturing the middle ground for groups who are misrepresented.

(2007: 69)

Critical literacy in schools will involve interrogating news reports with questions such as the following:

Generalisations. Are Muslims seen as basically all the same, or are they represented as being engaged in reflective disagreement and dialogue with each other, and with a range of different views?

A plague on them all? In so far as Muslims are seen as having disagreements with each other, for example between Shi'a and Sunni or between Sufi and Islamist, is the assumption that all are wrong, all as bad as each other? Or is there a much more nuanced and sensitive account of differences among Muslims, similar to the differences, deliberations and disagreements among non-Muslims?

Two kinds of Muslim? Are Muslims divided into two broad categories, 'good Muslims' (hard-working, decent, law-abiding and 'moderate') and 'bad Muslims' (mixing religion with politics, inclined to extremism and terrorism, making unreasonable demands)? Or is the multifaceted complexity of Islam, both in the present and the past, recognised and attended to?

Like or unlike? Are Muslims seen as totally 'other', separate from 'the West', or as both similar and interdependent, sharing a common humanity, a common set of aspirations and values, a common history and a common space? Are there stories in the media about 'ordinary' Muslims, people 'just like ourselves'?

Partners or enemies? Are Muslims seen as an aggressive enemy to be feared, opposed and defeated, or as cooperative partners with whom to work on shared problems, locally, nationally and internationally?

Really religious? Are Muslims seen as hypocritical in their religious beliefs and practices, using religion to justify things that cannot be justified, or simply to give themselves a sense of identity, or are they seen as sincere and genuine?

Identity as well as belief? Are Muslims represented as all holding certain theological beliefs, essentially, or is it recognised that being a Muslim is for some people more to do with ethno-religious identity, or affiliation to a broad tradition and heritage, than with holding specific beliefs?

Abusive language? Is immoderate language used, for example language that compares Muslims to animals, or that claims they are insane, or evil, or similar to people with severe medical conditions such as cancer and gangrene? Or are disagreement and criticism expressed with civility?

Recognition of power differences? Is no account made of the fact that Muslims have far less access to the media than do non-Muslims, and are therefore at a competitive disadvantage on an uneven playing field? Or is unequal freedom of expression recognised?

Attention to Muslim insights and arguments? Are Muslim criticisms of the so-called West rejected out of hand or are they considered and debated?

Double standards? Are double standards applied in descriptions and criticisms of Islam and the so-called West, or are criticisms even-handed?

Who gets to speak? Are Muslim voices sought out and quoted and is there a range of such voices? Are they given a fair hearing, or are they ridiculed or sidelined? And is it shown that many non-Muslims seek and express solidarity with Muslims on many issues?

Common sense? Are anti-Muslim comments, stereotypes and discourse seen as natural and 'common sense', or as problematic and to be challenged?

Complaints and complaining

Up to a point, news organisations are susceptible to pressure and to complaints, although as we have seen in chapter 5 this was not the case with the edition of *Panorama* devoted to the Muslim Council of Britain. Furthermore, the record of the Press Complaints Commission

(PCC) in the matter of complaints relating to press coverage of minorities of one kind or another is far from encouraging (Frost, 2004; Petley, 2006b). However, those who wish to complain should nonetheless consider the following courses of action:

If a paper has a readers' editor or ombudsman, then polite, factual, restrained letters and/or emails should be addressed to them. If not, then write direct to editors. Either way, use the very tactics which papers use to get their message across – drip-drip-drip. Editors need to be told as often as possible where their papers are going wrong.

The task is to 'censure not censor': don't try to censor opinions, but engage in debate, for example through letters to the editor or directly to the writers concerned. Remember the famous dictum that 'comment is free, but facts are sacred'. If the newspaper has got its facts wrong, then don't simply assert this but supply what you believe to be the true facts of the case. One does of course need to be aware that the authors of opinion columns (something of which British newspapers are not exactly short) are obviously in the business of venting their opinions. However, their opinions need to be based on facts, not rumour, supposition and myth.

If you don't get satisfaction, write to the PCC, making sure that your letter addresses the specific points and criteria in the PCC's code of practice. Bear in mind in particular the code's first clause, which states that:

> (i) The Press must take care not to publish inaccurate, misleading or distorted information, including pictures.
>
> (ii) A significant inaccuracy, misleading statement or distortion once recognised must be corrected, promptly and with due prominence, and – where appropriate – an apology published.
>
> (iii) The Press, while free to be partisan, must distinguish clearly between comment, conjecture and fact.

Make your complaint as widely known as possible. Contact rival newspapers, or post it on one of the growing number of websites which highlight press inaccuracy and misconduct, such as Liberal Conspiracy, Regret the Error or the Campaign for Press and Broadcasting Freedom. Newspapers repeatedly call for the 'naming and shaming' of offenders of one kind or another, but they very strongly dislike the same tactic being applied to them. In this way a climate of critical opinion is built up, which encourages others to complain as well.

Bear in mind that effective complaining requires organisation, both to monitor what is published and to ensure that complaints are formulated in the best possible way. Again, websites such as the above can be of enormous assistance here.

Contact the National Union of Journalists (NUJ) at either national or local level. The NUJ's executive membership and headquarters staff are very sympathetic to the plight of minorities ill-treated by newspapers. For example, the decision of the NUJ chapel at the *Daily Express* to complain to the PCC about inflammatory and distorted stories concerning asylum seekers which they were required to write shows vividly that there are journalists deeply unhappy at being required to write prejudicial articles.

If you don't get satisfaction from any of the above, consider approaching your MP.

Codes of professional practice

Those working in the media are not exactly short of codes of professional practice of one kind or another. The PCC code has already been mentioned, and it's also worth pointing out that clause 12 of the code states that: 'i) The press must avoid prejudicial or pejorative reference to an individual's race, colour, religion, gender, sexual orientation or to any physical or mental illness or disability. ii) Details of an individual's race, colour, religion, sexual orientation, physical or mental illness or disability must be avoided unless genuinely relevant to the story.'

Meanwhile the NUJ's code of conduct lays down that a journalist

strives to ensure that information disseminated is honestly conveyed, accurate and fair;

does her/his utmost to correct harmful inaccuracies;

differentiates between fact and opinion;

produces no material likely to lead to hatred or discrimination on the grounds of a person's age, gender, race, colour, creed, legal status, disability, marital status, or sexual orientation.

One should also note the publication *Reporting Diversity: how journalists can contribute to community cohesion*, published by the Society of Editors and the Media Trust (2006). Though not a formal code of practice, it contains a great deal of useful advice to journalists, and echoes many of the sentiments in this chapter. For example, the section entitled 'Why journalists have a role' argues that 'if Britain is to promote good relations between people with a wide range of identities and religions, it is editors and journalists who bear the greatest responsibility for depicting different communities accurately to the majority and to one another' (2006: 13). It also notes that this is not simply a matter for newspapers in areas with significant ethnic minority communities but also in those which are less diverse, since 'everyone needs to understand better the society of which they are a part' (2006: 13). In the report's view, this means:

working to establish regular contact with those communities and with the organisations that support them;

making themselves aware of the impact on individuals, communities and society as a whole of what they report and how they do it;

seeing their role as more than chronicling what happens. Journalists will want to see it also as breaking down barriers to understanding so that everyone can live together in harmony. (2006: 13)

Broadcast journalists are covered by the extremely elaborate Ofcom code, and, if they work for the BBC, by the Corporation's own editorial guidelines as well. Both of these are far too lengthy to summarise here, but in the present context it's worth noting that the latter (which have already been touched upon in chapter 5) include the assurance that 'we strive to reflect a wide range of opinion and explore a range and conflict of views so that no significant strand of thought is knowingly unreflected or under- represented' and the stipulation that 'we must ensure we avoid bias or an imbalance of views on controversial subjects'. Meanwhile the Ofcom code states that 'news, in whatever form, must be reported with due accuracy and presented with due impartiality', and that 'broadcasters must avoid unjust or unfair treatment of individuals or organisations in programmes'. It's also worth noting that the Communications Act 2003 requires public service broadcasters to provide 'a sufficient quantity of programmes that reflect the lives and concerns of different communities and cultural interests and traditions within the United Kingdom, and locally in different parts of the United Kingdom'.

Towards a conclusion

It should by now be entirely obvious that the concerns and issues raised in this chapter are by no means restricted to academics, NGOs, what the press loves to call the 'PC brigade', and the victims of media misreporting and victimisation. Clearly, they are also shared by responsible journalists, editors, regulators and others within the media industries themselves. This being the case, it would perhaps be helpful to draw towards a conclusion with a series of recommendations which we hope will stimulate further debate and action on the topics discussed in this book:

The media should regard it as their duty to promote informed debate about the nature of multiculturalism.

The media should pay more attention to obtaining and publishing a range of opinion among Muslims. By the same token, they should provide and publish the views and viewpoints of people who are not themselves Muslims but have positive perceptions of Muslims based on first-hand and substantial experience of dialogue and shared projects.

There is a need in all media organisations for more Muslims to be employed, particularly in senior gatekeeper and supervisory functions. At the same time attention must be paid to the experiences and perceptions of people of Muslim heritage who are already employed in the media, as described in chapter 9 of this book. In particular, news organisations should consider how best to give Muslim staff appropriate professional support and to prevent them being pigeon-holed as specialists in minority issues rather than concerned with the full spectrum of an organisation's output.

Reporters, editors and sub-editors need convenient access to sources of reliable factual information. The British Council's *British Muslims Media Guide* (Masood, 2006) should be widely distributed and available throughout media organisations and consideration should be given to requesting the British Council to re-create its contents as an interactive website, routinely updated.

The media should find opportunities to present Muslims as individuals whose stories are worth telling, rather than merely as examples of a generic problem.

The PCC has issued valuable though non-binding guidance on the use of inaccurate terminology in reporting on asylum seekers and refugees, and the BBC has issued such guidance in relation to coverage of terrorism. Consideration should be given to providing guidelines on reporting of issues affecting Muslims, for example with regard to words such as 'fundamentalist', 'radical', 'jihad', 'Islamist', 'extremist' and 'moderate'. Central government could valuably give a lead by clarifying the vocabulary that it will itself use in official documents and statements.

Broadcasters are required by Act of Parliament to ensure their news coverage is balanced and fair. However, this requirement relates only to the way in which a specific story or topic is covered, not to how it is selected in the first place. Many stories selected for broadcasting are in fact generated by items in the print media, which are not required to be impartial and which, as we have seen throughout this book, very frequently have an agenda where issues pertaining to multiculturalism are concerned. In this way the press frequently, and perhaps increasingly, sets the agenda for broadcasters. This is not to say that the broadcasters take the same biased view as many newspapers, as it is customary for them to interview people who take opposing views on a given subject, thus providing a greater measure of balance than in a newspaper. However, all too frequently the consequence is that anyone speaking out in favour of, say, multiculturalism, is on the back foot from the outset, having to react and respond to a negative agenda that has already been set, rather than being able determine the topics and terms of debate themselves. It is our view that broadcasters should more vigorously question the factual accuracy of stories in the press, and ask themselves whether they should deal with a story (however impartially) simply because it happens to be high on the news agenda of sections of the press.

If they are to contribute constructively to the debate, then, the mainstream media need to put their own house in order. In this, they need to be supported, encouraged and empowered by their readers, viewers and users, and also, where necessary, by government agency. We thus recommend that:

Organisations, projects and programmes concerned with race relations should see and treat anti-Muslim hostility as a form of racism, and as serious as other forms of racism.

The Equality and Human Rights Commission (EHRC) should focus explicitly on, among other concerns, combating anti-Muslim hostility and prejudice, both in society at large and in the media in particular.

The Department for Communities and Local Government (DCLG) should give a higher profile to combating anti-Muslim hostility in the media and the general climate of opinion.

Both Muslim and non-Muslim organisations should complain more frequently and persistently about distorted coverage of Islam and Muslims in the media.

Organisations and institutions concerned with education should give consideration to how they can develop (a) critical media literacy and (b) religious literacy in the programmes, courses and curricula that they provide.

On 18 March 2007 the Secretary of State for Communities and Local Government, Ruth Kelly, was quoted in the *Observer* to the effect that 'we urgently need a new approach to tackling the violent extremism that seeks to undermine our society and this approach must be based as much on winning hearts and minds as on security measures'. She also stated that there must be 'a new emphasis on local solutions' and that 'our aim must be not just to stop people committing violence but also to challenge the ideologies that drive them'. She acknowledged that successive governments, including the one of which she was herself a member, 'have not always got this balance right'. Governments have put too much faith in action, she added, 'not enough in debate'. The purpose of the debate, she continued, would be to challenge, isolate and neutralise 'ideologies of hatred' among 'a tiny minority' of Muslims. She also drew an analogy with far right extremism – 'the British public rejects their ugly message'.

As has been argued at various points in this book, the actual strategy chosen – *Prevent* – was ill-considered and self-defeating. However, Kelly's stress on debate as well as action was, and remains, very welcome. The mainstream media – not just the Muslim media – have a major role to play here. In particular, there needs to be substantial debate about the prejudices and anxieties – sometimes amounting to panic – among non-Muslims, and an honest, self-critical appraisal of the ways in which the media may be responsible for helping to generate the myths, fears and prejudices discussed in this book.

Notes

1 The demonisation of Islam and Muslims

1 This definition has frequently been quoted in ECRI documents since 2003 and frequently the word 'race' appears in inverted commas, though this was not how it appeared in the original document. There was a footnote: 'Since all human beings belong to the same species, ECRI rejects theories based on the existence of different "races". However, in this Recommendation ECRI uses this term in order to ensure that those persons who are generally and erroneously perceived as belonging to "another race" are not excluded from the protection provided for by the legislation.'

3 Images of Islam in the UK

1 The authors are grateful to the research team at Cardiff University: Lucie Apampa, Ingeborg Braseth, Jenny Calvert, Stephanie Chlond and Lucy Dominy, Jo Hunt and Steve O'Shea. Also to Channel 4 for commissioning the research and to their colleagues at the production company Quicksilver, especially Ed Watts and Chris Balding. The study was commissioned by Channel 4 for a *Dispatches* documentary entitled, *It Shouldn't Happen to a Muslim*, broadcast on 7 July 2008.

2 Channel 4, *Dispatches*, 7 July 2008.

3 Specifically: Islam! OR Muslim! OR Mosque OR Jihad OR Sharia OR Moslem OR Mullah W/3 Brit! OR GB OR UK OR Eng! OR Scot! OR Wales OR welsh OR London! OR Birmingham OR Manchester OR Newcastle OR Liverpool OR Cardiff OR Glasgow OR Edinburgh OR Burnley OR Bradford OR Oldham.

4 Indeed, while the encoding/decoding model is no longer fashionable, the much discussed limits of the idea of a preferred meaning have rather overshadowed its undoubted usefulness in this kind of analysis.

5 The 'moderate' reputation of the MCB, previously instrumental in granting it a status as a source for New Labour politicians after 1997, began to be challenged when the MCB leadership lost this status by refusing to support certain UK foreign policies, such as on Iraq and Afghanistan. See chapter 5 of this book for a detailed analysis of the role of the media in an episode of the campaign against the MCB.

4 'Political correctness gone mad'

1 See: https://excalibur.bnp.org.uk/acatalog/British_Society.html
2 See: https://excalibur.bnp.org.uk/acatalog/British_Society.html

5 'A question of leadership'

1 See: http://news.bbc.co.uk/1/hi/programmes/panorama/4727513.stm
2 See: http://news.bbc.co.uk/1/hi/programmes/panorama/4297490.stm
3 See:http://news.bbc.co.uk/newswatch/ukfs/hi/newsid_4160000/newsid_4162000/4162038.stm
4 See: http://www.mpacuk.org/vote/voting-fardh.html#ixzz0lNDM MmRw
5 See: http://news.bbc.co.uk/1/hi/programmes/panorama/4171950.stm (all further quotes from the programme are taken from this source).
6 See: http://news.bbc.co.uk/1/hi/england/beds/bucks/herts/4310545.stm
7 That Ware significantly overstates the power of the MCB, and seems indeed to display a somewhat paranoid attitude towards it, was displayed by his reaction in the *Sunday Telegraph*, 18 November 2007, in an article headed 'Am I the demoniser … or is it Ken's "experts"?', which was

occasioned by the publication of the Insted report for the Greater London Authority (Insted Consultancy, 2007) on which the present book is partly based. Noting that 'criticism of my *Panorama* programme made up a quarter of the report', and also noting that 'the three "experts on Islam" who helped to produce the report … all turn out to be from the MCB', Ware strongly implies (although characteristically he fails to state this outright) that it was they who wrote the section of the report dealing with his programme. However, had Ware bothered to consult the footnotes of the report he would have discovered that footnote 32 plainly states that 'this chapter is based on the work of Julian Petley'. For the record, none of the report's advisers who are associated with the MCB wrote *any* of the report, and my only communication with the MCB in the context of the *Panorama* programme was to ask Inayat Bunglawala for a copy of the Council's letter of complaint to the BBC. Exactly the same innuendo had appeared a few days earlier in a column by Nick Cohen in the London *Evening Standard*, 14 November, which argued that 'a large chunk of the report was a devious attack on a *Panorama* exposé of the Muslim Council of Britain'. Again noting that three of those involved in the report were 'from the MCB', Cohen put two and two together to make anything other than four, claiming that: 'At a cost of £30,000 to the taxpayer, Livingstone was allowing the MCB and its friends to rubbish a well-sourced and balanced documentary and dressing up the results as an impartial study.' Readers of this chapter will have to judge for themselves whether it is 'devious' and whether Ware's documentary is 'balanced', but the suggestion in both of these articles seems to be that any criticism of the programme, and any attempt to explain the true nature and function of the MCB, *must* emanate from the MCB or its 'friends' – presumably because any unbiased observer (such as Ware?) would see straight through the Council. Whatever the case, I would contend that Ware's characteristic attempt to smear the GLA report in the *Sunday Telegraph* serves only to back up my analysis of his particular journalistic methods in this chapter.

8   See: http://news.bbc.co.uk/1/hi/programmes/panorama/4162514.stm
9   See: http://www.newstatesman.com/blogs/martin-bright/2007/07/government-islam-muslim-debate

7 Muslim women and veiled threats

1 There is no single garment that equates to the veil. The word '*hijab*' comes from the Arabic for veil, but there are different hijab garments or combinations of garments that relate to different nationalities, regions, ethnic and class backgrounds. The *shayla* is a long rectangular scarf wrapped around the head and pinned to the shoulder. The *al-amira* is a two-piece veil consisting of a close fitting cap and a tube-like scarf. The *chador*, worn by Iranian women when outside the house, is a full body-cloak. It is often accompanied by a smaller headscarf underneath. The *niqab* is a veil for the face that leaves the area around the eyes clear. The *burka* covers the entire face and body, leaving just a mesh screen to see through. In English there are three spellings for *burka*. We have used *burka* except when quoting from articles where the spelling is either *burqa* or *burkha* (significantly, certain newspapers are inconsistent in their spellings of the word).

2 See:http://georgewbush-whitehouse.archives.gov/news/releases/2001/11/20011117.html

3 On this issue, for example, see some excellent case studies of diversities of this practice, and of its meaning and contention, in *Fashion Theory*, 11: 2/3, 2007.

Bibliography

Abu-Lughod, Lila (2006) 'The Muslim women: the power of images and the danger of pity', 1 September (http://www.eurozine.com/articles/2006-09-01-abulughod-en.html).

Ahmed, Akbar (1992) *Postmodernism and Islam: predicament and promise*, New York: Routledge.

Ahmed, Leila (1992) *Women and Gender in Islam: historical roots of a modern debate*, New Haven, CT: Yale University Press.

Ajegbo, Keith (2007) *Curriculum Review: Diversity and Citizenship*, London: Department for Education and Skills.

Akram, Javid and Robin Richardson (2009) 'Citizenship education for all or preventing violent extremism for some? Choices and challenges for schools', *Race Equality Teaching* 27(3), pp. 49–55.

Al-Azmeh, Aziz (2007) 'Afterword', in Aziz Al-Azmeh and Effie Fokas (eds) *Islam in Europe: diversities, identities and influence*, Cambridge: Cambridge University Press, pp. 208–15.

Al-Hassani, Sunduss (2006) *Islamophobia in Europe: shadow report 2005*, Brussels: European Network Against Racism (http://p9445.typo3server.info/uploads/media/2005_en.pdf).

Al-Kateb, Abdullah (2005) 'Who labels who? A reply to Ehsan Masood', *Open Democracy*, 13 September (http://www.opendemocracy.net/conflict-terrorism/muslim_community_2828.jsp).

Al-Shaikh-Ali, Anas (2009) 'Public opinion and political influence: issues in contemporary popular fiction', in Wanda Krause (ed.) *Citizenship, Security and Democracy: Muslim engagement with the West*, London: Association of Muslim Social Scientists, pp. 47–70.

Allen, Christopher (2005) 'From race to religion: the new face of discrimination', in Tahir Abbas (ed.) *Muslim Britain: communities under pressure*, London: Zed Press, pp. 49–65.

—— (2010), *Islamophobia,* Farnham: Ashgate

Allen, Christopher and Jørgen Nielsen (2002) *Summary Report on Islamophobia in the EU after 11 September 2001*, Vienna: European Monitoring Centre on Racism and Xenophobia.

Ameli, Saied, Syed Marandi, Sameera Ahmed, Kara Seyfeddin and Arzu Merali (2007) *The British Media and Muslim Representation: the ideology of demonisation*, London: Islamic Human Rights Commission (Summary at: http://www.ihrc.org.uk/file/BMEG_VOL6.pdf).

American-Arab Anti-Discrimination Committee (2008) *Defamation in the Media and Popular Culture*, Washington, DC: American-Arab Anti-Discrimination Committee.

An-Nisa Society (2009) *An-Nisa Society's initial response to Contest 2's Prevent Strategy*, London: An-Nisa Society.

Ansari, Abidullah (2005) 'Postscript: panning *Panorama*', *Q News*, November, pp. 15–16.

Ansari, Humayan (2004) *'The Enemy Within': Muslims in Britain since 1800*, London: Hurst.

—— (2005) 'Attitudes to jihad, martyrdom and terrorism', in Tahir Abbas (ed.) *Muslim Britain: communities under pressure*, London: Zed Books, pp. 144–63.

Bevelander, Pieter and Jonas Otterbeck (2008) 'Young people's attitudes towards Muslims in Sweden', *Journal of Ethnic and Racial Studies* 33(3), pp. 1–22.

Birt, Jonathan (2005) 'Lobbying and marching: British Muslims and the state', in Tahir Abbas (ed.) *Muslim Britain: communities under pressure*, London: Zed Books, pp. 92–106.

Birt, Yahya (2006a) 'British emigration and the Muslim question' (http://www.yahyabirt.com/?p=47, accessed 2 April 2010).

—— (2006b) 'Notes on Islamophobia' (http://www.yahyabirt.com/?p=48, accessed 27 March 2010).

—— (2008) 'British Muslims and the Muslim Council of Britain: the next decade', *Open Democracy* 7 July (http://www.opendemocracy.net/article/the-next-ten-years-british-muslims-and-the-muslim-council-of-britain).

Birt, Yahya (2009a) 'Promoting virulent envy: reconsidering the UK's terrorist prevention strategy', *Rusi Journal* 154(4), pp. 52–8.

Birt, Yahya (2009b) 'Islamophobia in the construction of British Muslim identity politics', in Peter Hopkins and Richard Gale (eds) *Muslims in Britain: race, place and identities,* Edinburgh: Edinburgh University Press, pp. 210–11.

Bright, Martin (2006) *When Progressives Treat with Reactionaries: the British state's flirtation with radical Islamism,* London: Policy Exchange.

Brown, Gordon (2004) British Council Annual Lecture, 7 July (http://www.hm-treasury.gov.uk/press_63_04.htm).

Browne, Anthony (2006) *The Retreat of Reason: political correctness and the corruption of public debate in modern Britain,* 2nd edn, London: Institute for the Study of Civil Society.

Bunzi, Matti (2007) *Antisemitism and Islamophobia: hatreds old and new in Europe,* Chicago: Chicago University Press.

Buruma, Ian (2006) *Murder in Amsterdam: the death of Theo Van Gogh and the limits of tolerance,* London: Atlantic Books.

Cantle, Ted (chair) (2001) *Community Cohesion: a report of the independent review team,* London: Home Office.

Cesari, Jocelyne (2006) 'Muslims in Europe after 9/11: why the term Islamophobia is more a predicament than an explanation' (http://www.libertysecurity.org/article1167.html, accessed 30 November 2007).

Choudhury, Tufyal (2006) *The Role of Muslim Identity Politics in Radicalisation: a study in progress,* London: Department for Communities and Local Government.

Clark, Tony (chair) (2001) *Burnley Speaks, Who Listens?* Burnley Metropolitan Council.

Cohen, Stanley (2002 [1972]) *Folk Devils and Moral Panics: the creation of mods and rockers,* 3rd edn, London: Routledge.

Commission on British Muslims and Islamophobia (1997) *Islamophobia: a challenge for us all,* London: Runnymede Trust.

—— (2004) *Islamophobia: issues, challenges and action,* Stoke on Trent: Trentham Books.

Commission on the Future of Multi-Ethnic Britain (2000) *The Future of Multi-ethnic Britain,* London: Profile Books.

Cottle, Simon (ed.) (2000) *Ethnic Minorities in the Media: changing cultural boundaries,* Buckingham: Open University Press.

Curran, James, Ivor Gaber and Julian Petley (2005) *Culture Wars: the media and the British left*, Edinburgh: Edinburgh University Press.

Davies, Nick (2008) *Flat Earth News*, London: Chatto & Windus.

Davis, Aeron (2003) 'Whither mass media and power? Evidence for a critical elite theory alternative', *Media, Culture & Society* 25(5), pp. 669–90.

Dirlik, Arif (2002) 'Rethinking colonialism: globalisation, postcolonialism, and the nation', *Interventions* 4(3), pp. 428–48.

Dyer, Richard (1997) *White: essays on race and culture*, London: Routledge.

ECRI (European Commission against Racism and Intolerance) (2003) *ECRI General Policy Recommendation No. 7 on National Legislation to Combat Racism and Racial Discrimination*, adopted 13 December 2002, Strasbourg: Council of Europe.

El Hamel, Chouki (2002) 'Muslim diaspora in Western Europe: the Islamic headscarf (*hijab*), the media and Muslims' integration in France', *Citizenship Studies* 6(3), pp. 293–308.

Engage (2009) *A Pocket Guide to Media and Politics*, UK: Engage (http://www.iengage.org.uk/images/stories/pocketguide.pdf).

Equality and Human Rights Commission (2009) *Parliamentary Briefing on the Equality Bill, House of Lords Second Reading*, 15 December, Manchester: Equality and Human Rights Commission.

(ECRI) (2009) *Combating Racism and Intolerance*, Strasbourg: European Commission against Racism and Intolerance.

European Union Agency for Fundamental Human Rights (2006) *Muslims in the European Union: discrimination and Islamophobia*, Vienna: FRA/EUMC (http://eumc.europa.eu/eumc/material/pub/muslim/Manifestations_EN.pdf).

European Union Agency for Fundamental Rights (2009) *European Union Minorities and Discrimination Survey: data in focus report 2: Muslims*, Vienna: European Union Agency for Fundamental Rights.

Ezzerhouni, Dahou (2010) 'L'islamophobie, un racisme apparu avec les colonisations', *Algérie-Focus* 3 February.

Fairclough, Norman (1995) *Media Discourse*, London: Edward Arnold.

Fekete, Liz (2006) 'Enlightened fundamentalism? Immigration, feminism and the right', *Race & Class* 48(2), pp. 1–22.

—— (2008) *Integration, Islamophobia and Civil Rights in Europe*, London: Institute of Race Relations.

—— (2009) *A Suitable Enemy: racism, migration and Islamophobia in Europe*, London: Pluto Press.

Field, Clive (2007) 'Islamopbobia in contemporary Britain: the evidence of the opinion polls, 1988–2006', *Islam and Christian–Muslim Relations* 18(4), pp. 447–77.

Fukuyama, Francis (2006) 'Neoconservatism has evolved into something I can no longer support' (http://newagebd.com/2006/feb/23/oped.html).

Githens-Mazer, Jonathan and Robert Lambert (2010) *Islamophobia and Anti-Muslim Hate Crime: a London case study*, Exeter: European Muslim Research Centre.

Globescan (2007) 'Global poll finds that religion and culture are not to blame for tensions between Islam and the West', London: BBC World Service (http://news.bbc.co.uk/1/shared/bsp/hi/pdfs/19_02_07_islam.pdf).

Gohir, Shaista (2006) *Understanding the Other Perspective: Muslim and non-Muslim relations*, London: Muslim Voice UK.

Gole, Nilufer (1997) 'The gendered nature of the public sphere', *Public Culture* 10(1), pp. 61–81.

Goodhart, David (2004) 'Too diverse?', *Prospect* February (also available as 'Discomfort of strangers' at http://www.guardian.co.uk/politics/2004/feb/24/race.eu).

Gottschalk, Peter and Gabriel Greenberg (2008) *Islamophobia: making Muslims the enemy*, Lanham, MD: Rowman and Littlefield.

Gove, Michael (2006) *Celsius 7/7: how the West's policy of appeasement has provoked yet more fundamentalist terror – and what has to be done now*, London: Weidenfeld & Nicolson.

Gramsci, Antonio (1971) *Selections from the Prison Notebooks of Antonio Gramsci*, ed. and trans. Quintin Hoare and Geoffrey Nowell-Smith, London: Lawrence & Wishart.

Greenslade, Roy (2005) *Seeking Scapegoats: the coverage of asylum in the UK press*, London: Institute for Public Policy Research.

Gross, Bernhard, Kerry Moore and Terry Threadgold (2007) *Broadcast News Coverage of Asylum April to October 2006: caught between human rights and public safety*, Cardiff: Cardiff School of Journalism, Media and Cultural Studies.

Hall, Stuart (1980) 'Encoding/decoding', in Stuart Hall, Dorothy Hobson, Andrew Lowe *et al.* (eds) *Culture, Media, Language*, London: Hutchinson, pp. 128–38.

Hamdan, Karima (2009) 'Contest 2 and the great white whale', 28 March (www.ummapulse.com).

HM Government (2009) *Pursue, Prevent, Protect, Prepare: the United Kingdom's strategy for countering international terrorism*, London: The Stationery Office.

Hollar, Julie and Jim Naureckas (eds) (2008) *Smearcasting: how Islamophobes spread fear, bigotry and misinformation*, New York: Fairness & Accuracy In Reporting (http://www.smearcasting.com/pdf/FAIR_Smearcasting_Final.pdf).

Home Office (2001) *Building Cohesive Communities: a report of the ministerial group on public order and community cohesion*, London: Home Office.

Hopkins, Peter and Richard Gale (eds) (2009) *Muslims in Britain: race, place and identities*, Edinburgh: Edinburgh University Press.

House of Commons Communities and Local Government Committee (2010) *Preventing Violent Extremism: sixth report of session 2009–10*, London: The Stationery Office.

House of Lords Select Committee on Religious Offences in England and Wales (2002) *Oral Evidence 425*, 23 October, London: The Stationery Office.

Hull, Andy and Ian Kearns (2009) 'Stopping bombs and standing up for what we believe in', *Institute for Public Policy Research* 7 April (http://www.ippr.org.uk/articles/?id=3460).

Huntington, Samuel (1996) *The Clash of Civilizations and the Remaking of World Order*, New York: Touchstone.

—— (2004) *Who Are We? The challenges to America's national identity*, New York: Simon & Schuster.

Insted Consultancy (2007) *The Search for Common Ground: Muslims, non-Muslims and the UK media*, London: Greater London Authority.

Institute for Public Policy Research (2010) *Exploring the Roots of BNP Support*, London: Institute for Public Policy Research.

International Helsinki Federation for Human Rights (2005) *Intolerance and Discrimination against Muslims in the EU: developments since September 11*, Vienna: IHF (http://www.ihf-hr.org/viewbinary/viewdocument.php?doc_id=6237).

IPSOS (2009) *Sondage: dans quelle mesure les Belges sont-ils tolérants par rapport aux minorités ethniques?* Brussels: Centre pour égalité des chances et la lutte contre le racisme.

Islam, Iyanatul (2005) *The Political Economy of Islamophobia and the Global Discourse on Islam*, Regional Outlook Paper No. 3, Griffith Asia Institute, Queensland.

Islamic Society of Britain (2009) 'Memorandum on preventing violent extremism', in *Pursue, Prevent, Protect, Prepare: the United Kingdom's strategy for countering international terrorism*, London: The Stationery Office, pp. 193–7.

Kabbani, Rana (1994) *Imperial Fictions: Europe's myths of the Orient*, London: Pandora Press.

Kepel, Gilles (2005) 'Europe's answer to Londonistan', *Open Democracy* 23 August (http://www.opendemocracy.net/conflict-terrorism/londonistan_2775.jsp).

Khan, Humera (2002) 'The next intifada', *Q-News* July/August.

Khan, Khalida (2009) *Preventing Violent Extremism (PVE) and PREVENT: a response from the Muslim community*, London: An-Nisa Society.

Khiabany, Gholam and Milly Williamson (2008) 'Veiled bodies – naked racism: culture, politics and race in the *Sun*', *Race & Class* 50(2), pp. 69–88.

Kitzinger, Jenny (2000) 'Media templates: patterns of association and the (re)construction of meaning over time', *Media, Culture & Society* 22(1), pp. 61–84.

Kramer, Martin (2003) 'Coming to terms: fundamentalists or Islamists?', *Middle East Quarterly* 10(2), pp. 65–77 (http://www.geocities.com/martinkramerorg/Terms.htm).

Krause, Wanda (ed.) (2009) *Citizenship, Security and Democracy: Muslim engagement with the West*, London: Association of Muslim Social Scientists.

Kumar, Deepa (2010) 'Green scare: the making of the new Muslim enemy', *Dissident Voice* 17 April (http://dissidentvoice.org/2010/04/green-scare-the-making-of-the-new-muslim-enemy/).

Kundnani, Arun (2001) 'From Oldham to Bradford: the violence of the violated', Institute of Race Relations, 1 October (http://www.irr.org.uk/2001/october/ak000003.html).

—— (2006) 'Integrationism: the politics of anti-Muslim racism', *Race & Class* 48(4), pp. 24–44.

—— (2007) *The End of Tolerance: racism in 21st century Britain*, London: Pluto Press.

—— (2008) 'How thinktanks are shaping the political agenda on Muslims in Britain', Institute of Race Relations, 2 September (http://www.irr.org.uk/2008/september/ak000003.html).

—— (2009) *Spooked: how not to prevent violent extremism*, London: Institute of Race Relations.

Leadership Group on US–Muslim Engagement (2009 [2008]) *Changing Course: a new direction for U.S. relations with the Muslim world*, 2nd edn, Washington, DC: Search for Common Ground and Consensus Building Institute.

LeGendre, Paul, Michael McClintock and Michael Posner (2007) *Islamophobia: 2007 hate crime report*, New York and Washington, DC: Human Rights First.

Lewis, Justin (2005) 'The power of myths: the war on terror and military might, in Hillel Nossek, Annabelle Sreberny and Prasun Sonwalkar (eds) *Media and Political Violence*, Cresskill, NJ: Hampton Press, pp. 341–54.

Lewis, Justin, Sanna Inthorn and Karin Wahl-Jorgensen (2005) *Citizens or Consumers? The media and the decline of political participation*, Maidenhead: Open University Press.

Lewis, Philip (2007) *Young, British and Muslim*, London: Continuum Publishing.

Lewis, Reina (2007) 'Veils and sales: Muslims and the spaces of postcolonial fashion retail', *Fashion Theory* 11(4), pp. 423–42.

Living History Forum (2006) *Islamophobia Report (English summary)*, Stockholm: Living History Forum (http://www.levandehistoria.se/files/islamophobia_englishsummary.pdf).

Lloyd, John (2004) *What the Media Are Doing to Our Politics*, London: Constable.

Macdonald, Myra (2003) *Exploring Media Discourse*, London: Edward Arnold.

Maher, Shiraz and Martyn Frampton (2009) *Choosing Our Friends Wisely: criteria for engagement with Muslim groups*, London: Policy Exchange.

Malik, Kenan (2005) 'The Islamophobia myth', *Prospect* February, pp. 28–31 (also available at http://www.kenanmalik.com/essays/prospect_islamophobia.html).

Malik, Maleiha (ed.) (2010) *Anti-Muslim Prejudice in the West, Past and Present*, London: Routledge.

Masood, Ehsan (2005) 'British Muslims must stop the war', *Open Democracy* (http://www.opendemocracy.net/debates/article.jsp?id=2&debateId=124&articleId=2786).

—— (2006) *British Muslims Media Guide*, London: British Council.

—— (2008) *Our Shared Europe: swapping treasures, sharing losses, celebrating futures*, London: British Council (http://www.ourshaedeurope.org/documents/OSE_report.pdf).

McLaughlin, Eugene and Sarah Neal (2004) 'Misrepresenting the multicultural nation: the policy-making process, news media management and the Parekh Report', *Policy Studies* 25(3), pp. 155–74.

Meer, Nasar and Tariq Modood (2009) 'The multicultural state we're in: Muslims, "multiculture" and the "civic re-balancing" of British multiculturalism', *Political Studies* 57(3), pp. 473–97.

Meer, Nasar, Claire Dwyer and Tariq Modood (2010) 'Embodying nationhood? Conceptions of British national identity, citizenship, and gender in the "Veil Affair" ', *Sociological Review* 58(1), pp. 84–111.

Miliband, David (2009) *Our Shared Future: building coalitions and winning consent*, lecture at Oxford Centre for Islamic Studies, 21 May (http://www.fco.gov.uk/en/news/latest-news/?view=Speech&id=18709688).

Mirza, Munira, Abi Sentihilkumaran and Aa'far Zein (2007) *Living Apart Together: British Muslims and the paradox of multiculturalism*, London: Policy Exchange.

Modood, Tariq (1992) *Not Easy Being British: colour, culture and citizenship*, Stoke-on-Trent: Trentham Books for the Runnymede Trust.

—— (2005) *Multicultural Politics: racism, ethnicity and Muslims in Britain*, Edinburgh: Edinburgh University Press.

—— (2006) 'The liberal dilemma: integration or vilification?', *Open Democracy* 8 (February) (http://www.opendemocracy.net/faith-terrorism/liberal_dilemma_3249.jsp).

Moore, Kerry, Paul Mason and Justin Lewis (2008) *Images of Islam in the UK: the representation of British Muslims in the national print news media 2000–2008*, Cardiff School of Journalism, Media and Cultural Studies (http://www.cardiff.ac.uk/jomec/resources/08channel4-dispatches.pdf).

MORI (2006) *Careers in Print Media: what people from ethnic minorities think*, London: Market and Opinion Research International (for the Commission for Racial Equality).

Morley, David (1980) *The 'Nationwide' Audience*, London: British Film Institute.

Muslim Council of Britain (2007) *Meeting the Needs of Muslim Pupils in State Schools: information and guidance*, London: Muslim Council of Britain (http://www.mcb.org.uk/downloads/Schoolinfoguidance.pdf).

National Centre for Social Research (2010) *British Social Attitudes* (http://www.natcen.ac.uk/study/british-social-attitudes).

Nimer, Mohamed (2007) *Islamophobia and Anti-Americanism: causes and remedies*, Beltsville, MD: Amana Publications.

Obama, Barack (2009) 'New beginning', speech given in Cairo, 4 June.

Oborne, Peter (2007) *The Triumph of the Political Class*, London: Simon & Schuster.

Oborne, Peter and James Jones (2008) *Muslims Under Siege: alienating vulnerable communities*, Human Rights Centre, University of Essex (http://www.channel4.com/news/media/pdfs/Muslims_under_siege_LR.pdf).

Office for Democratic Institutions and Human Rights (2004) *International Action against Racism, Xenophobia, Antisemitism and Intolerance in the OSCE Region: a comparative study*, Warsaw: Organisation for Security and Cooperation in Europe.

—— (2006) *The Representation of Muslims in Public Discourse,* report on a roundtable, Warsaw, 9 May (http://www.osce.org/documents/odihr/2006/05/22829_en.pdf).

—— (2008) *Combating Intolerance and Discrimination against Muslims in the Field of Education*, report on a meeting 3–4 June, Warsaw: Office for Democratic Institutions and Human Rights (http://tandis.odihr.pl/content/conferences/0806-asmus-rep.pdf).

Omaar, Rageh (2006) *Only Half of Me: being a Muslim in Britain*, London: Viking.

O'Neill, Brendan (2005) 'Creating the enemy: how a risk-averse West has inflamed the terrorism it fears', *Spiked* 18 July (http://www.spiked-online.com/Printable/0000000CA492.htm).

Open Democracy (2005) *What Happened? What Changed? What Now?* Report on a symposium, 3 August (http://www.opendemocracy.net/conflict-terrorism/chatham_house_2729.jsp).

Open Society Institute (2009) *Muslims in Europe: a report on 11 EU cities*, New York, London and Budapest: Open Society Institute.

Organization of the Islamic Conference (2008) *First OIC Observatory Report on Islamophobia: May 2007–March 2008*, Jeddah: Organization of the Islamic Conference.

—— (2009) *Second OIC Observatory Report on Islamophobia: June 2008–April 2009,* Jeddah: Organization of the Islamic Conference (http://www.oic-oci.org/uploads/file/Islamphobia/Islamophobia_rep_May_23_25_2009.pdf).

Orhun, Ömür (2007) *Combating Intolerance and Discrimination against Muslims: protecting and promoting human rights and human dignity within the context of diversity*, Warsaw: OSCE Yearbook (http://tandis.odihr.pl/documents/04992.pdf).

Orhun, Ömür (2008) *Report on Combating Intolerance and Discrimination against Muslims*, Warsaw: Office for Democratic Institutions and Human Rights (http://www.osce.org/documents/pr/2008/11/35260_en.pdf).

Parekh, Bikhu (2000) *The Future of Multi-ethnic Britain*, London: Profile Books.

Parekh, Bhikhu (2008) *A New Politics of Identity: political principles for an interdependent world*, Basingstoke: Macmillan.

Peach, Ceri (2005) 'Muslims in the UK', in Tahir Abbas (ed.) *Muslim Britain: communities under pressure*, London: Zed Books, pp. 18–30.

Petley, Julian (2001) 'A case of mistaken identity', *Index on Censorship* 30(3), pp. 20–9.

—— (2006a) 'The retreat of reason', *Index on Censorship* 35(4), pp. 8–14.

—— (2006b) 'Still no redress from the PCC', in Elizabeth Poole and John E. Richardson (eds) *Muslims and the News Media*, London: I.B. Tauris, pp. 53–62.

Pew Global Attitudes Project (2006) *The Great Divide: how Westerners and Muslims view each other*, Washington, DC: Pew Research Center (http://pewglobal.org/reports/pdf/253.pdf).

Phillips, Kevin (2006) *American Theocracy: the perils of radical religion, oil, and borrowed money in the 21st century*, London: Viking Penguin.

Phillips, Melanie (2008 [2006]) *Londonistan: how Britain has created a terrorist state within*, London: Gibson Square.

Phillips, Trevor (2005) 'After 7/7: sleep-walking to segregation', speech given 22 September at the Manchester Council for Community Relations.

Philo, Greg and Mike Berry (2004) *Bad News from Israel*, London: Pluto Press.

Poole, Elizabeth (2002) *Reporting Islam: media representations of British Muslims*, London: I.B. Tauris.

—— (2006) 'The effects of September 11 and the war in Iraq on British newspaper coverage', in Elizabeth Poole and John E. Richardson (eds) *Muslims and the News Media*, London: I.B. Tauris, pp. 89–102.

Poole, Elizabeth and John E. Richardson (eds) (2006) *Muslims and the News Media*, London: I.B. Tauris.

Prince Alwaleed Bin Talal Center for Muslim-Christian Understanding (2008) *Islamophobia and the Challenges of Pluralism in the 21st Century*, ACMCU Occasional Papers, Georgetown University.

Richardson, John E. (2004) *(Mis)Representing Islam: the racism and rhetoric of British broadsheet newspapers*, Amsterdam: John Benjamins.

—— (2006) 'On delineating "reasonable" and "unreasonable" criticisms of Muslims', Fifth-Estate-Online (http://www.fifth-estate-online.co.uk/criticsm/ondelineatingreasonableandunreasonable.html).

Richardson, Robin (2007) ' "How dare they?" Islamophobia, the media and an educational resource', *Race Equality Teaching* 25(2), pp. 21–30.

Ritchie, David (chair) (2001) *Oldham Independent Review*, Oldham Metropolitan Council.

Rokeach, Milton (1960) *The Open and Closed Mind*, New York: Basic Books.

Rose, Martin (2009) *A Shared Past for a Shared Future: European Muslims and history-making*, London: Association of Muslim Social Scientists and British Council.

Roy, Olivier (2008) *Al Qaeda in the West as a Youth Movement: the power of a narrative*, MICROCON Policy Working Paper 2, Institute of Development Studies, University of Sussex.

Said, Edward (1985) 'Orientalism reconsidered', *Race & Class* 27(2), pp. 1–15.

—— (1993) *Culture and Imperialism*, London: Chatto & Windus.

—— (1995 [1978]) *Orientalism: western conceptions of the Orient*, London: Routledge & Kegan Paul.

—— (1997) *Covering Islam: how the media and the experts determine how we see the rest of the world*, London: Vintage.

—— (2001) *Reflections on Exile and Other Essays*, London: Granta.

—— (2003) 'Preface', in *Orientalism: western conceptions of the Orient*, London, Penguin.

Samuels, Andrew (2006) 'The fascination of fundamentalism', summary of a lecture (http://www.andrewsamuels.com/index.php?view=article&catid=3%3AArticles+And+Lectures&id=11%3AThe+Fascination+of+Fundamentalism&option=com_content&Itemid=4).

Sayyid, Bobby S. and Abdoolkarim Vakil (2010) *Thinking through Islamophobia*, London: Hurst.

Scatamburlo, Valerie L. (1998) *Soldiers of Misfortune: the New Right's culture war and the politics of political correctness*, New York: Peter Lang.

Search for Common Ground (2008) *Media Kit for Common Ground Training*, New York: Search for Common Ground.

Sims, Paul (2009) 'Mills and minarets', *New Humanist* May/June.

Sivanandan, Ambalavaner (2010) 'Fighting anti-Muslim racism: an interview with A. Sivanandan', Institute of Race Relations, 15 March (http://www.irr.org.uk/2010/march/ha000031.html).

Society of Editors/Media Trust (2006) *Reporting Diversity: how journalists can contribute to community cohesion*, Cambridge/London: Society of Editors/Media Trust.

Sreberny, Annabelle (2004) 'Unsuitable coverage: the media, the veil, and regimes of representation', in Tasha G. Oren and Patrice Petro (eds) *Global Currents: Media and Technology Now*, Chapel Hill, NC: Rutgers University Press.

Stabile, Carol and Deepa Kumar (2005) 'Unveiling imperialism: media, gender and the war on Afghanistan', *Media, Culture & Society* 27(5), pp. 765–82.

Tarlo, Emma (2007) 'Islamic cosmopolitanism: the sartorial biographies of three Muslim women in London', *Fashion Theory* 11(2/3), pp. 143–72.

Thanki, Ashika and Monica McKay (2006) *Why Ethnic Minority Workers Leave London's Print Journalism Sector*, London: Working Lives Research Unit for the Commission for Racial Equality.

Thobani, Sunera (2007) 'White wars: Western feminisms and the "War on Terror"', *Feminist Theory* 8(2), pp. 169–85.

United States Department of Homeland Security (2008) 'Terminology to define the terrorists: recommendations from American Muslims', memorandum (http://www.dhs.gov/xabout/structure/gc_1212591972165.shtm).

Vakil, Abdoolkarim (2008) 'Is the Islam in Islamophobia the same as the Islam in anti-Islam, or, when is it Islamophobia time?', in Bobby S. Sayyid and Abdoolkarim Vakil (eds) *Thinking through Islamophobia*, University of Leeds seminar papers (http://www.ces.uc.pt/e-cadernos/media/ecadernos3/Vakil.pdf).

Vakulenko, Anastasia (2007) '"Islamic Headscarves" and the European Convention on Human Rights: an intersectional perspective', *Social and Legal Studies* 16(2), pp. 183–99.

Van Dijk, Tjeuk (2000) 'New(s) racism: a discourse analytical approach', in Simon Cottle (ed.) *Ethnic Minorities and the Media*, Buckingham: Open University Press, pp. 31–49.

Watson, Helen (1994) 'Women and the veil: personal responses to global process', in Akbar S. Ahmed and Hastings Donnan (eds) *Islam, Globalisation, and Postmodernity*, London: Routledge, pp. 141–59.

Weller, Paul, Alice Feldman and Kingsley Purdam (2001) *Religious Discrimination in England and Wales*, Home Office Research Study 220: Research Development and Statistics Directorate, London: Home Office.

Werbner, Prina (2007) 'Veiled interventions in pure space: honour, shame and embodied struggles among Muslims in Britain and France', *Theory, Culture & Society* 24(2), pp. 161–86.

Williams, Rowan (2002) *Writing in the Dust: reflections on 11th September and its aftermath*, London: Hodder & Stoughton.

Whitaker, Brian (2002) 'Islam and the British press after September 11', talk given at the Central London Mosque, 20 June (http://www.al-bab.com/media/articles/bw020620.htm).

Wilson, Amrit (2007) 'The forced marriage debate and the British state', *Race & Class* 49(1), pp. 25–38.

Wilson, John K. (1995) *The Myth of Political Correctness: the conservative attack on higher education*, Durham, NC: Duke University Press.

Yalonis, Chris (2005) *Western Perception of Islam and Muslims*, State of Kuwait: Ministry of Awqaf and Islamic Affairs.

Yaqoob, Salma (2008) 'Government's PVE agenda is failing to tackle extremism', *Muslim News* 28 November (http://www.muslimnews.co.uk/paper/index.php?article=3795).

Yegenoglu, Meyda (1998) *Colonial Fantasies: towards a feminist reading of Orientalism*, Cambridge: Cambridge University Press.

Zubaida, Sami (2003) 'Islam in Europe', *Critical Quarterly* 45(1/2), pp. 88–98.

Index

Note: Page numbers for tables are shown in italics.